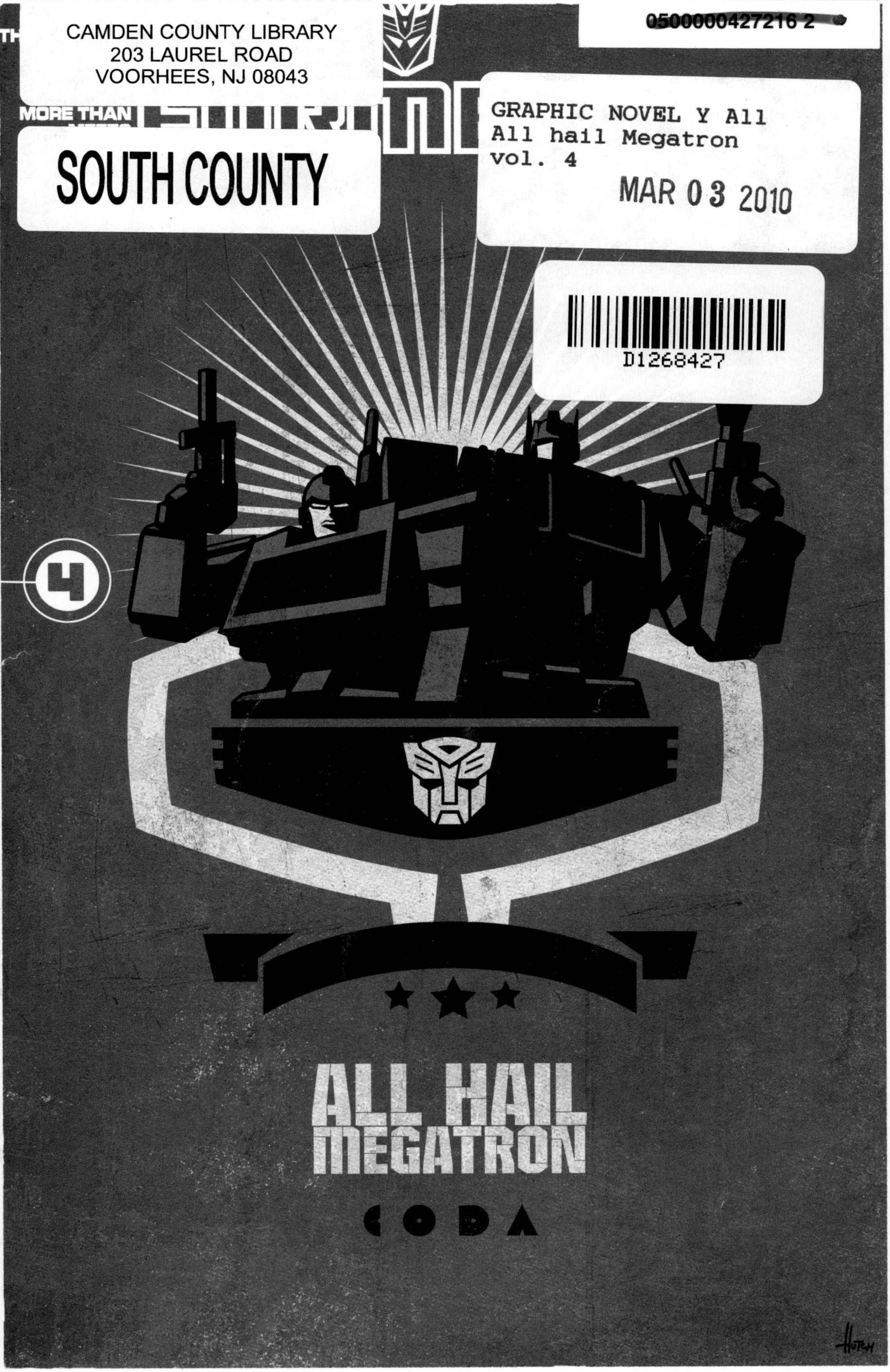
MORE THAN
4
ALL HAIL
MEGATRON
CODA
HUTCH

"Old Ways"
Written by Simon Furman
Art by Don Figueroa
Colors by James Brown

"Uneasy Lies the Head"
Written by Mike Costa
Art by Chee Yang Ong
Colors by Moose Baumann

"Replay"
Written by Shane McCarthy
Art by Emiliano Santalucia
Colors by Josh Burcham

"Rebirth"
Written by Andy Schmidt
Art by Andrew Griffith
Colors by Josh Burcham

"Everything In Its Right Place"
Written by Nick Roche
Art by Nick Roche
Colors by Kris Carter

"Lost & Found"
Written by Denton J. Tipton
Art by Casey Coller
Colors by Joana Lafuente

"The Man of Steel"
Written by Mike Costa
Art by Guido Guidi
Colors by Josh Burcham

"Hidden"
Written by Zander Cannon
Art by Chee Yang Ong
Colors by Moose Baumann

Lettering by Chris Mowry

Original Series Edits by
Andy Schmidt & Denton J. Tipton

Original Series Assistant Editor
Carlos Guzman

Collection Edits by
Justin Eisinger and Mariah Huehner

Collection Design by
Chris Mowry

Special thanks to Hasbro's Aaron Archer, Michael Kelly, Amie Lozanski, Val Roca, Ed Lane, Michael Provost, Erin Hillman, Jos Huxley, Samantha Lomow, and Michael Verrecchia for their invaluable assistance.

IDW Publishing
Operations:
Ted Adams, Chief Executive Officer
Greg Goldstein, Chief Operating Officer
Matthew Ruzicka, CPA, Chief Financial Officer
Alan Payne, VP of Sales
Lorelei Bunjes, Dir. of Digital Services
AnnaMaria White, Marketing & PR Manager
Marci Hubbard, Executive Assistant
Alonzo Simon, Shipping Manager
Angela Loggins, Staff Accountant

Editorial:
Chris Ryall, Publisher/Editor-in-Chief
Scott Dunbier, Editor, Special Projects
Andy Schmidt, Senior Editor
Bob Schreck, Senior Editor
Justin Eisinger, Editor
Kris Oprisko, Editor/Foreign Lic.
Denton J. Tipton, Editor
Tom Waltz, Editor
Mariah Huehner, Associate Editor
Carlos Guzman, Editorial Assistant

Design:
Robbie Robbins, EVP/Sr. Graphic Artist
Neil Uyetake, Art Director
Chris Mowry, Graphic Artist
Amauri Osorio, Graphic Artist
Gilberto Lazcano, Production Assistant
Shawn Lee, Production Assistant

Licensed By:

ISBN: 978-1-60010-592-0
12 11 10 09 1 2 3 4

www.idwpublishing.com

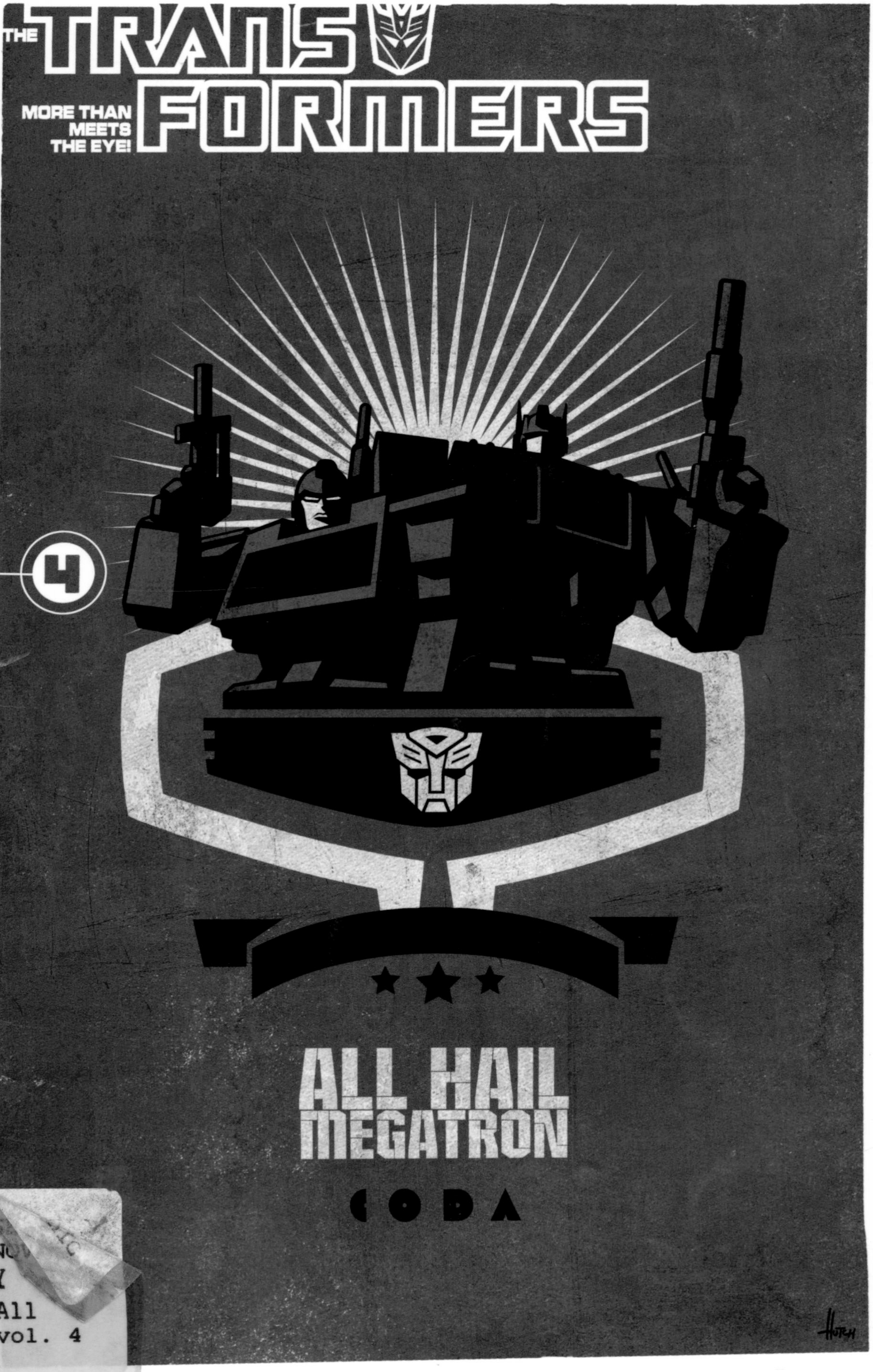
THE TRANSFORMERS
MORE THAN MEETS THE EYE!
4
ALL HAIL MEGATRON
CODA
HUTCH

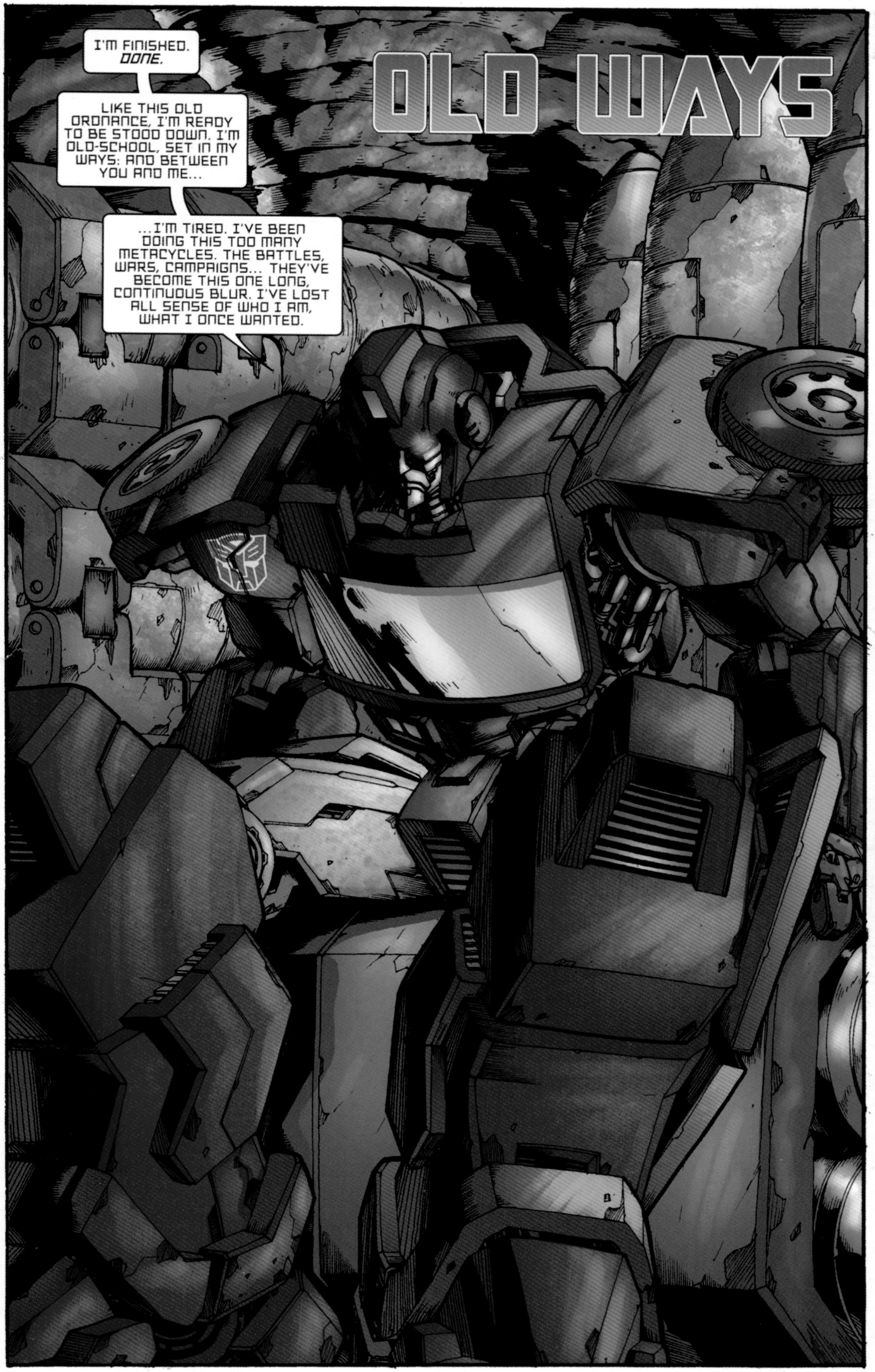
OLD WAYS
I'M FINISHED. *DONE.*
LIKE THIS OLD ORDNANCE, I'M READY TO BE STOOD DOWN. I'M OLD-SCHOOL, SET IN MY WAYS: AND BETWEEN YOU AND ME...
...I'M TIRED. I'VE BEEN DOING THIS TOO MANY METACYCLES. THE BATTLES, WARS, CAMPAIGNS... THEY'VE BECOME THIS ONE LONG, CONTINUOUS BLUR. I'VE LOST ALL SENSE OF WHO I AM, WHAT I ONCE WANTED.

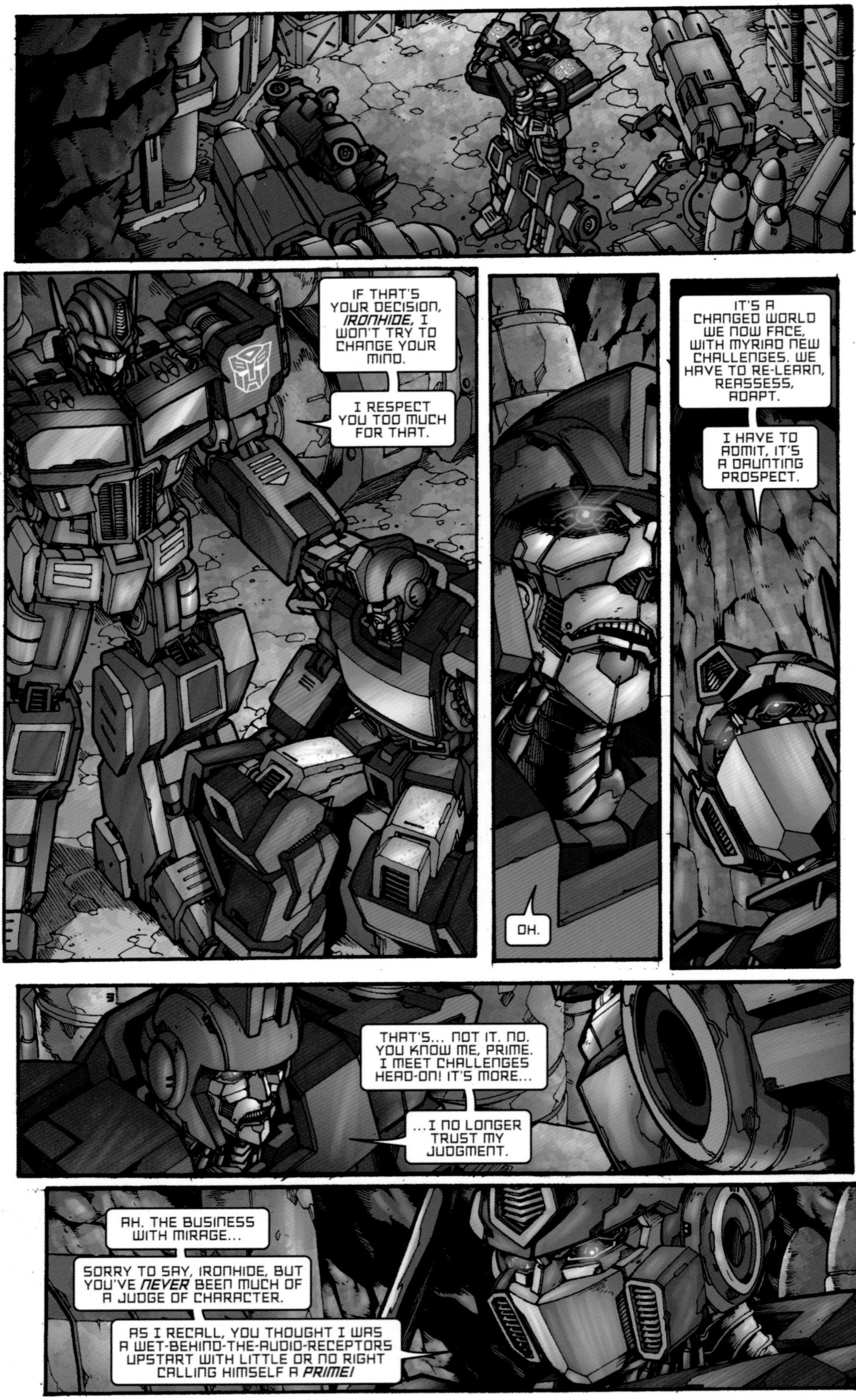
IF THAT'S YOUR DECISION, *IRONHIDE*, I WON'T TRY TO CHANGE YOUR MIND.
I RESPECT YOU TOO MUCH FOR THAT.
OH.
IT'S A CHANGED WORLD WE NOW FACE, WITH MYRIAD NEW CHALLENGES. WE HAVE TO RE-LEARN, REASSESS, ADAPT.
I HAVE TO ADMIT, IT'S A DAUNTING PROSPECT.
THAT'S... NOT IT. NO. YOU KNOW ME, PRIME. I MEET CHALLENGES HEAD-ON! IT'S MORE...
...I NO LONGER TRUST MY JUDGMENT.
AH. THE BUSINESS WITH MIRAGE...
SORRY TO SAY, IRONHIDE, BUT YOU'VE *NEVER* BEEN MUCH OF A JUDGE OF CHARACTER.
AS I RECALL, YOU THOUGHT I WAS A WET-BEHIND-THE-AUDIO-RECEPTORS UPSTART WITH LITTLE OR NO RIGHT CALLING HIMSELF A *PRIME!*

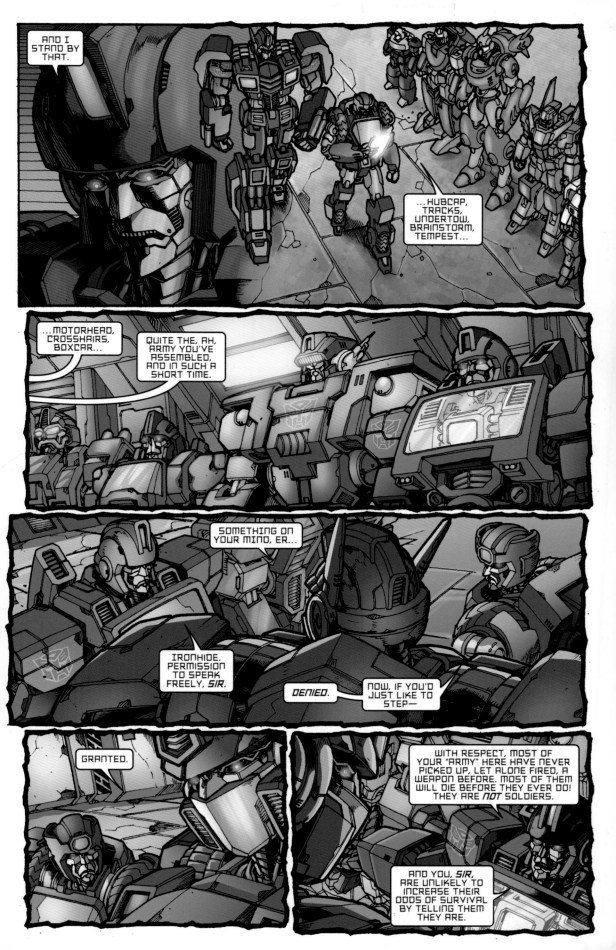

AND I STAND BY THAT.

...HUBCAP, TRACKS, UNDERTOW, BRAINSTORM, TEMPEST...

...MOTORHEAD, CROSSHAIRS, BOXCAR...

QUITE THE, AH, ARMY YOU'VE ASSEMBLED, AND IN SUCH A SHORT TIME.

SOMETHING ON YOUR MIND, ER...

IRONHIDE. PERMISSION TO SPEAK FREELY, *SIR.*

DENIED.

NOW, IF YOU'D JUST LIKE TO STEP—

GRANTED.

WITH RESPECT, MOST OF YOUR "ARMY" HERE HAVE NEVER PICKED UP, LET ALONE FIRED, A WEAPON BEFORE. MOST OF THEM WILL DIE BEFORE THEY EVER DO! THEY ARE *NOT* SOLDIERS.

AND YOU, *SIR,* ARE UNLIKELY TO INCREASE THEIR ODDS OF SURVIVAL BY TELLING THEM THEY ARE.

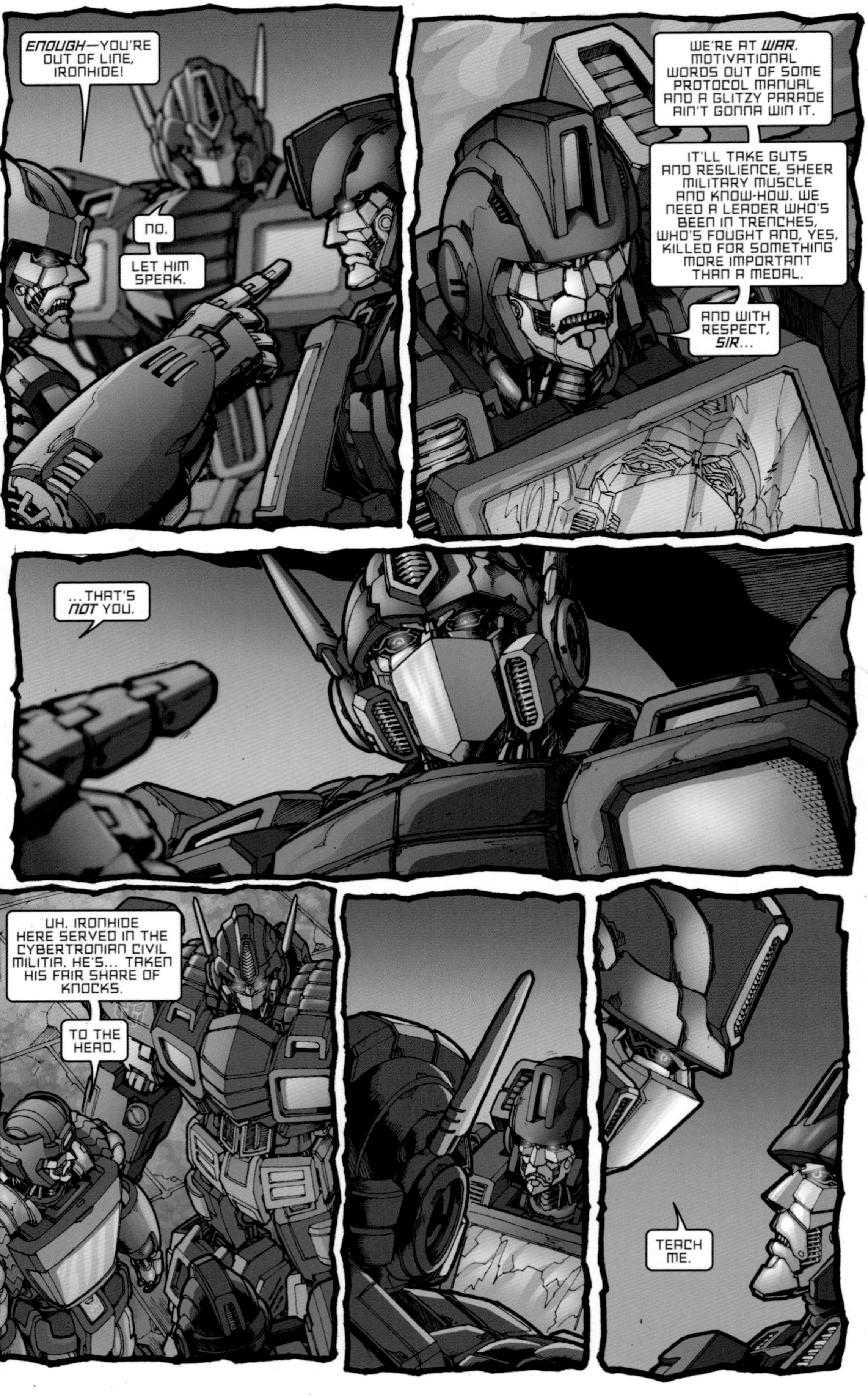
ENOUGH—YOU'RE OUT OF LINE, IRONHIDE!
NO.
LET HIM SPEAK.
WE'RE AT WAR. MOTIVATIONAL WORDS OUT OF SOME PROTOCOL MANUAL AND A GLITZY PARADE AIN'T GONNA WIN IT.
IT'LL TAKE GUTS AND RESILIENCE, SHEER MILITARY MUSCLE AND KNOW-HOW. WE NEED A LEADER WHO'S BEEN IN TRENCHES, WHO'S FOUGHT AND, YES, KILLED FOR SOMETHING MORE IMPORTANT THAN A MEDAL.
AND WITH RESPECT, SIR...
...THAT'S NOT YOU.
UH. IRONHIDE HERE SERVED IN THE CYBERTRONIAN CIVIL MILITIA. HE'S... TAKEN HIS FAIR SHARE OF KNOCKS.
TO THE HEAD.
TEACH ME.

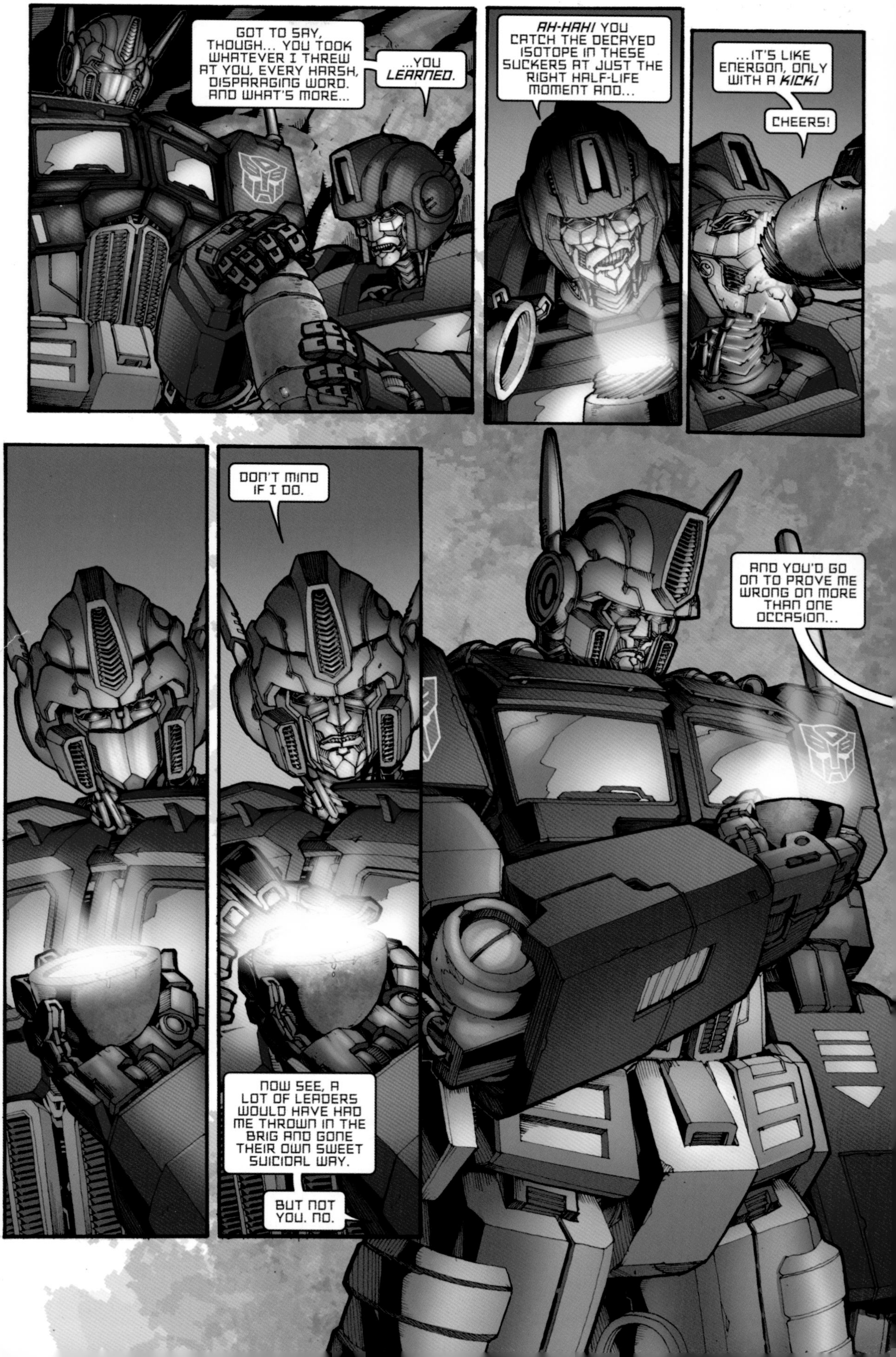
GOT TO SAY, THOUGH... YOU TOOK WHATEVER I THREW AT YOU, EVERY HARSH, DISPARAGING WORD. AND WHAT'S MORE...
...YOU *LEARNED*.
AH-HAH! YOU CATCH THE DECAYED ISOTOPE IN THESE SUCKERS AT JUST THE RIGHT HALF-LIFE MOMENT AND...
...IT'S LIKE ENERGON, ONLY WITH A *KICK!*
CHEERS!
DON'T MIND IF I DO.
NOW SEE, A LOT OF LEADERS WOULD HAVE HAD ME THROWN IN THE BRIG AND GONE THEIR OWN SWEET SUICIDAL WAY.
BUT NOT YOU. NO.
AND YOU'D GO ON TO PROVE ME WRONG ON MORE THAN ONE OCCASION...

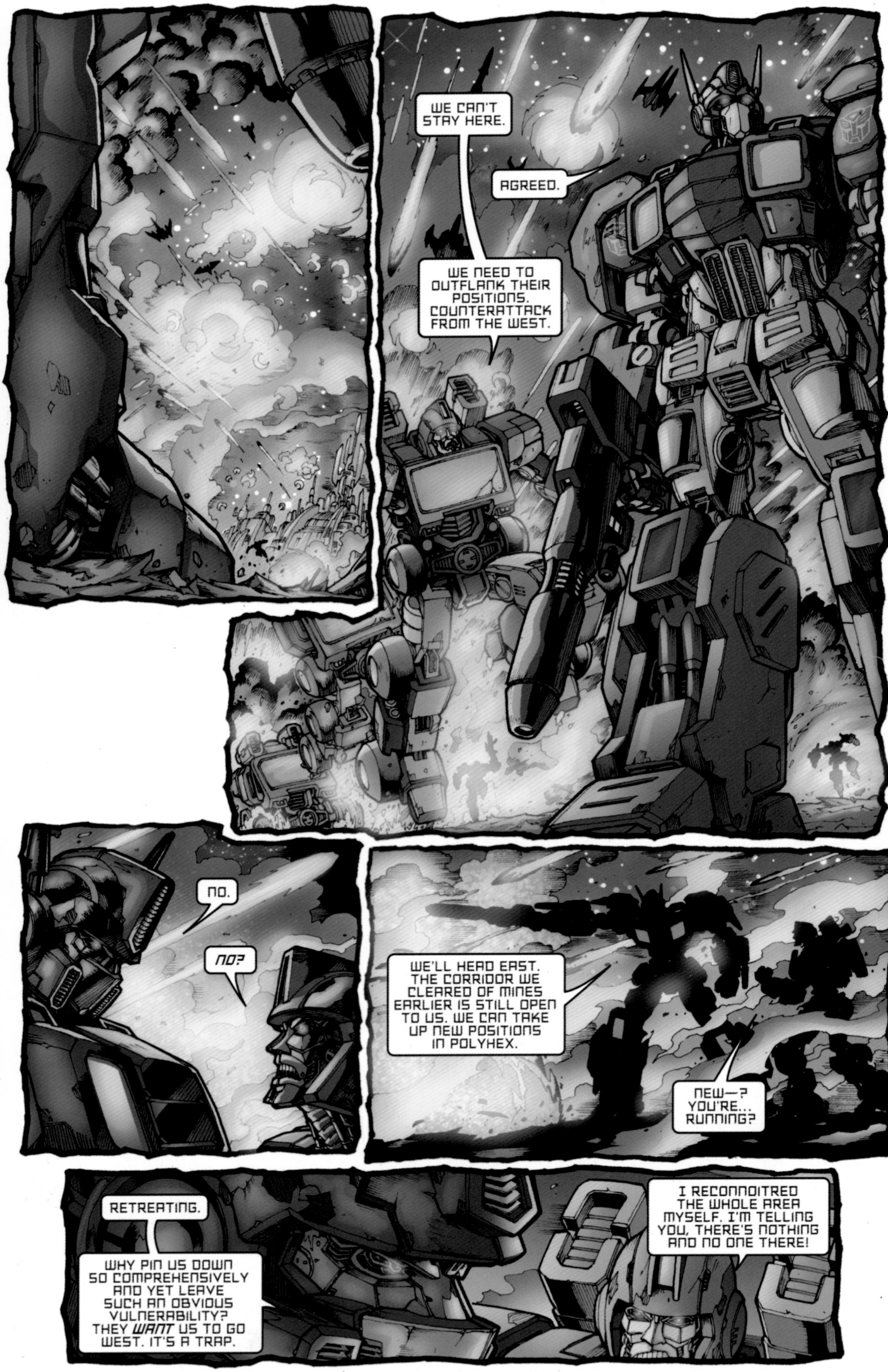

WE CAN'T STAY HERE.
AGREED.
WE NEED TO OUTFLANK THEIR POSITIONS. COUNTERATTACK FROM THE WEST.
NO.
NO?
WE'LL HEAD EAST. THE CORRIDOR WE CLEARED OF MINES EARLIER IS STILL OPEN TO US. WE CAN TAKE UP NEW POSITIONS IN POLYHEX.
NEW—? YOU'RE... RUNNING?
RETREATING.
WHY PIN US DOWN SO COMPREHENSIVELY AND YET LEAVE SUCH AN OBVIOUS VULNERABILITY? THEY *WANT* US TO GO WEST. IT'S A TRAP.
I RECONNOITRED THE WHOLE AREA MYSELF. I'M TELLING YOU, THERE'S NOTHING AND NO ONE THERE!

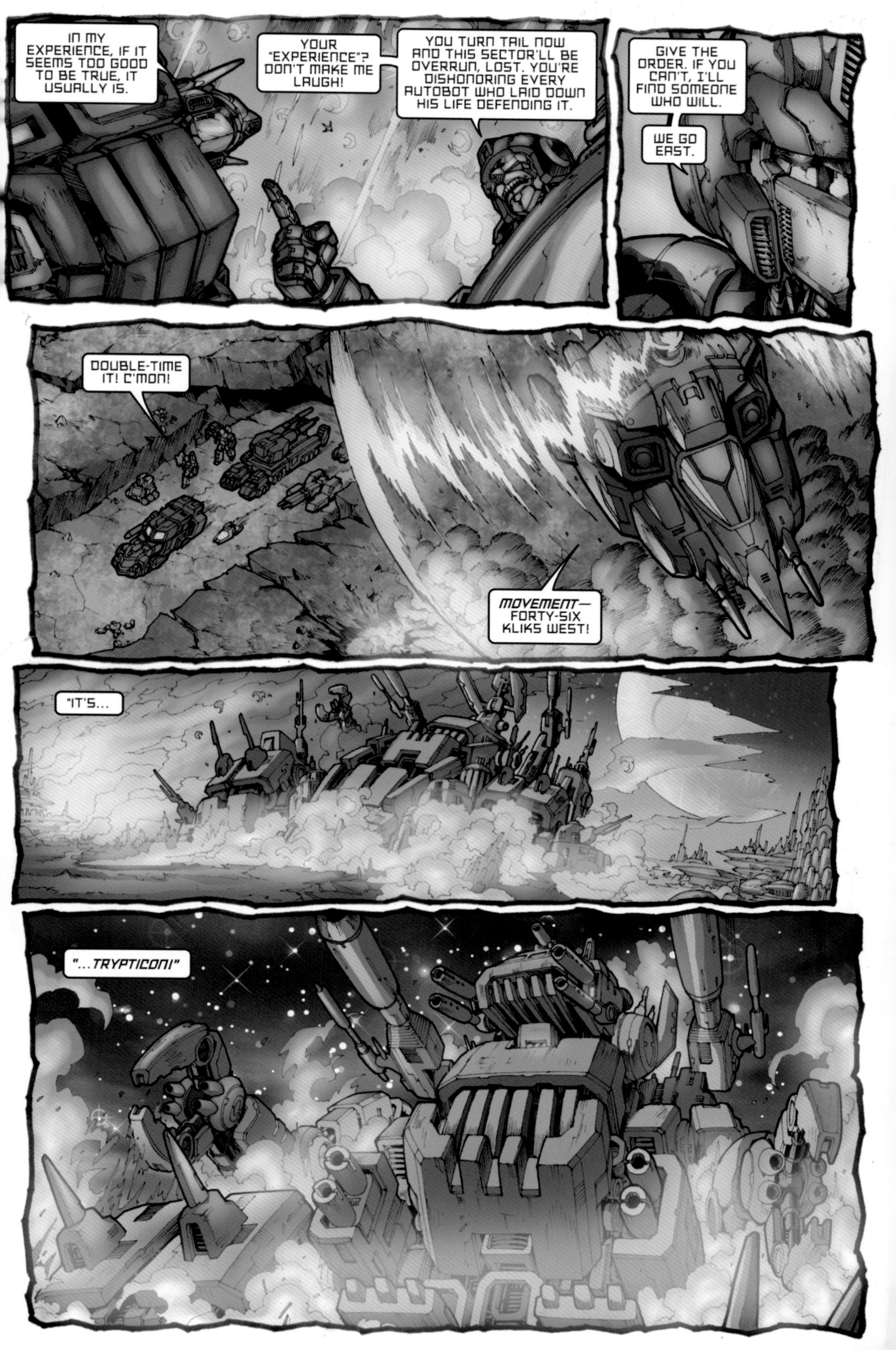

IN MY EXPERIENCE, IF IT SEEMS TOO GOOD TO BE TRUE, IT USUALLY IS.
YOUR "EXPERIENCE"? DON'T MAKE ME LAUGH!
YOU TURN TAIL NOW AND THIS SECTOR'LL BE OVERRUN, LOST. YOU'RE DISHONORING EVERY AUTOBOT WHO LAID DOWN HIS LIFE DEFENDING IT.
GIVE THE ORDER. IF YOU CAN'T, I'LL FIND SOMEONE WHO WILL.
WE GO EAST.
DOUBLE-TIME IT! C'MON!
MOVEMENT— FORTY-SIX KLIKS WEST!
"IT'S...
"...*TRYPTICON!*"

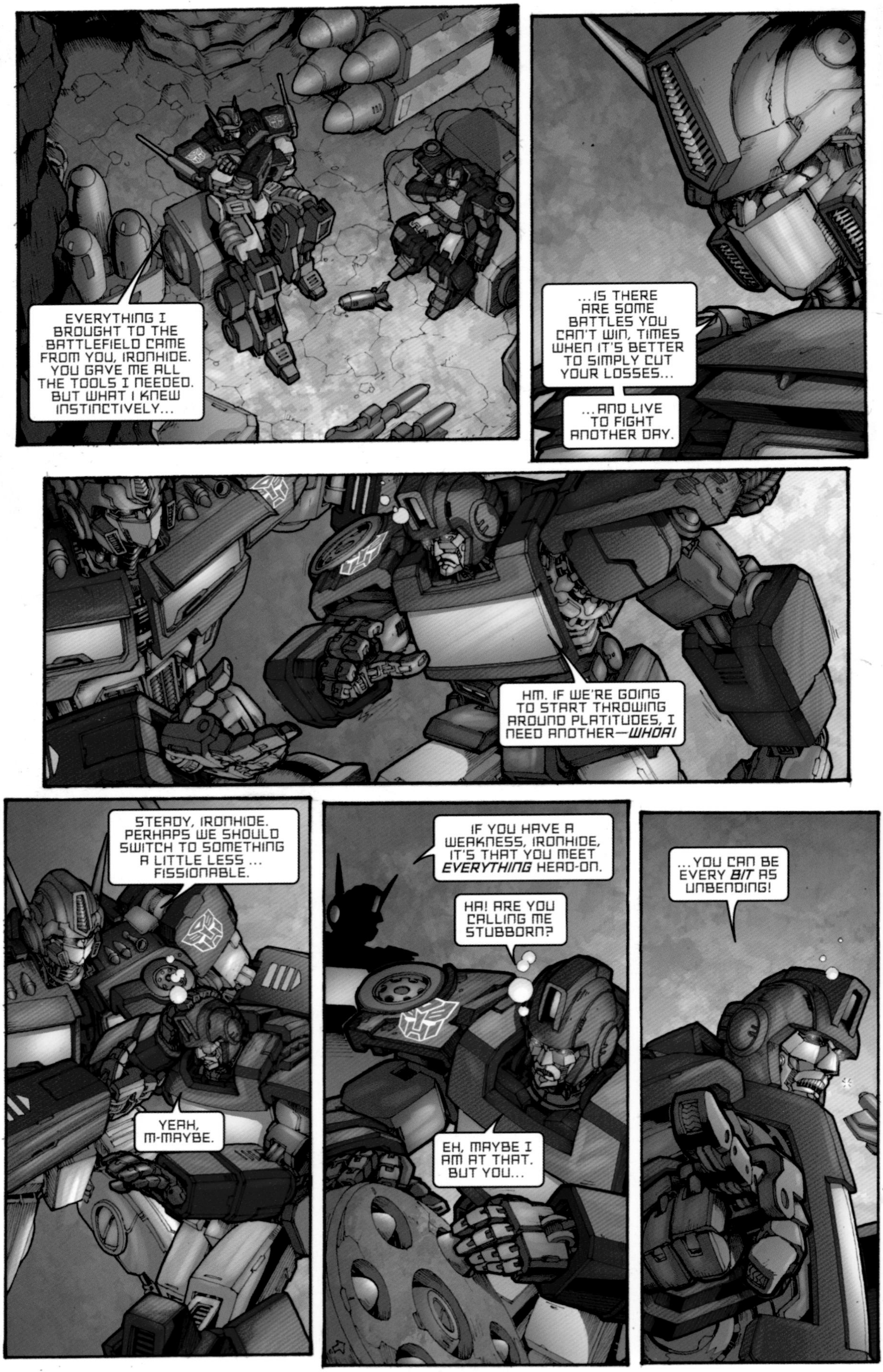
EVERYTHING I BROUGHT TO THE BATTLEFIELD CAME FROM YOU, IRONHIDE. YOU GAVE ME ALL THE TOOLS I NEEDED. BUT WHAT I KNEW INSTINCTIVELY...
...IS THERE ARE SOME BATTLES YOU CAN'T WIN, TIMES WHEN IT'S BETTER TO SIMPLY CUT YOUR LOSSES...
...AND LIVE TO FIGHT ANOTHER DAY.
HM. IF WE'RE GOING TO START THROWING AROUND PLATITUDES, I NEED ANOTHER—WHOA!
STEADY, IRONHIDE. PERHAPS WE SHOULD SWITCH TO SOMETHING A LITTLE LESS ... FISSIONABLE.
YEAH, M-MAYBE.
IF YOU HAVE A WEAKNESS, IRONHIDE, IT'S THAT YOU MEET EVERYTHING HEAD-ON.
HA! ARE YOU CALLING ME STUBBORN?
EH, MAYBE I AM AT THAT. BUT YOU...
...YOU CAN BE EVERY BIT AS UNBENDING!

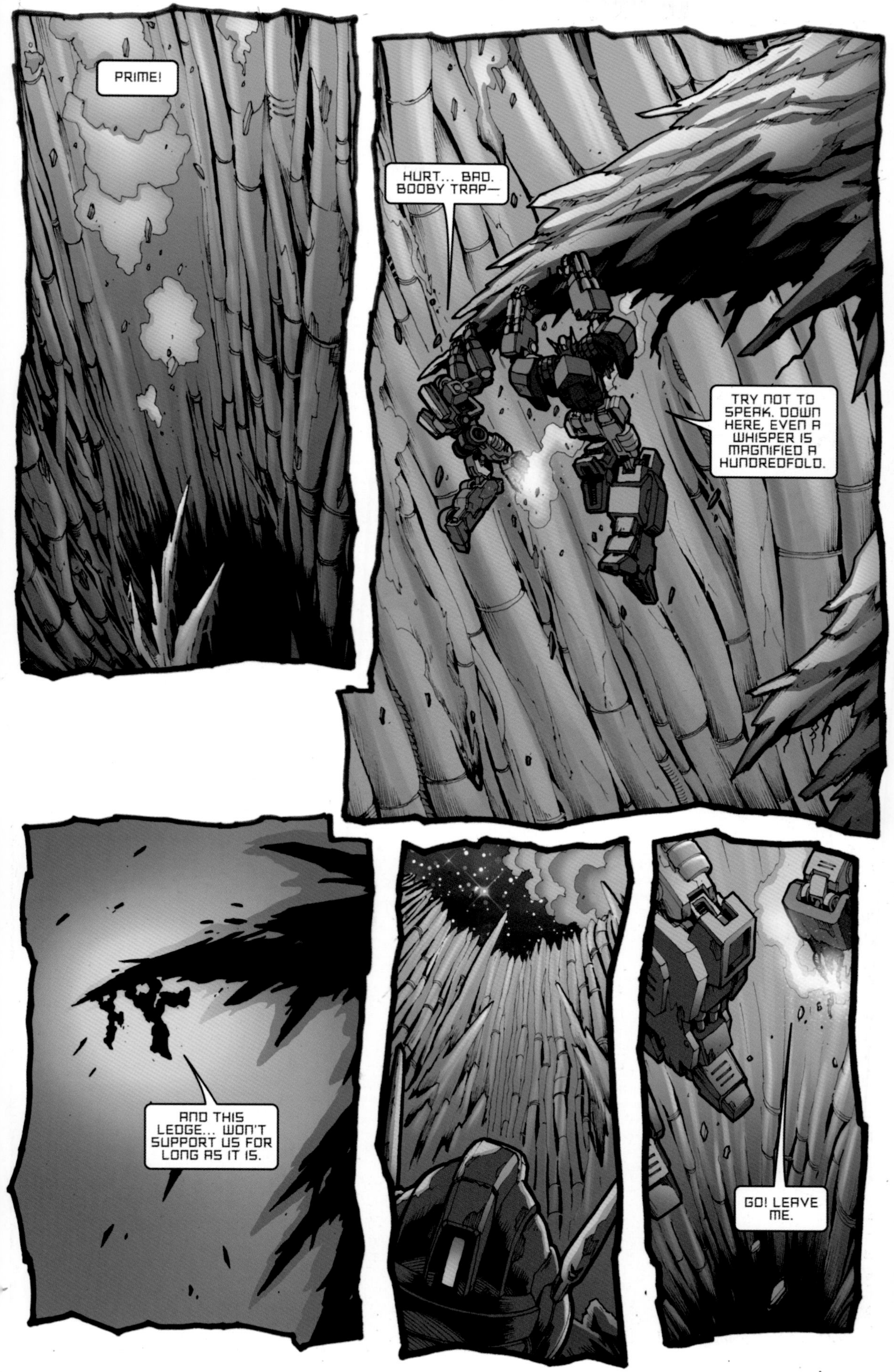
PRIME!
HURT... BAD. BOOBY TRAP—
TRY NOT TO SPEAK. DOWN HERE, EVEN A WHISPER IS MAGNIFIED A HUNDREDFOLD.
AND THIS LEDGE... WON'T SUPPORT US FOR LONG AS IT IS.
GO! LEAVE ME.

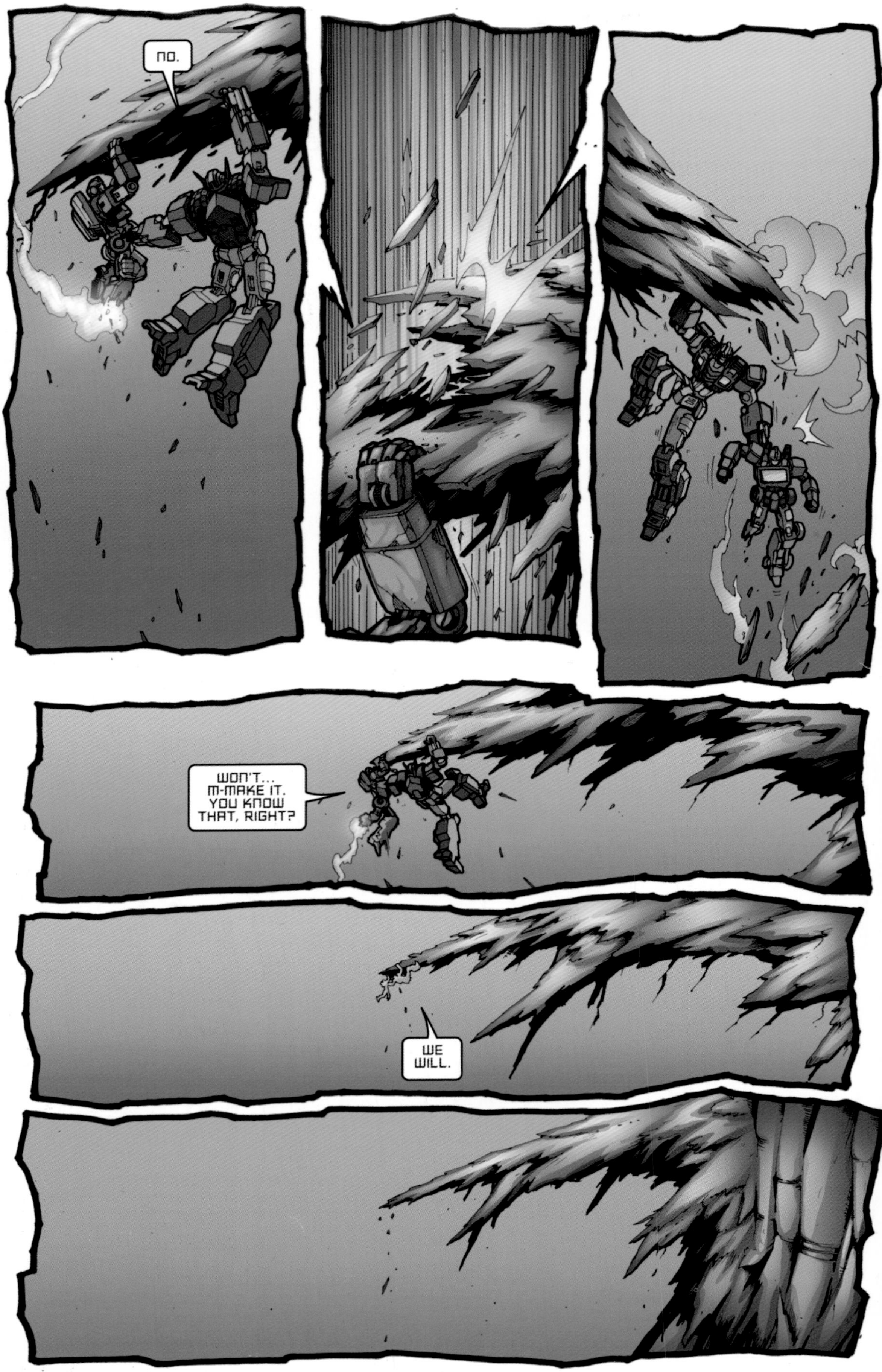
NO.
WON'T... M-MAKE IT. YOU KNOW THAT, RIGHT?
WE WILL.

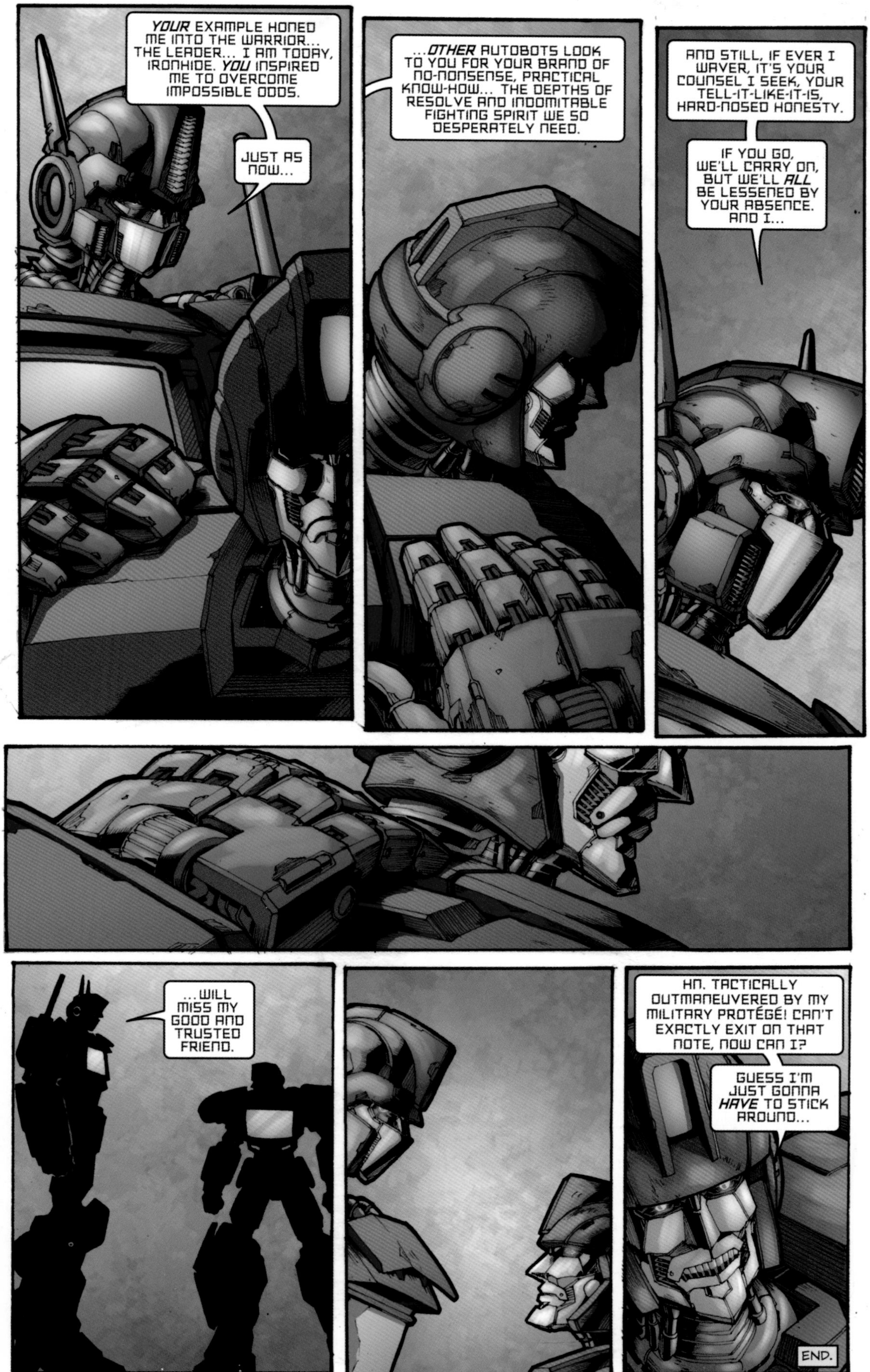
YOUR EXAMPLE HONED ME INTO THE WARRIOR... THE LEADER... I AM TODAY, IRONHIDE. YOU INSPIRED ME TO OVERCOME IMPOSSIBLE ODDS.
JUST AS NOW...
...OTHER AUTOBOTS LOOK TO YOU FOR YOUR BRAND OF NO-NONSENSE, PRACTICAL KNOW-HOW... THE DEPTHS OF RESOLVE AND INDOMITABLE FIGHTING SPIRIT WE SO DESPERATELY NEED.
AND STILL, IF EVER I WAVER, IT'S YOUR COUNSEL I SEEK, YOUR TELL-IT-LIKE-IT-IS, HARD-NOSED HONESTY.
IF YOU GO, WE'LL CARRY ON, BUT WE'LL ALL BE LESSENED BY YOUR ABSENCE. AND I...
...WILL MISS MY GOOD AND TRUSTED FRIEND.
HN. TACTICALLY OUTMANEUVERED BY MY MILITARY PROTÉGÉ! CAN'T EXACTLY EXIT ON THAT NOTE, NOW CAN I?
GUESS I'M JUST GONNA HAVE TO STICK AROUND...
END.

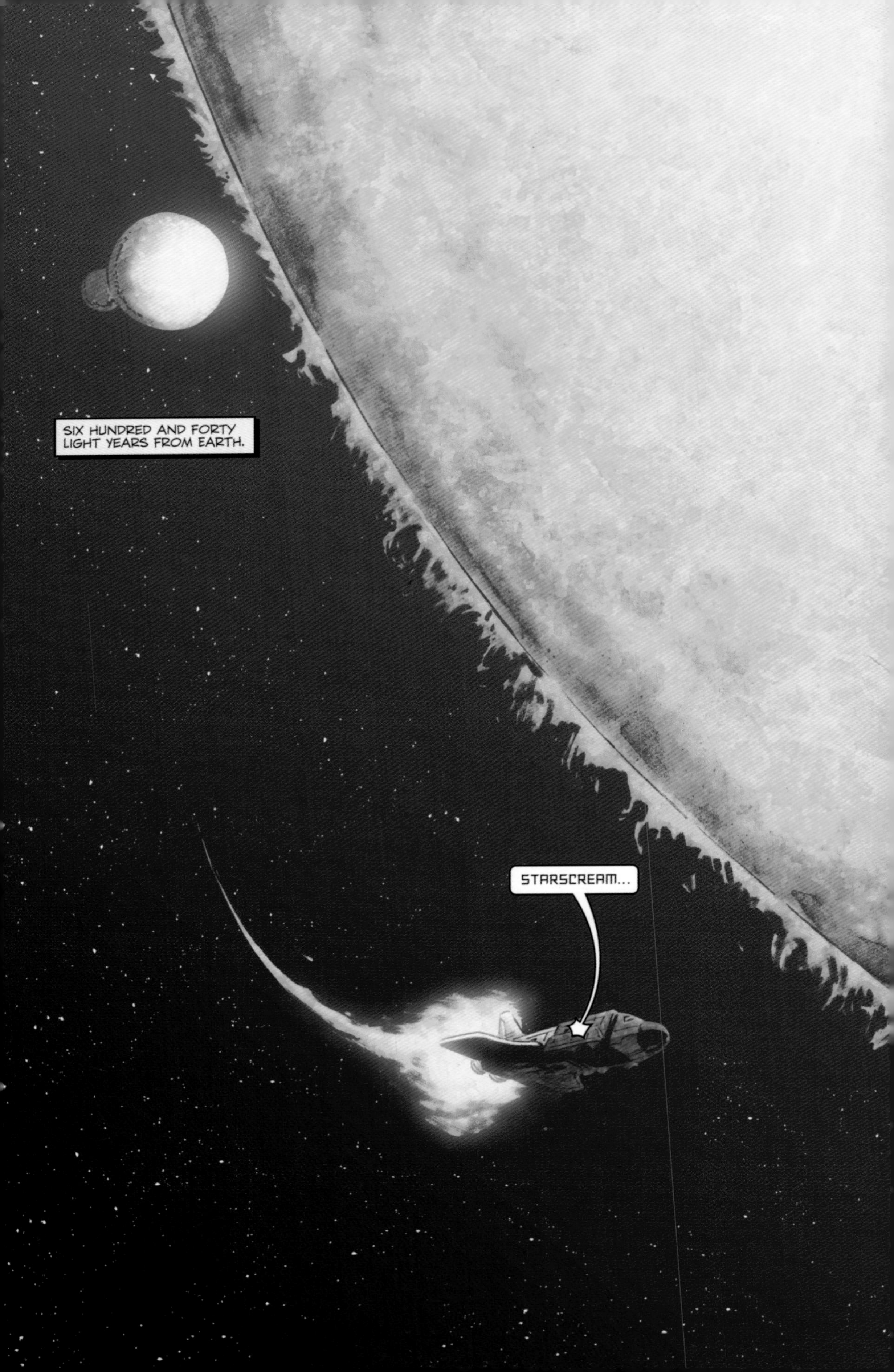
SIX HUNDRED AND FORTY LIGHT YEARS FROM EARTH.
STARSCREAM...

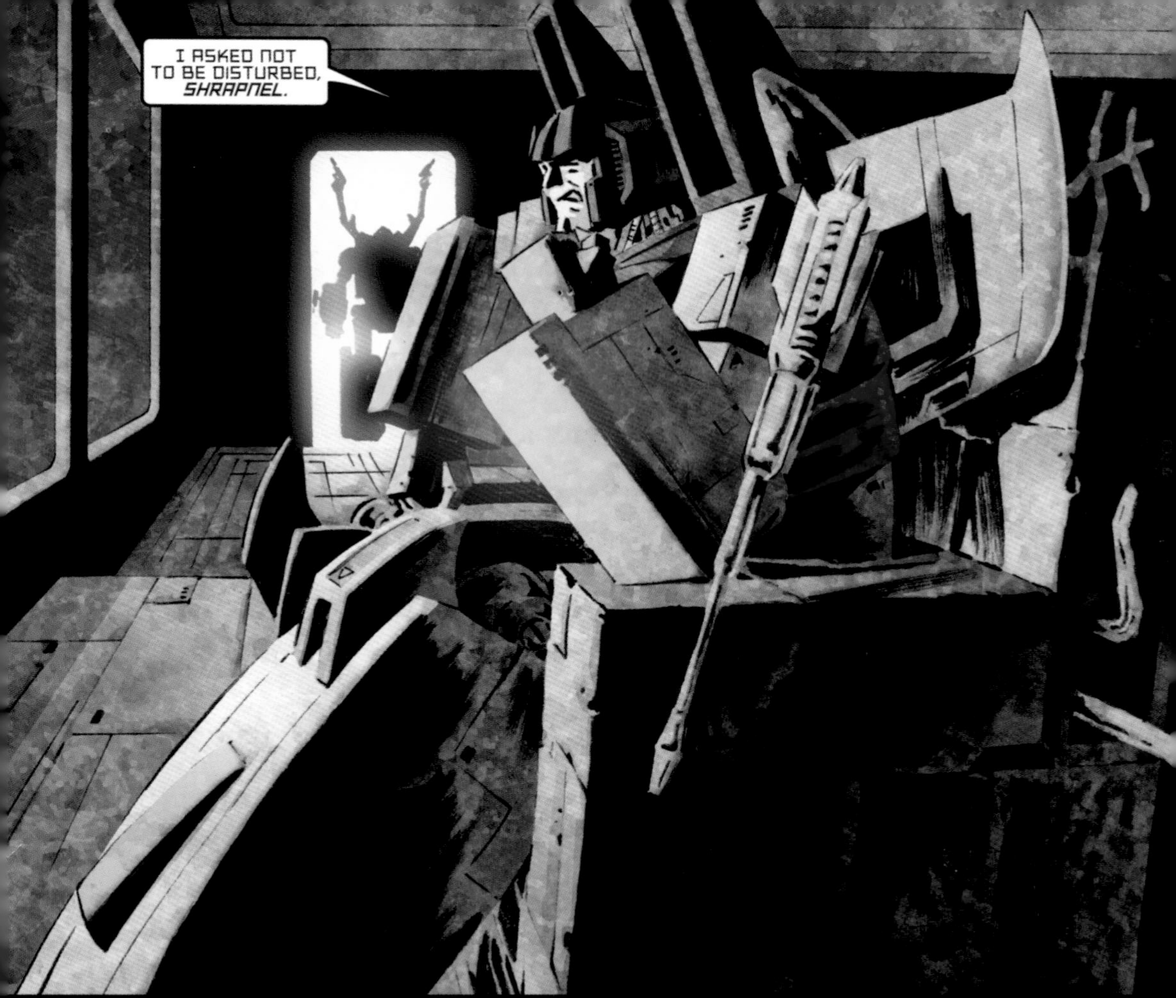
I ASKED NOT TO BE DISTURBED, *SHRAPNEL*.

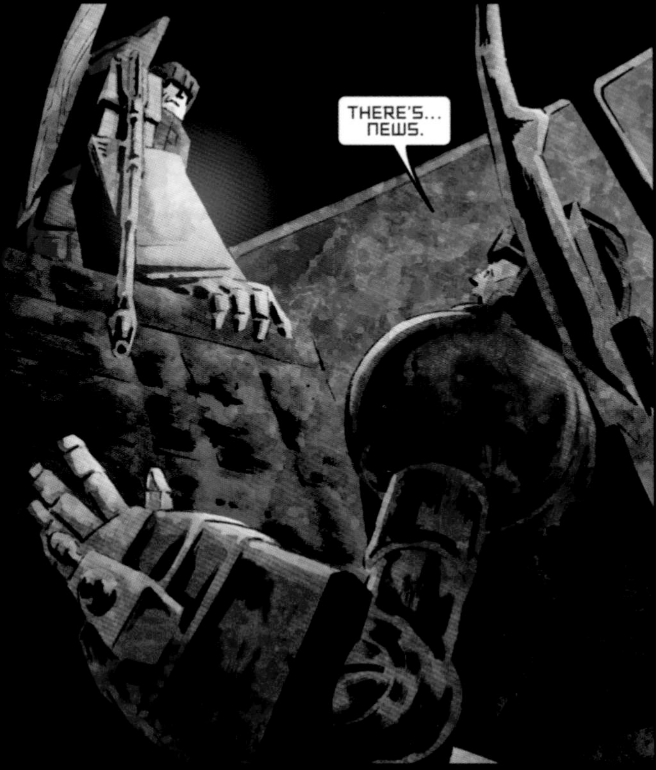
THERE'S... NEWS.

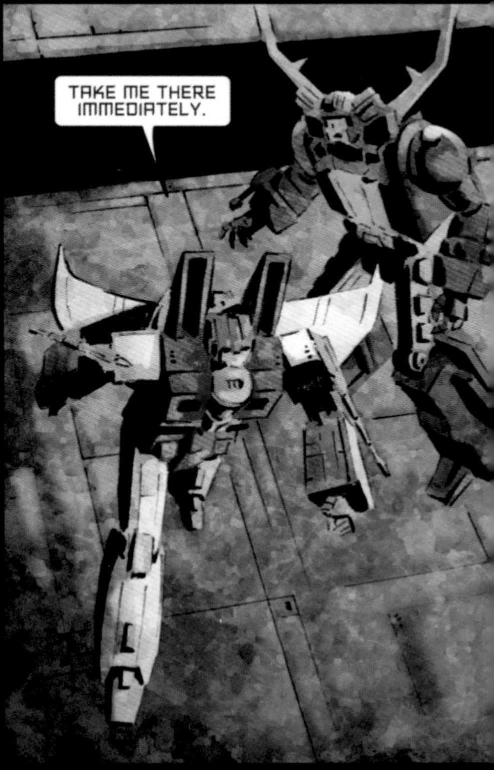
TAKE ME THERE IMMEDIATELY.

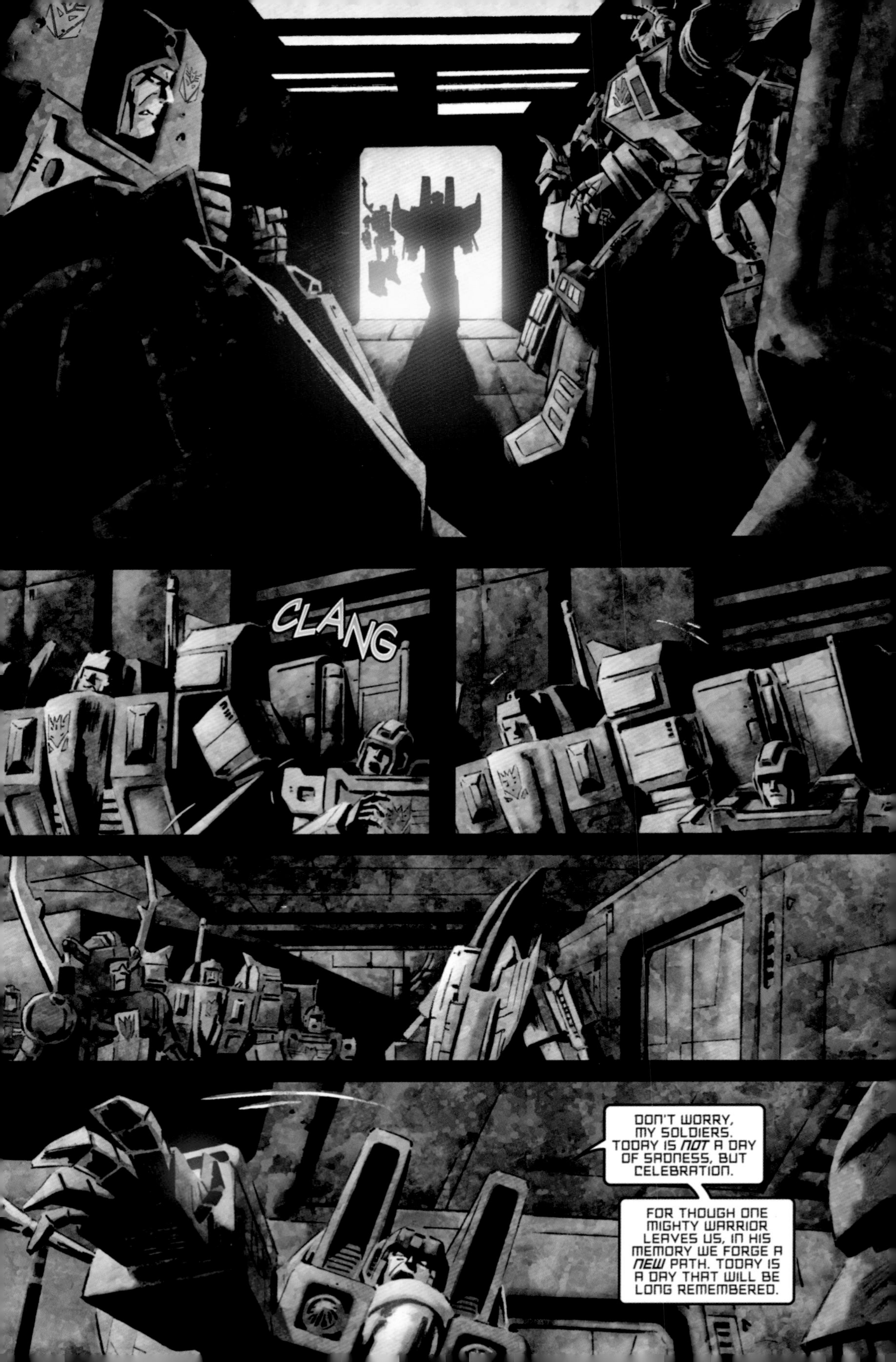
CLANG
DON'T WORRY, MY SOLDIERS. TODAY IS *NOT* A DAY OF SADNESS, BUT CELEBRATION.
FOR THOUGH ONE MIGHTY WARRIOR LEAVES US, IN HIS MEMORY WE FORGE A *NEW* PATH. TODAY IS A DAY THAT WILL BE LONG REMEMBERED.

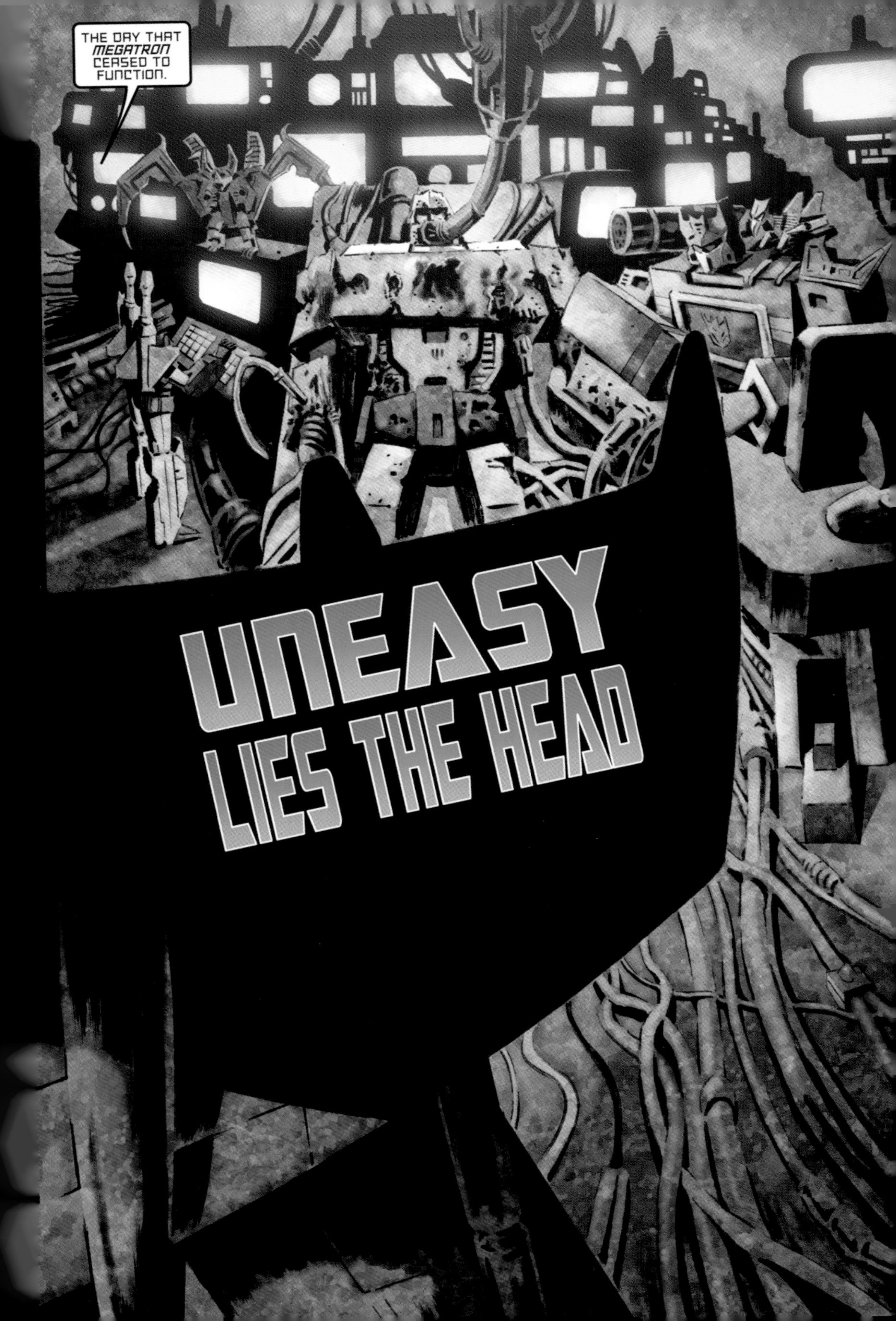

THE DAY THAT MEGATRON CEASED TO FUNCTION.
UNEASY LIES THE HEAD

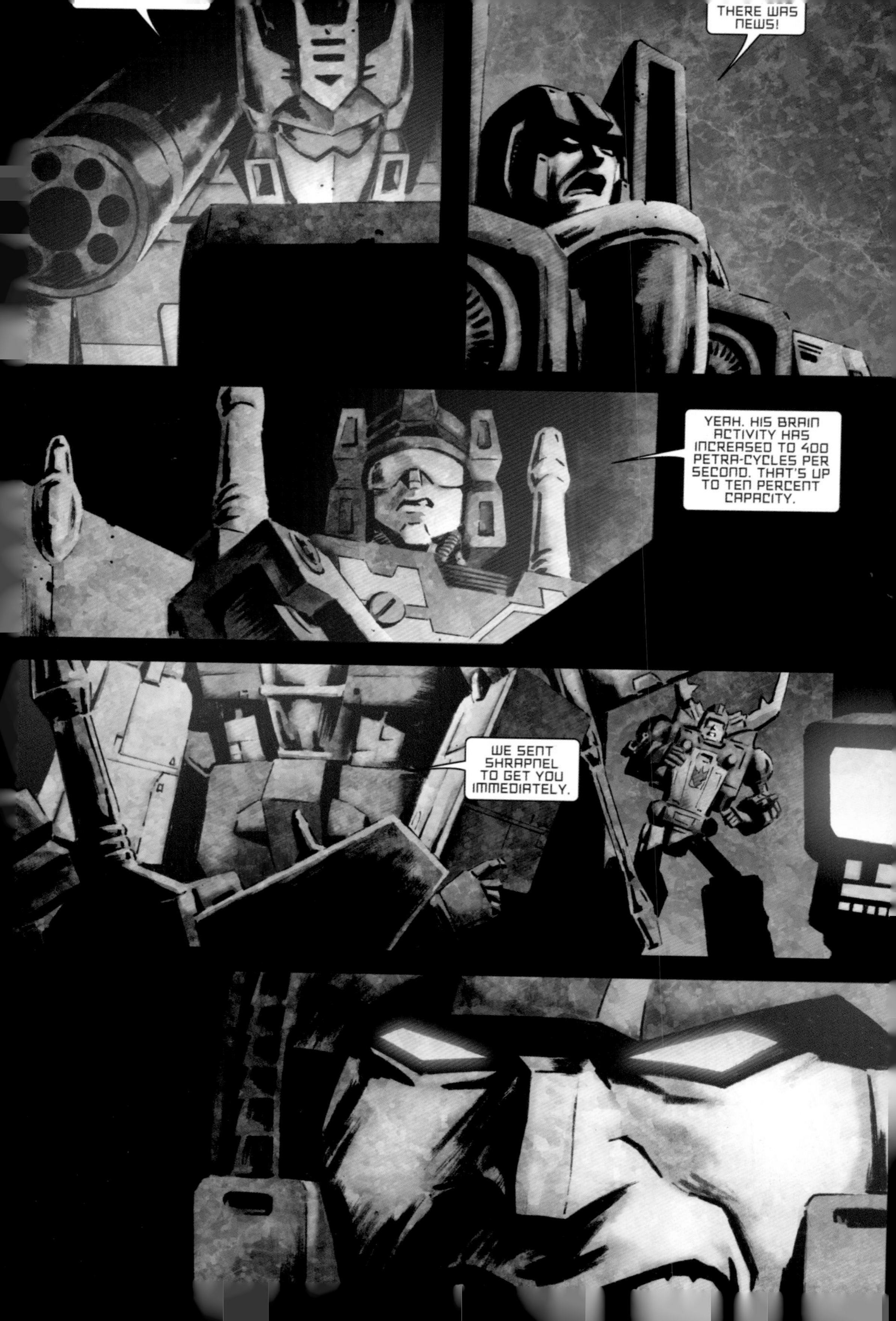
THERE WAS NEWS!
YEAH. HIS BRAIN ACTIVITY HAS INCREASED TO 400 PETRA-CYCLES PER SECOND. THAT'S UP TO TEN PERCENT CAPACITY.
WE SENT SHRAPNEL TO GET YOU IMMEDIATELY.

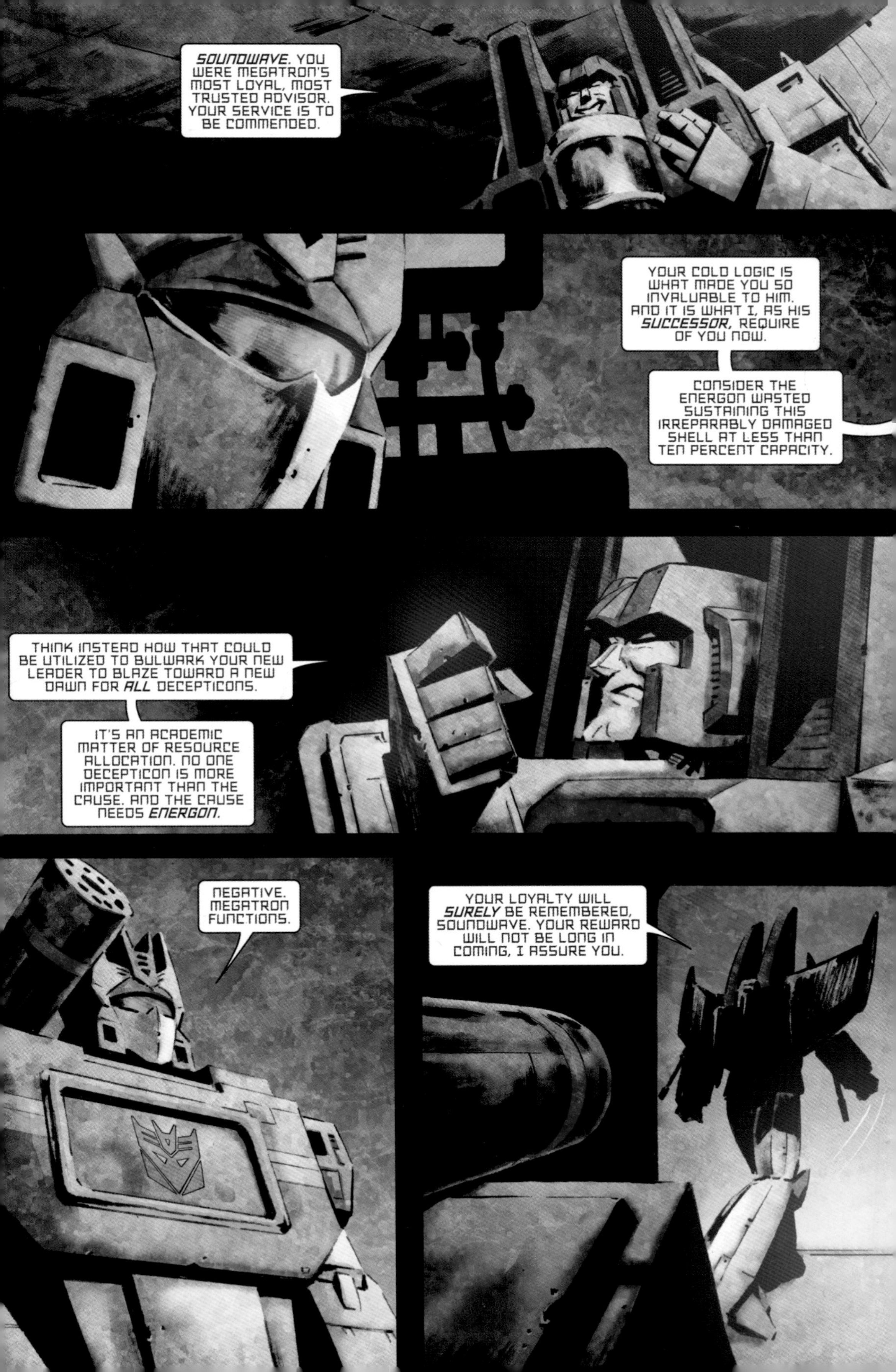
SOUNDWAVE. YOU WERE MEGATRON'S MOST LOYAL, MOST TRUSTED ADVISOR. YOUR SERVICE IS TO BE COMMENDED.
YOUR COLD LOGIC IS WHAT MADE YOU SO INVALUABLE TO HIM. AND IT IS WHAT I, AS HIS SUCCESSOR, REQUIRE OF YOU NOW.
CONSIDER THE ENERGON WASTED SUSTAINING THIS IRREPARABLY DAMAGED SHELL AT LESS THAN TEN PERCENT CAPACITY.
THINK INSTEAD HOW THAT COULD BE UTILIZED TO BULWARK YOUR NEW LEADER TO BLAZE TOWARD A NEW DAWN FOR ALL DECEPTICONS.
IT'S AN ACADEMIC MATTER OF RESOURCE ALLOCATION. NO ONE DECEPTICON IS MORE IMPORTANT THAN THE CAUSE. AND THE CAUSE NEEDS ENERGON.
NEGATIVE. MEGATRON FUNCTIONS.
YOUR LOYALTY WILL SURELY BE REMEMBERED, SOUNDWAVE. YOUR REWARD WILL NOT BE LONG IN COMING, I ASSURE YOU.

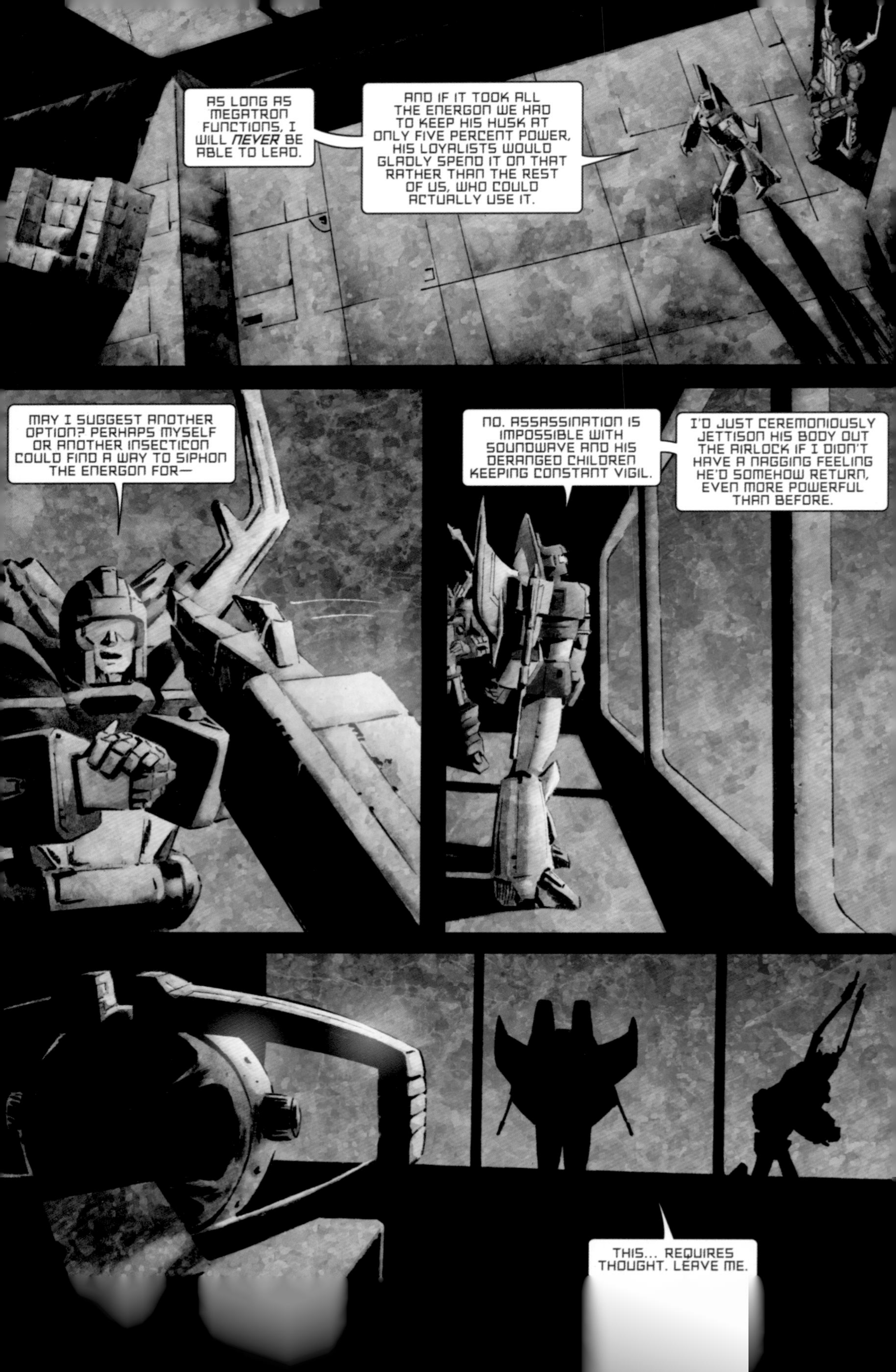
AS LONG AS MEGATRON FUNCTIONS, I WILL *NEVER* BE ABLE TO LEAD.
AND IF IT TOOK ALL THE ENERGON WE HAD TO KEEP HIS HUSK AT ONLY FIVE PERCENT POWER, HIS LOYALISTS WOULD GLADLY SPEND IT ON THAT RATHER THAN THE REST OF US, WHO COULD ACTUALLY USE IT.
MAY I SUGGEST ANOTHER OPTION? PERHAPS MYSELF OR ANOTHER INSECTICON COULD FIND A WAY TO SIPHON THE ENERGON FOR—
NO. ASSASSINATION IS IMPOSSIBLE WITH SOUNDWAVE AND HIS DERANGED CHILDREN KEEPING CONSTANT VIGIL.
I'D JUST CEREMONIOUSLY JETTISON HIS BODY OUT THE AIRLOCK IF I DIDN'T HAVE A NAGGING FEELING HE'D SOMEHOW RETURN, EVEN MORE POWERFUL THAN BEFORE.
THIS... REQUIRES THOUGHT. LEAVE ME.

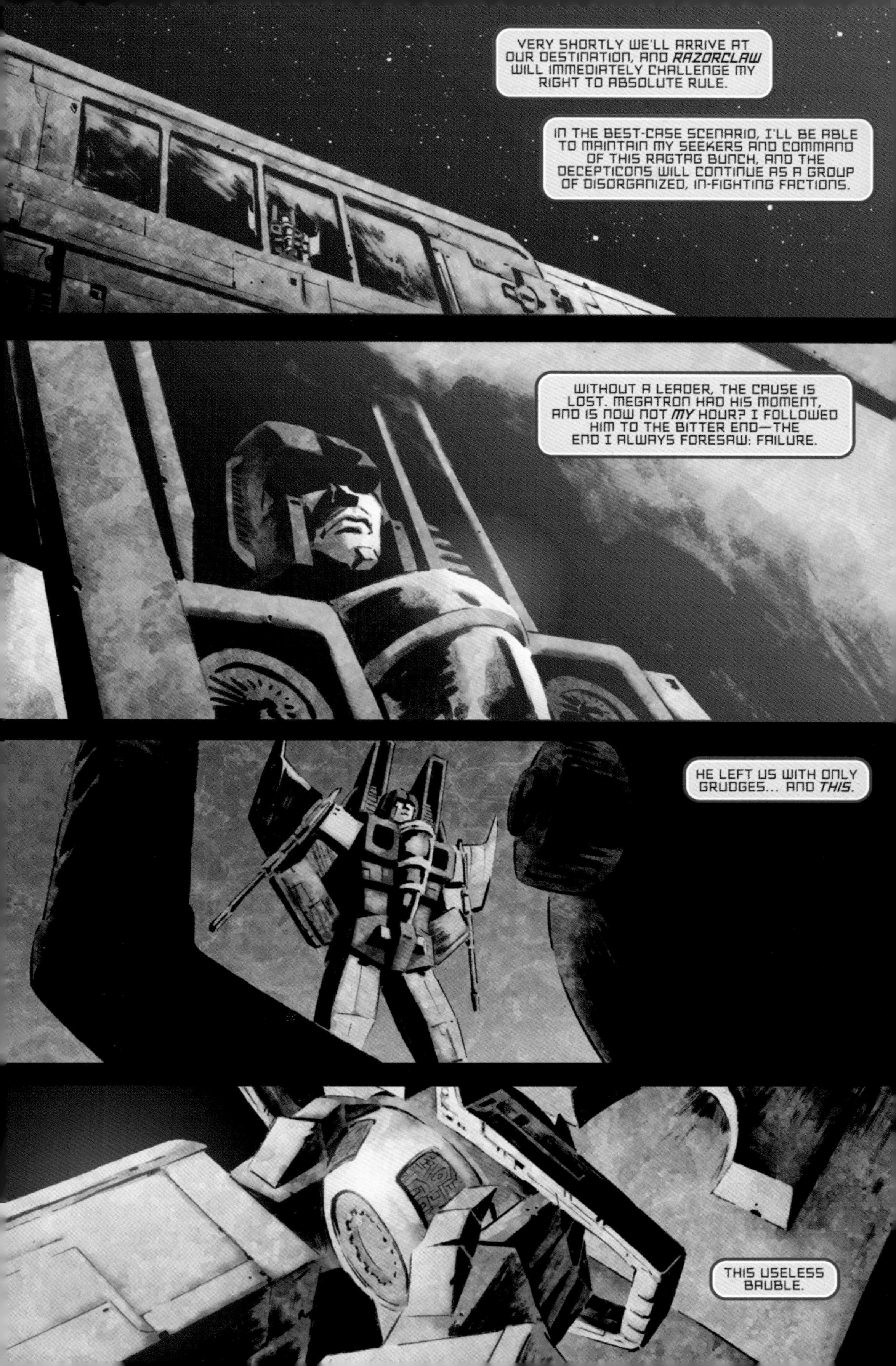
VERY SHORTLY WE'LL ARRIVE AT OUR DESTINATION, AND *RAZORCLAW* WILL IMMEDIATELY CHALLENGE MY RIGHT TO ABSOLUTE RULE.
IN THE BEST-CASE SCENARIO, I'LL BE ABLE TO MAINTAIN MY SEEKERS AND COMMAND OF THIS RAGTAG BUNCH, AND THE DECEPTICONS WILL CONTINUE AS A GROUP OF DISORGANIZED, IN-FIGHTING FACTIONS.
WITHOUT A LEADER, THE CAUSE IS LOST. MEGATRON HAD HIS MOMENT, AND IS NOW NOT *MY* HOUR? I FOLLOWED HIM TO THE BITTER END—THE END I ALWAYS FORESAW: FAILURE.
HE LEFT US WITH ONLY GRUDGES... AND *THIS*.
THIS USELESS BAUBLE.

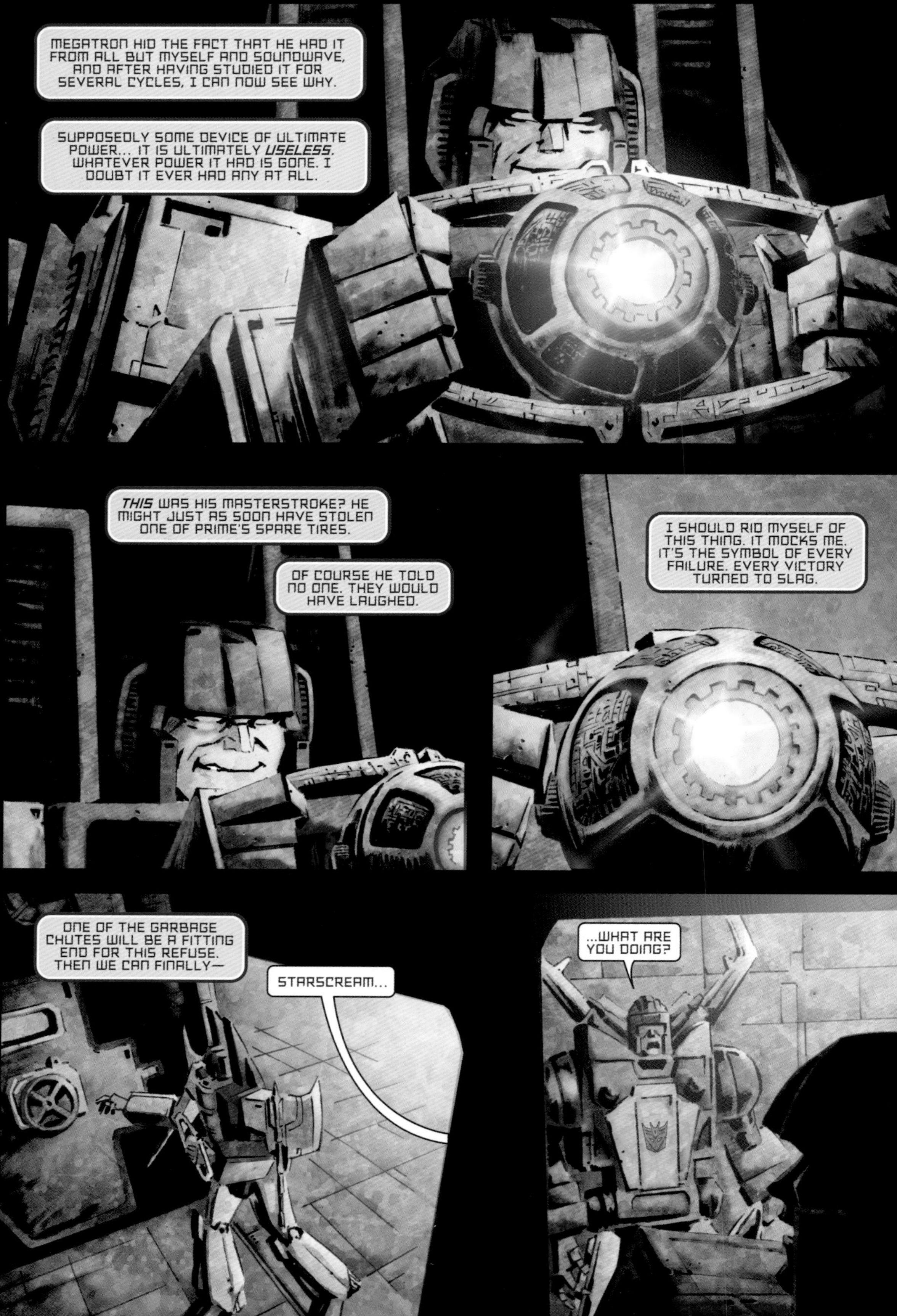
MEGATRON HID THE FACT THAT HE HAD IT FROM ALL BUT MYSELF AND SOUNDWAVE, AND AFTER HAVING STUDIED IT FOR SEVERAL CYCLES, I CAN NOW SEE WHY.
SUPPOSEDLY SOME DEVICE OF ULTIMATE POWER... IT IS ULTIMATELY *USELESS.* WHATEVER POWER IT HAD IS GONE. I DOUBT IT EVER HAD ANY AT ALL.
THIS WAS HIS MASTERSTROKE? HE MIGHT JUST AS SOON HAVE STOLEN ONE OF PRIME'S SPARE TIRES.
OF COURSE HE TOLD NO ONE. THEY WOULD HAVE LAUGHED.
I SHOULD RID MYSELF OF THIS THING. IT MOCKS ME. IT'S THE SYMBOL OF EVERY FAILURE. EVERY VICTORY TURNED TO SLAG.
ONE OF THE GARBAGE CHUTES WILL BE A FITTING END FOR THIS REFUSE. THEN WE CAN FINALLY—
STARSCREAM...
...WHAT ARE YOU DOING?

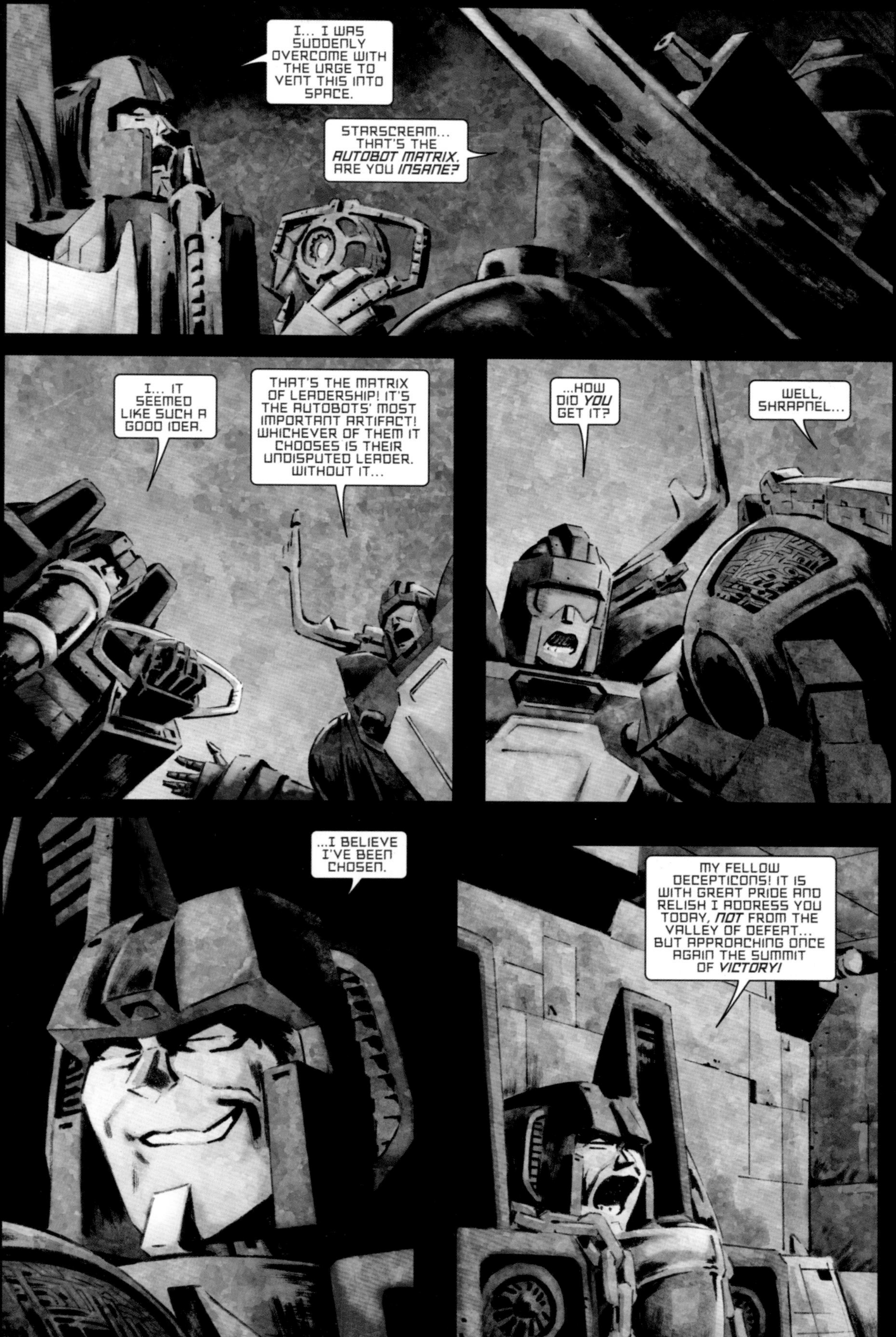

I... I WAS SUDDENLY OVERCOME WITH THE URGE TO VENT THIS INTO SPACE.
STARSCREAM... THAT'S THE *AUTOBOT MATRIX.* ARE YOU *INSANE?*
I... IT SEEMED LIKE SUCH A GOOD IDEA.
THAT'S THE MATRIX OF LEADERSHIP! IT'S THE AUTOBOTS' MOST IMPORTANT ARTIFACT! WHICHEVER OF THEM IT CHOOSES IS THEIR UNDISPUTED LEADER. WITHOUT IT...
...HOW DID *YOU* GET IT?
WELL, SHRAPNEL...
...I BELIEVE I'VE BEEN CHOSEN.
MY FELLOW DECEPTICONS! IT IS WITH GREAT PRIDE AND RELISH I ADDRESS YOU TODAY, *NOT* FROM THE VALLEY OF DEFEAT... BUT APPROACHING ONCE AGAIN THE SUMMIT OF *VICTORY!*

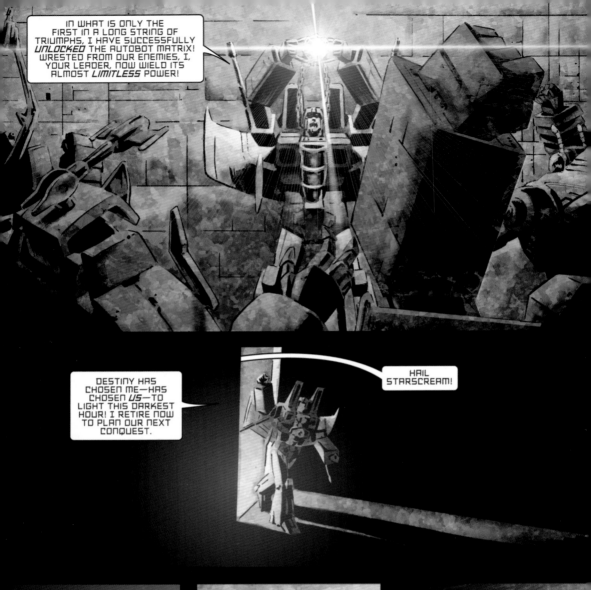

IN WHAT IS ONLY THE FIRST IN A LONG STRING OF TRIUMPHS, I HAVE SUCCESSFULLY *UNLOCKED* THE AUTOBOT MATRIX! WRESTED FROM OUR ENEMIES, I, YOUR LEADER, NOW WIELD ITS ALMOST *LIMITLESS* POWER!

DESTINY HAS CHOSEN ME—HAS CHOSEN *US*—TO LIGHT THIS DARKEST HOUR! I RETIRE NOW TO PLAN OUR NEXT CONQUEST.

HAIL STARSCREAM!

HAIL! HAIL!

HAIL! HAIL!

HAIL! HAIL!

THE END.

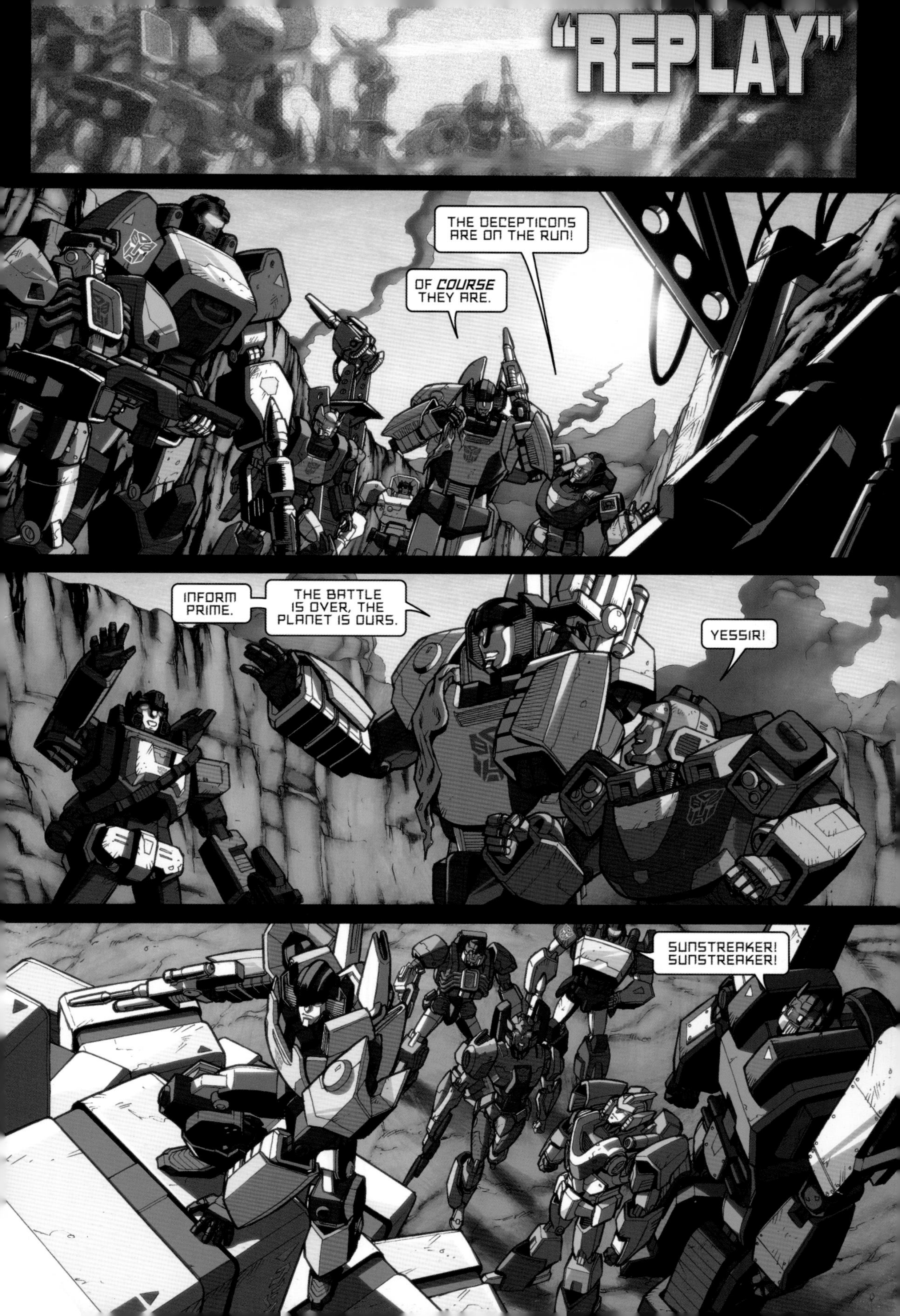
"REPLAY"
THE DECEPTICONS ARE ON THE RUN!
OF COURSE THEY ARE.
INFORM PRIME.
THE BATTLE IS OVER, THE PLANET IS OURS.
YESSIR!
SUNSTREAKER! SUNSTREAKER!

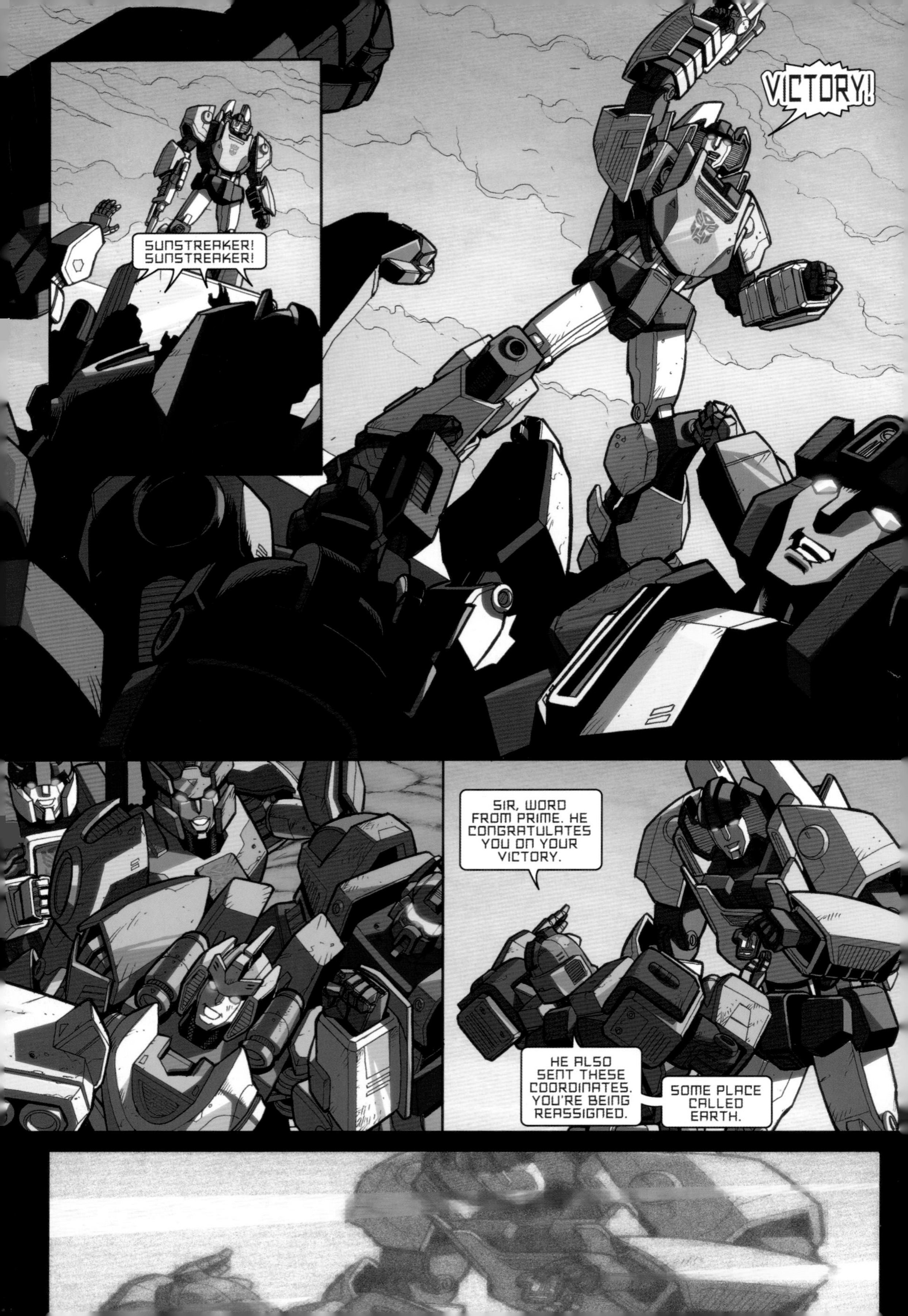
SUNSTREAKER! SUNSTREAKER!
VICTORY!
SIR, WORD FROM PRIME. HE CONGRATULATES YOU ON YOUR VICTORY.
HE ALSO SENT THESE COORDINATES. YOU'RE BEING REASSIGNED.
SOME PLACE CALLED EARTH.

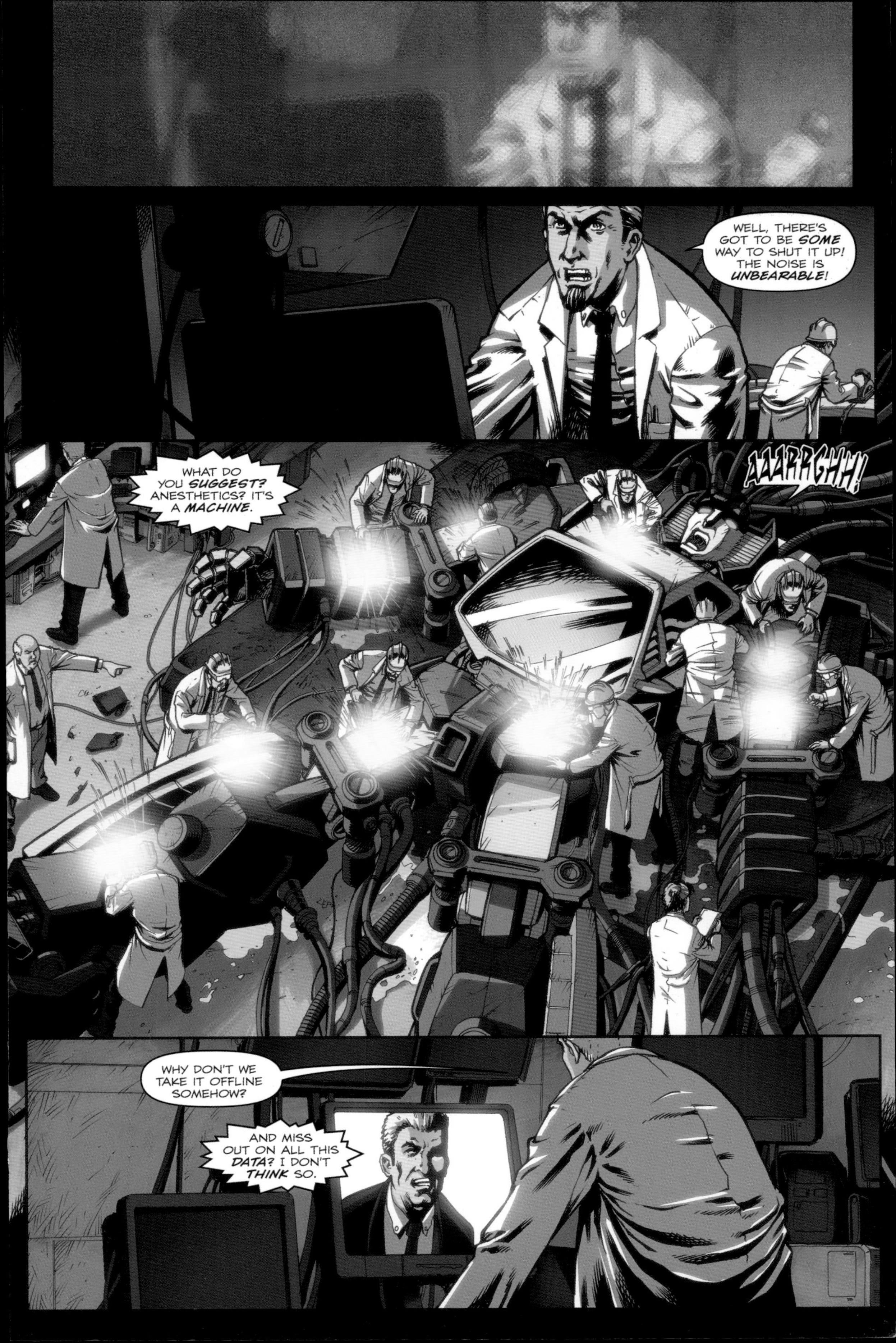
WELL, THERE'S GOT TO BE SOME WAY TO SHUT IT UP! THE NOISE IS UNBEARABLE!
WHAT DO YOU SUGGEST? ANESTHETICS? IT'S A MACHINE.
AAARRGHH!
WHY DON'T WE TAKE IT OFFLINE SOMEHOW?
AND MISS OUT ON ALL THIS DATA? I DON'T THINK SO.

I WANT ALL THE READINGS WE CAN *GET* ON THESE THINGS.

IT'S A *MACHINE*, DOUGLAS, A PIECE OF *METAL*. IT'S NOT AS THOUGH IT CAN FEEL PAIN LIKE *WE* DO.

IT'S AN *AUTOMATED* RESPONSE.

THEN GET YOURSELF SOME *EARPLUGS* AND GET *ON* WITH IT.

I DON'T CARE ABOUT *THAT*, IT'S JUST *DISTRACTING*.

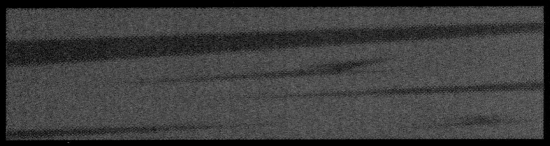

NO, DON'T.

WHAT?

DON'T, IT'S... IT'S *LOOKING* AT ME.

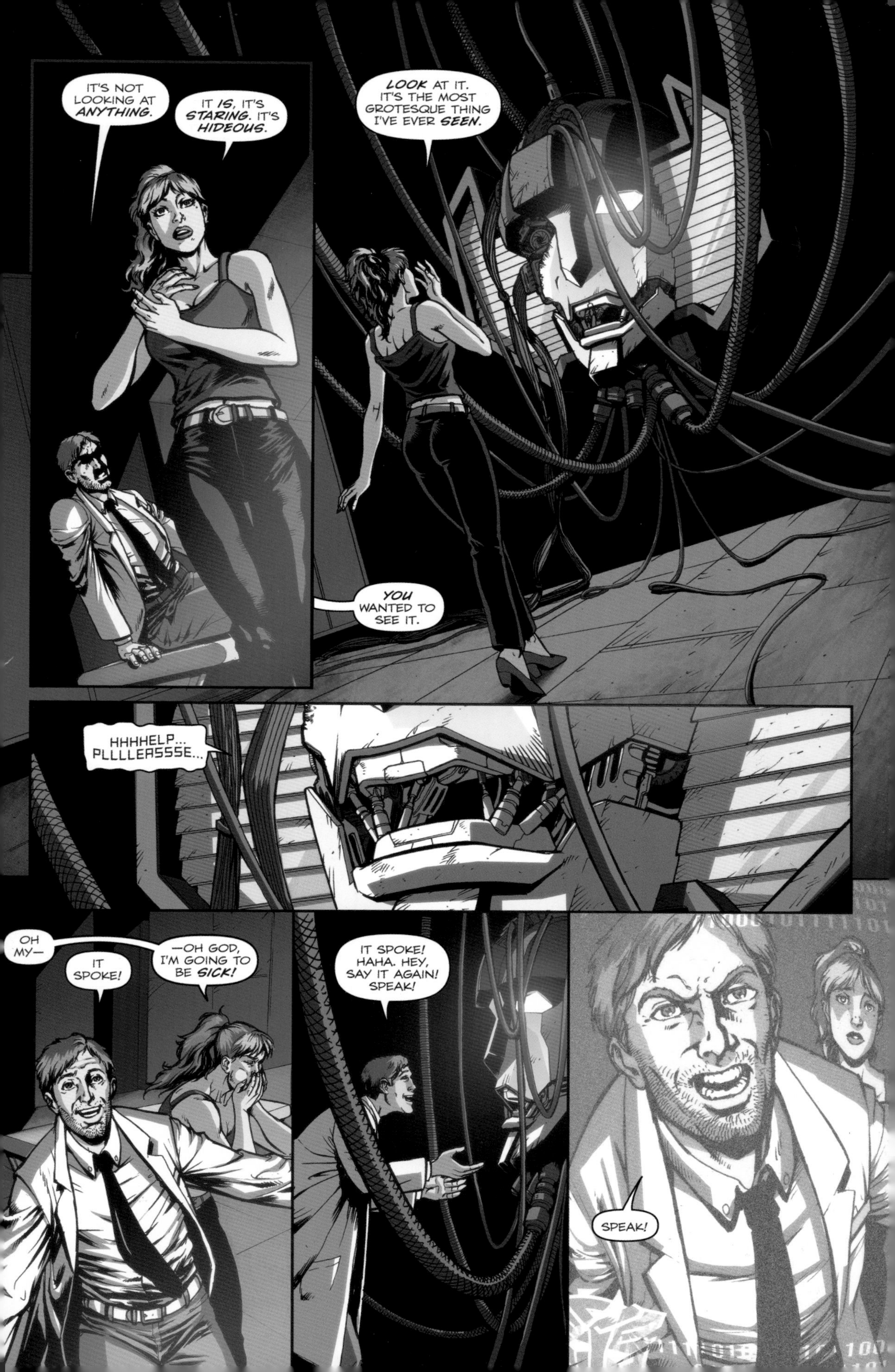
IT'S NOT LOOKING AT ANYTHING.
IT IS, IT'S STARING. IT'S HIDEOUS.
LOOK AT IT. IT'S THE MOST GROTESQUE THING I'VE EVER SEEN.
YOU WANTED TO SEE IT.
HHHHELP... PLLLLEASSSE...
OH MY—
IT SPOKE!
—OH GOD, I'M GOING TO BE SICK!
IT SPOKE! HAHA. HEY, SAY IT AGAIN! SPEAK!
SPEAK!

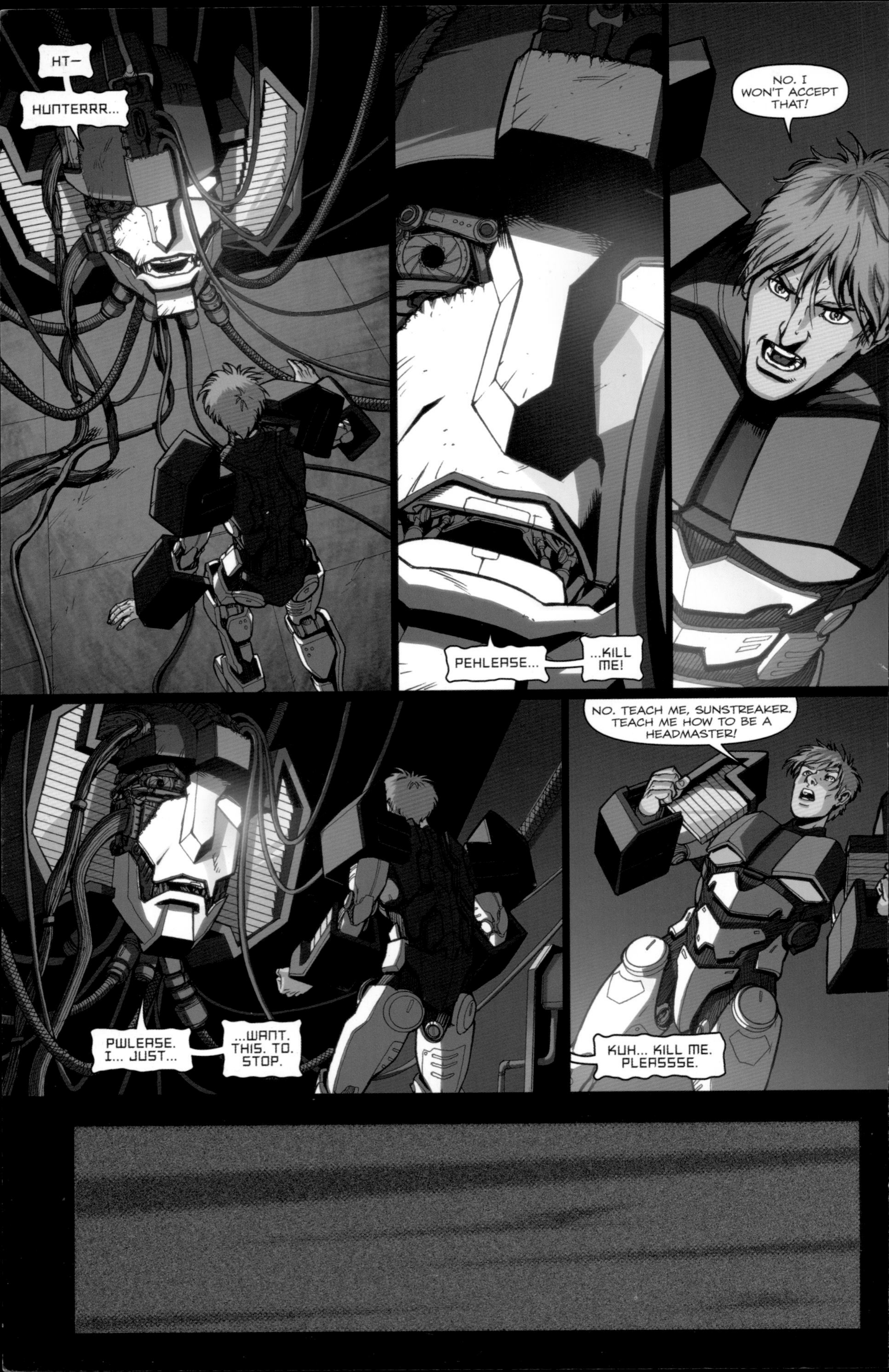

HT—
HUNTERRR...
PEHLEASE...
...KILL ME!
NO. I WON'T ACCEPT THAT!
PWLEASE. I... JUST...
...WANT. THIS. TO. STOP.
NO. TEACH ME, SUNSTREAKER. TEACH ME HOW TO BE A HEADMASTER!
KUH... KILL ME. PLEASSSE.

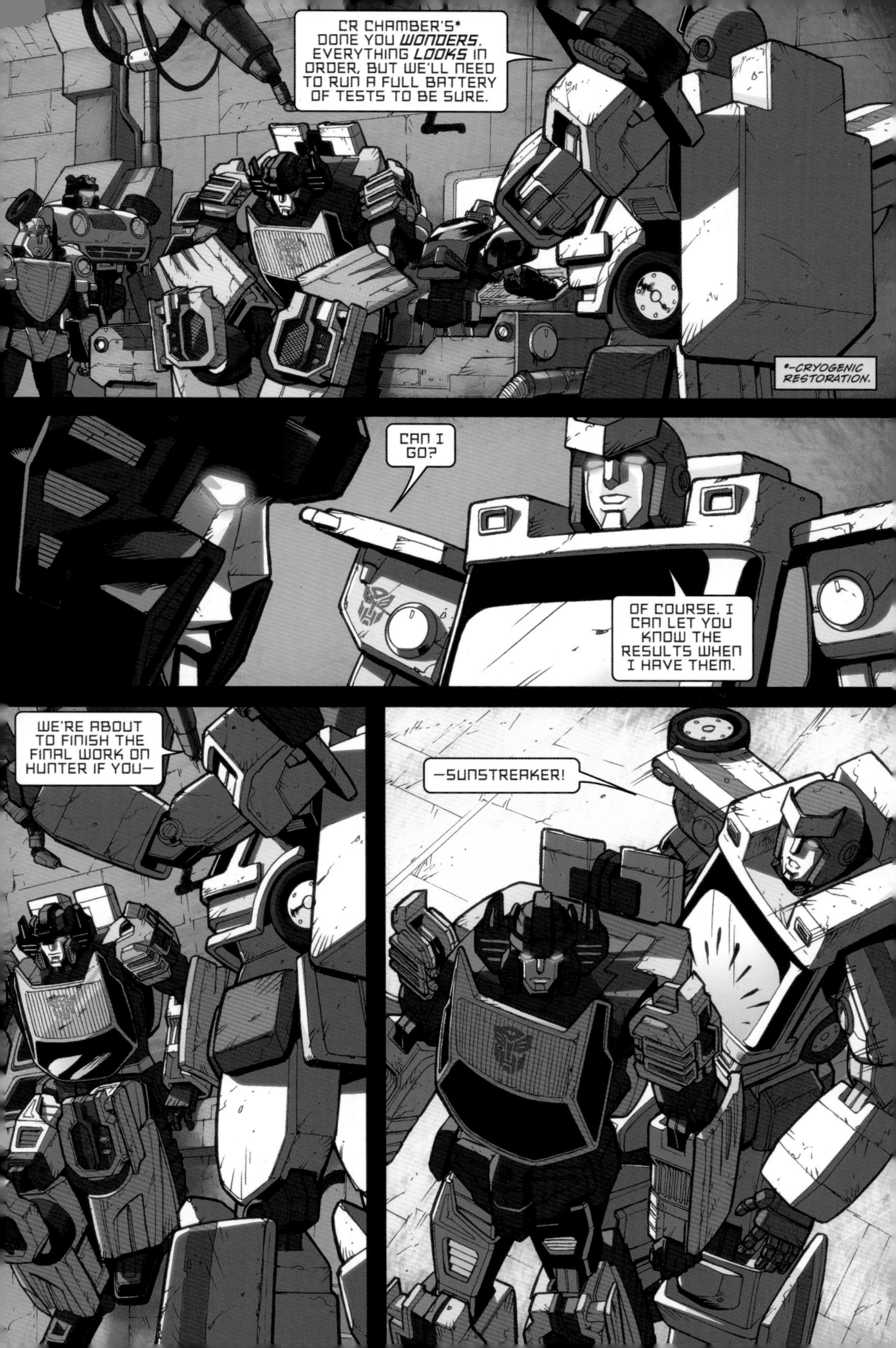
CR CHAMBER'S* DONE YOU WONDERS. EVERYTHING LOOKS IN ORDER, BUT WE'LL NEED TO RUN A FULL BATTERY OF TESTS TO BE SURE.
*--CRYOGENIC RESTORATION.
CAN I GO?
OF COURSE. I CAN LET YOU KNOW THE RESULTS WHEN I HAVE THEM.
WE'RE ABOUT TO FINISH THE FINAL WORK ON HUNTER IF YOU--
--SUNSTREAKER!

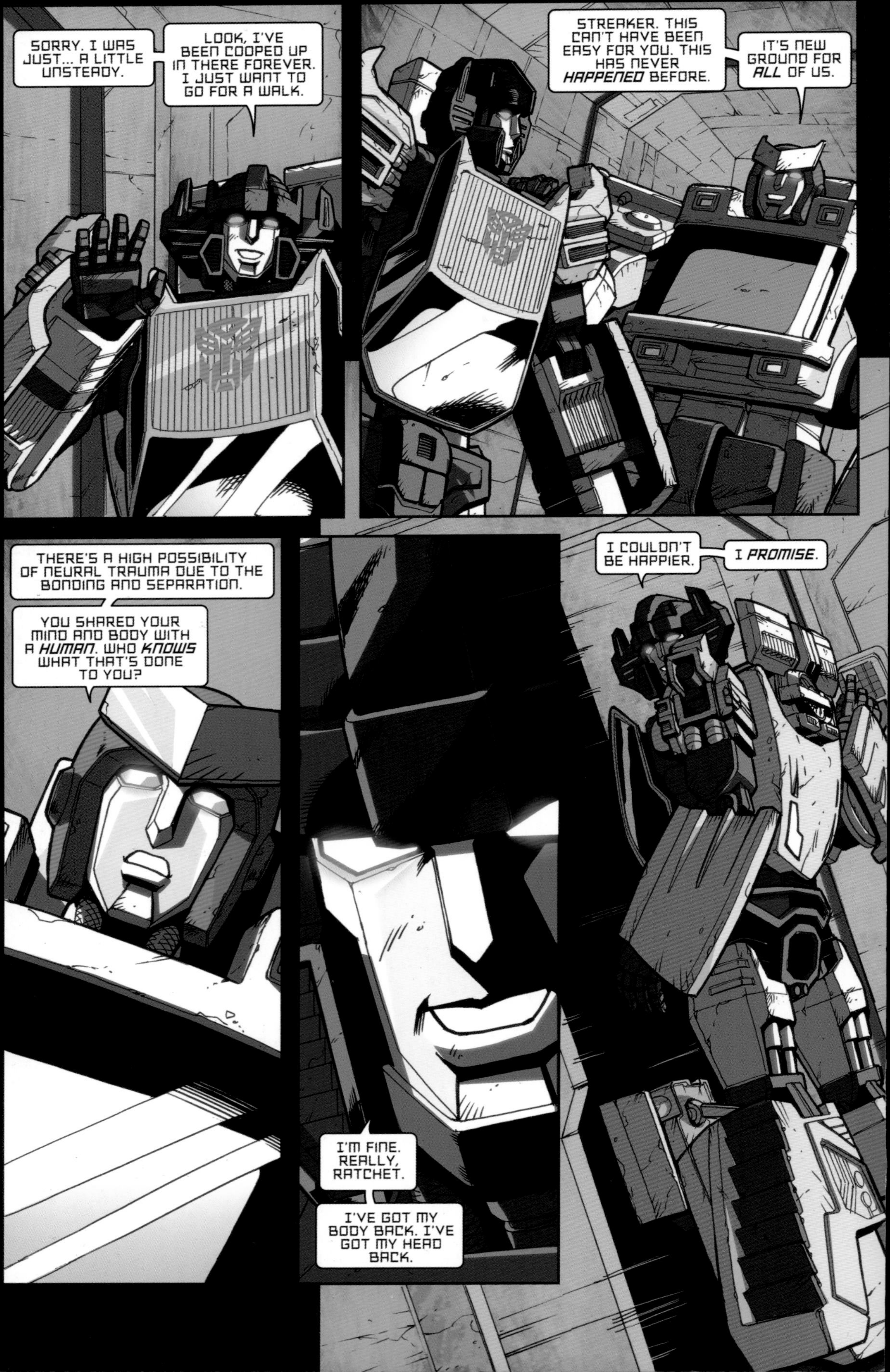
SORRY. I WAS JUST... A LITTLE UNSTEADY.
LOOK, I'VE BEEN COOPED UP IN THERE FOREVER. I JUST WANT TO GO FOR A WALK.
STREAKER. THIS CAN'T HAVE BEEN EASY FOR YOU. THIS HAS NEVER HAPPENED BEFORE.
IT'S NEW GROUND FOR ALL OF US.
THERE'S A HIGH POSSIBILITY OF NEURAL TRAUMA DUE TO THE BONDING AND SEPARATION.
YOU SHARED YOUR MIND AND BODY WITH A HUMAN. WHO KNOWS WHAT THAT'S DONE TO YOU?
I'M FINE. REALLY, RATCHET.
I'VE GOT MY BODY BACK. I'VE GOT MY HEAD BACK.
I COULDN'T BE HAPPIER.
I PROMISE.

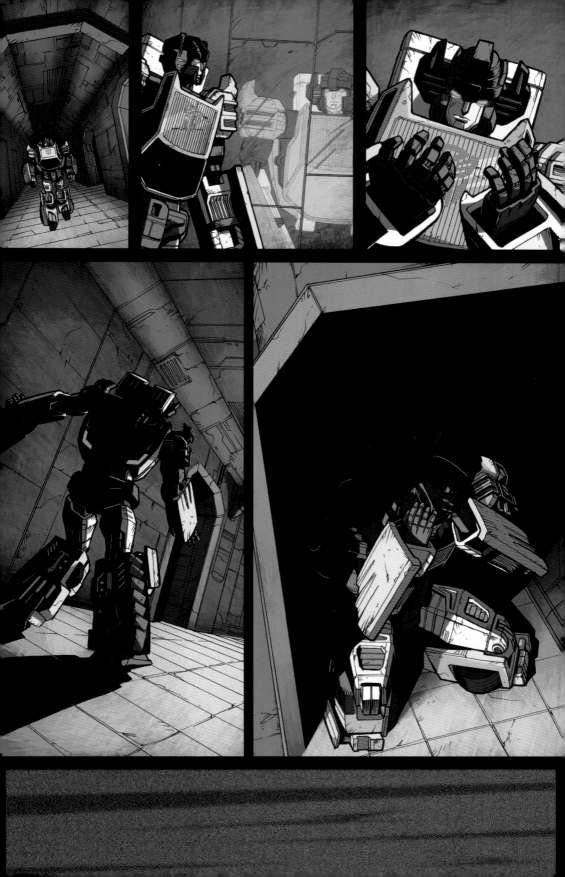

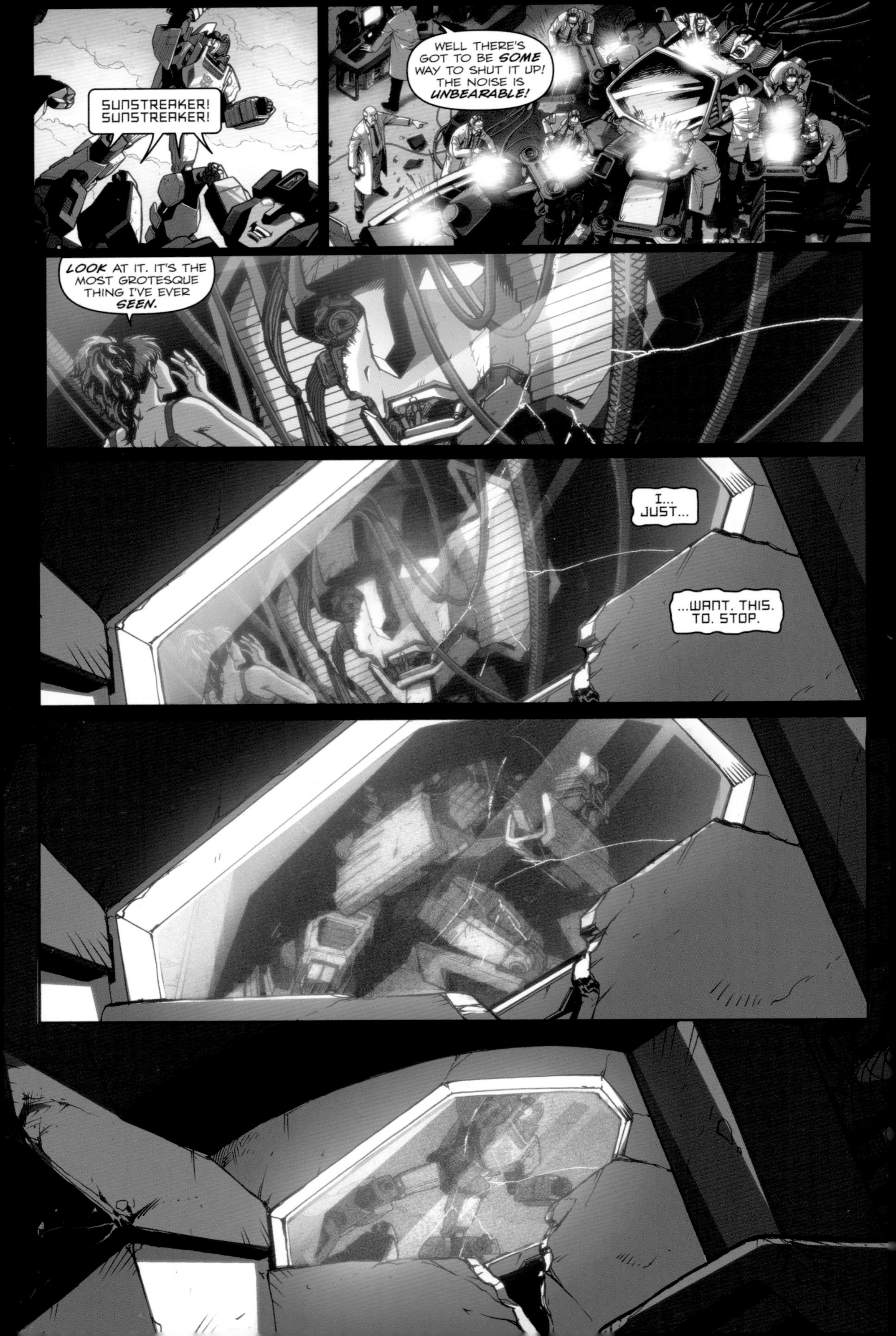

SUNSTREAKER! SUNSTREAKER!
WELL THERE'S GOT TO BE SOME WAY TO SHUT IT UP! THE NOISE IS UNBEARABLE!
LOOK AT IT. IT'S THE MOST GROTESQUE THING I'VE EVER SEEN.
I... JUST...
...WANT. THIS. TO. STOP.

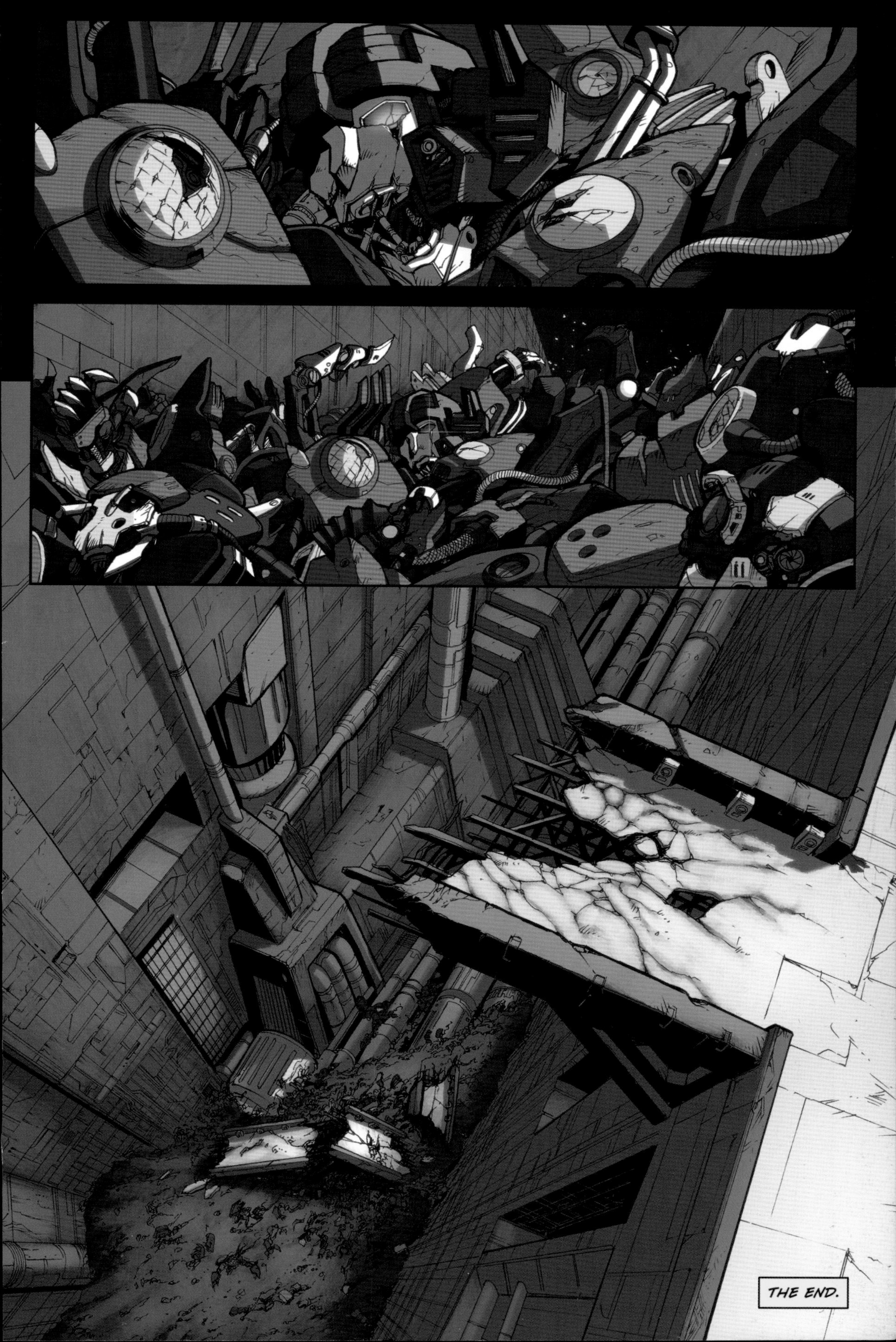
THE END.

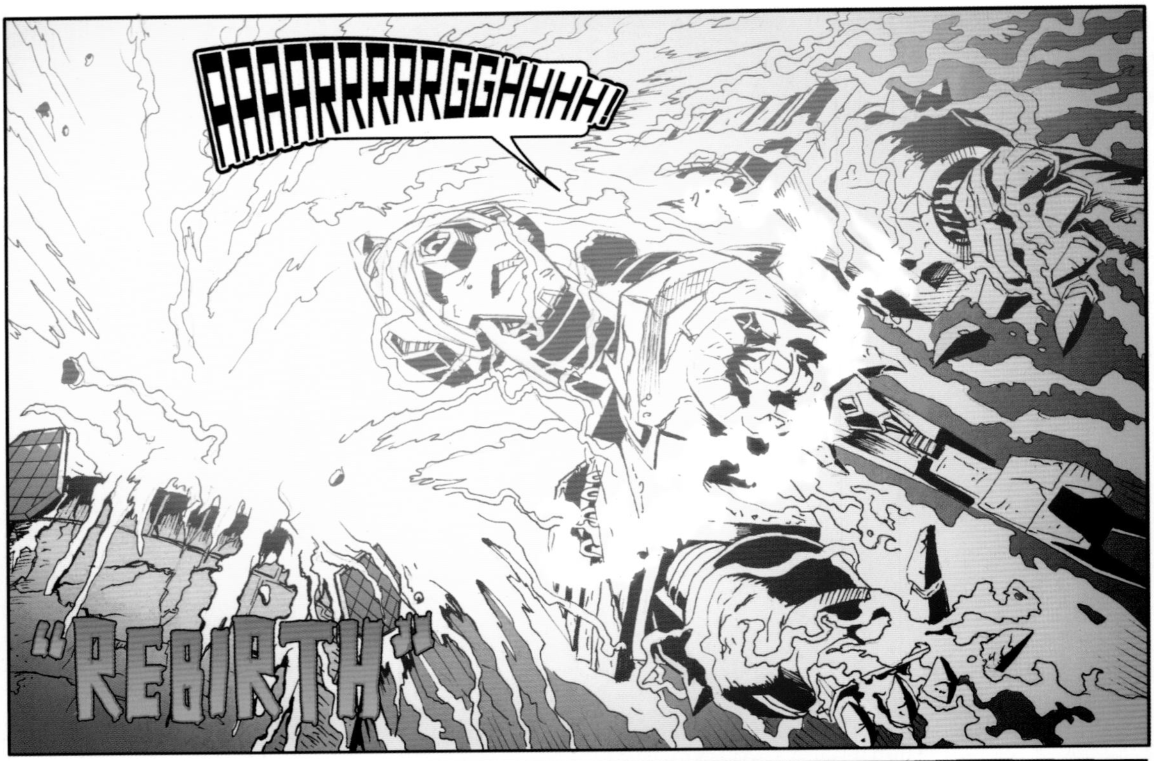
AAAARRRRRGGHHHH!
"REBIRTH"
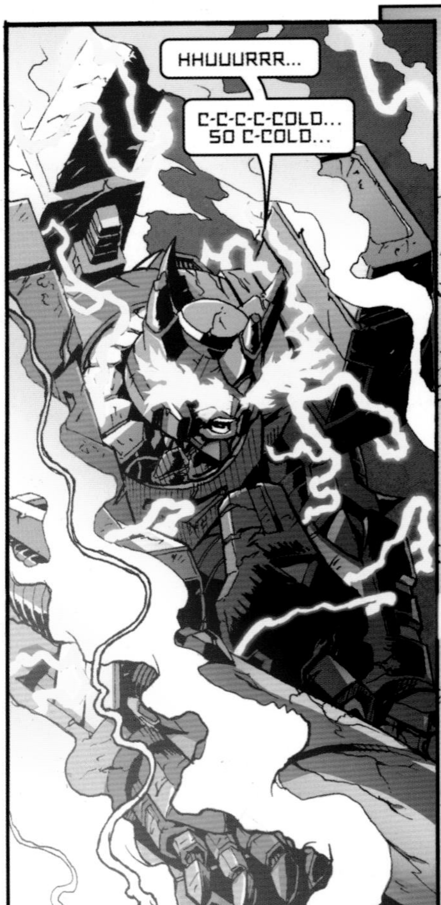
HHUUURRR...
C-C-C-C-COLD... SO C-COLD...
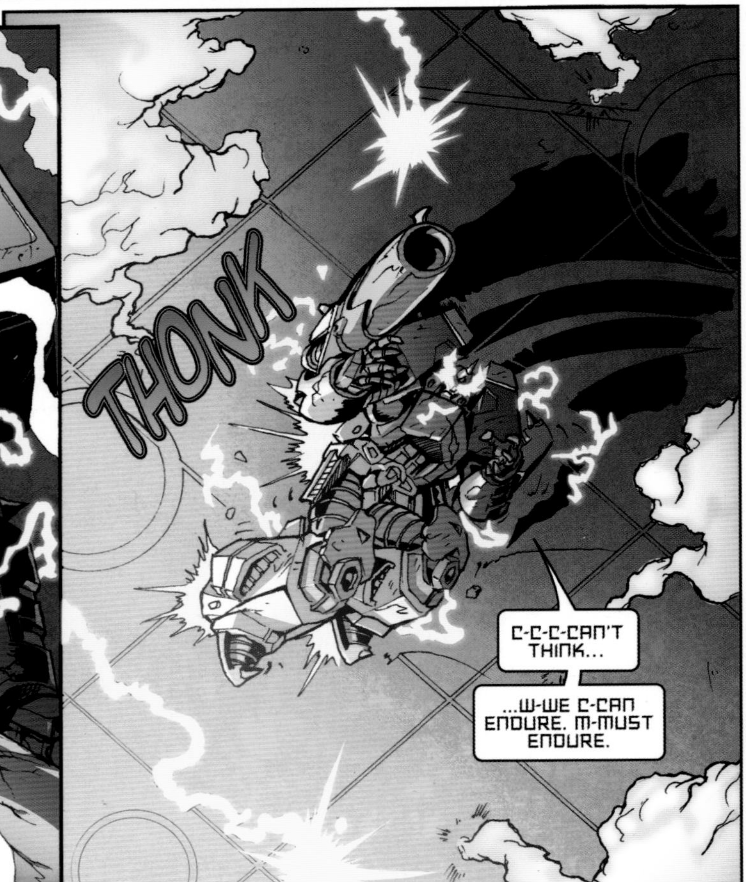
THONK
C-C-C-CAN'T THINK...
...W-WE C-CAN ENDURE. M-MUST ENDURE.

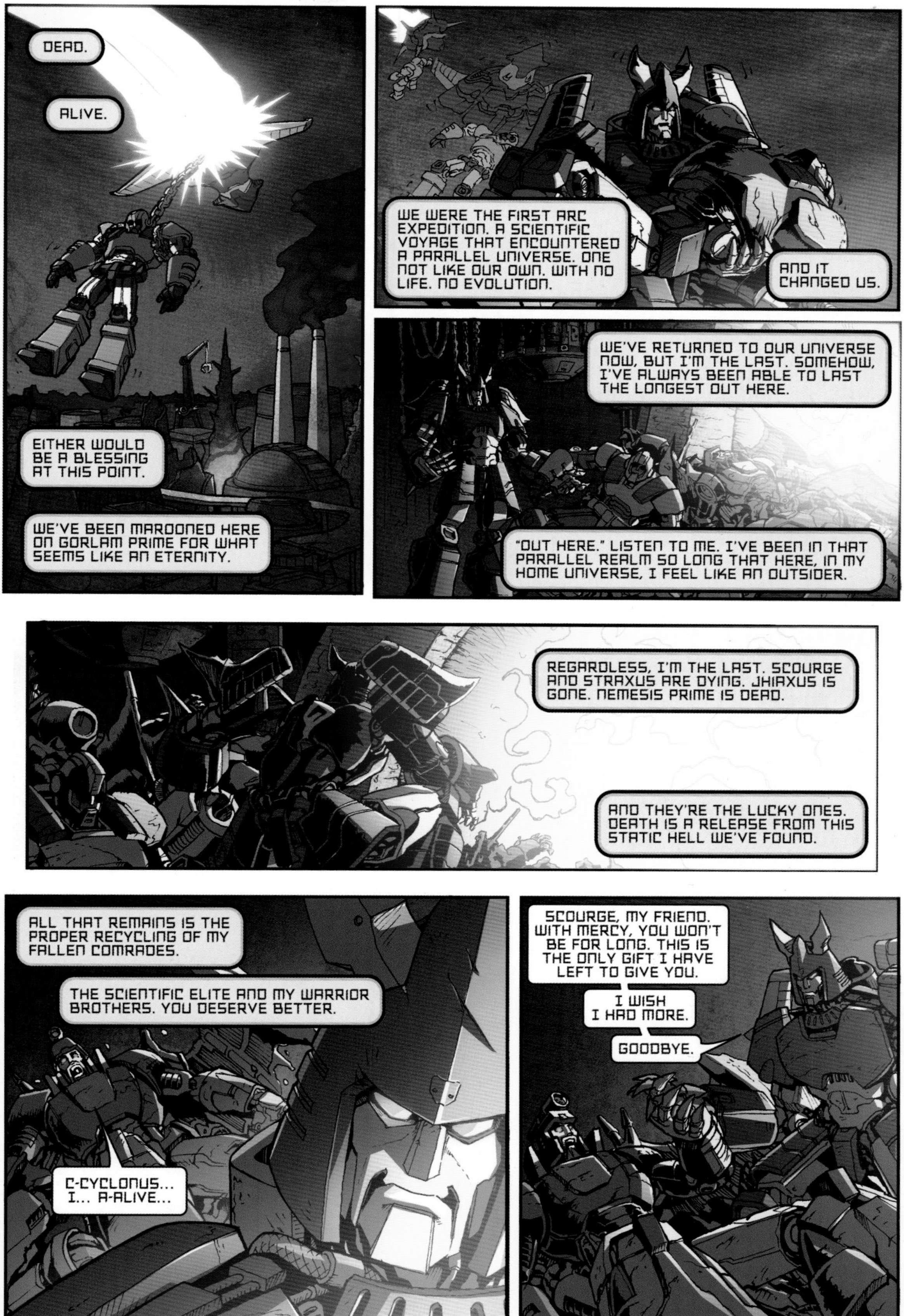
DEAD.
ALIVE.
EITHER WOULD BE A BLESSING AT THIS POINT.
WE'VE BEEN MAROONED HERE ON GORLAM PRIME FOR WHAT SEEMS LIKE AN ETERNITY.
WE WERE THE FIRST ARC EXPEDITION. A SCIENTIFIC VOYAGE THAT ENCOUNTERED A PARALLEL UNIVERSE. ONE NOT LIKE OUR OWN. WITH NO LIFE. NO EVOLUTION.
AND IT CHANGED US.
WE'VE RETURNED TO OUR UNIVERSE NOW, BUT I'M THE LAST. SOMEHOW, I'VE ALWAYS BEEN ABLE TO LAST THE LONGEST OUT HERE.
"OUT HERE." LISTEN TO ME. I'VE BEEN IN THAT PARALLEL REALM SO LONG THAT HERE, IN MY HOME UNIVERSE, I FEEL LIKE AN OUTSIDER.
REGARDLESS, I'M THE LAST. SCOURGE AND STRAXUS ARE DYING. JHIAXUS IS GONE. NEMESIS PRIME IS DEAD.
AND THEY'RE THE LUCKY ONES. DEATH IS A RELEASE FROM THIS STATIC HELL WE'VE FOUND.
ALL THAT REMAINS IS THE PROPER RECYCLING OF MY FALLEN COMRADES.
THE SCIENTIFIC ELITE AND MY WARRIOR BROTHERS. YOU DESERVE BETTER.
C-CYCLONUS... I... A-ALIVE...
SCOURGE, MY FRIEND. WITH MERCY, YOU WON'T BE FOR LONG. THIS IS THE ONLY GIFT I HAVE LEFT TO GIVE YOU.
I WISH I HAD MORE.
GOODBYE.

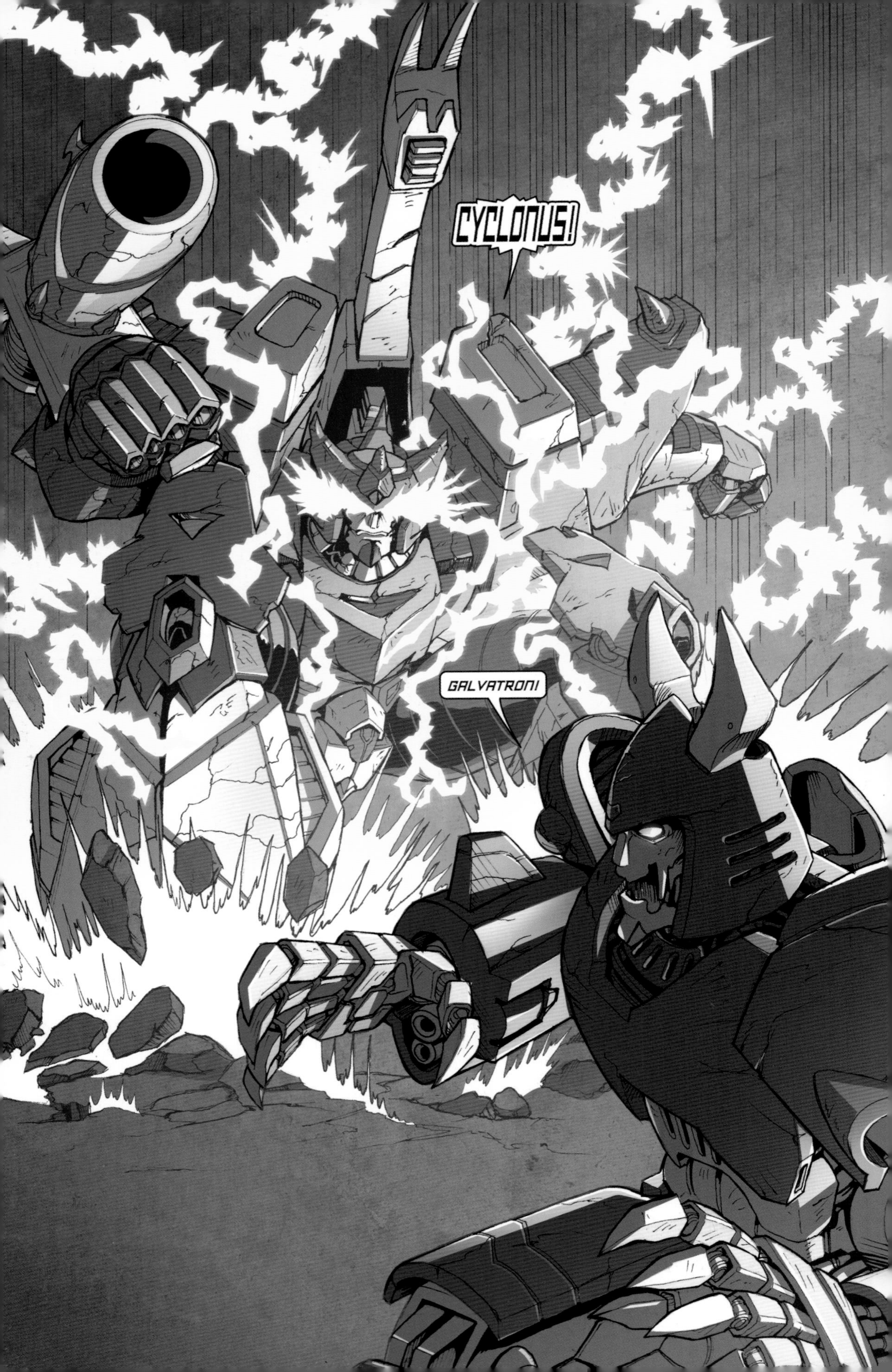
CYCLONUS!
GALVATRON!

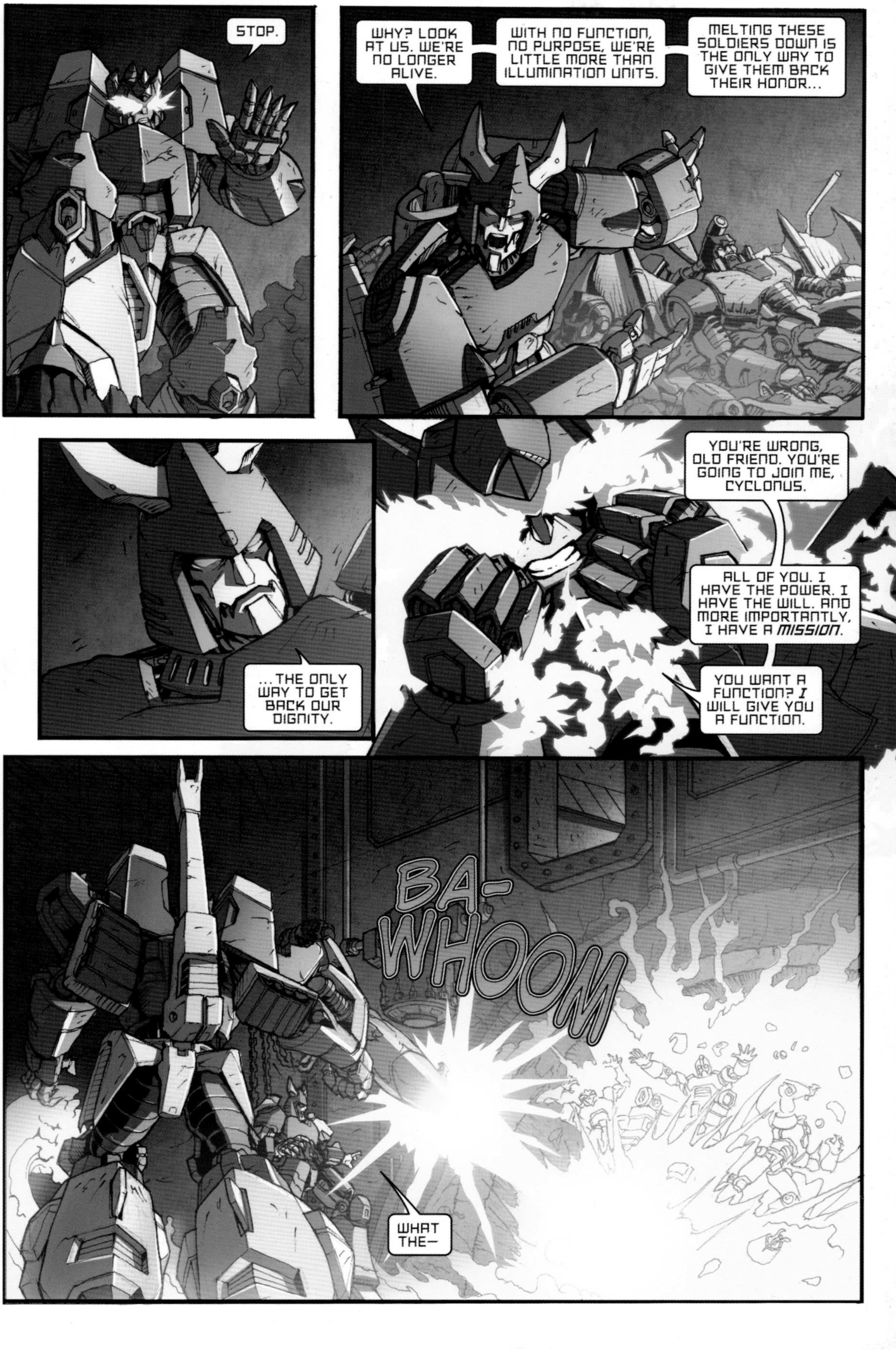
STOP.
WHY? LOOK AT US. WE'RE NO LONGER ALIVE.
WITH NO FUNCTION, NO PURPOSE, WE'RE LITTLE MORE THAN ILLUMINATION UNITS.
MELTING THESE SOLDIERS DOWN IS THE ONLY WAY TO GIVE THEM BACK THEIR HONOR...
...THE ONLY WAY TO GET BACK OUR DIGNITY.
YOU'RE WRONG, OLD FRIEND. YOU'RE GOING TO JOIN ME, CYCLONUS.
ALL OF YOU. I HAVE THE POWER. I HAVE THE WILL. AND MORE IMPORTANTLY, I HAVE A *MISSION*.
YOU WANT A FUNCTION? *I* WILL GIVE YOU A FUNCTION.
BA-WHOOM
WHAT THE—

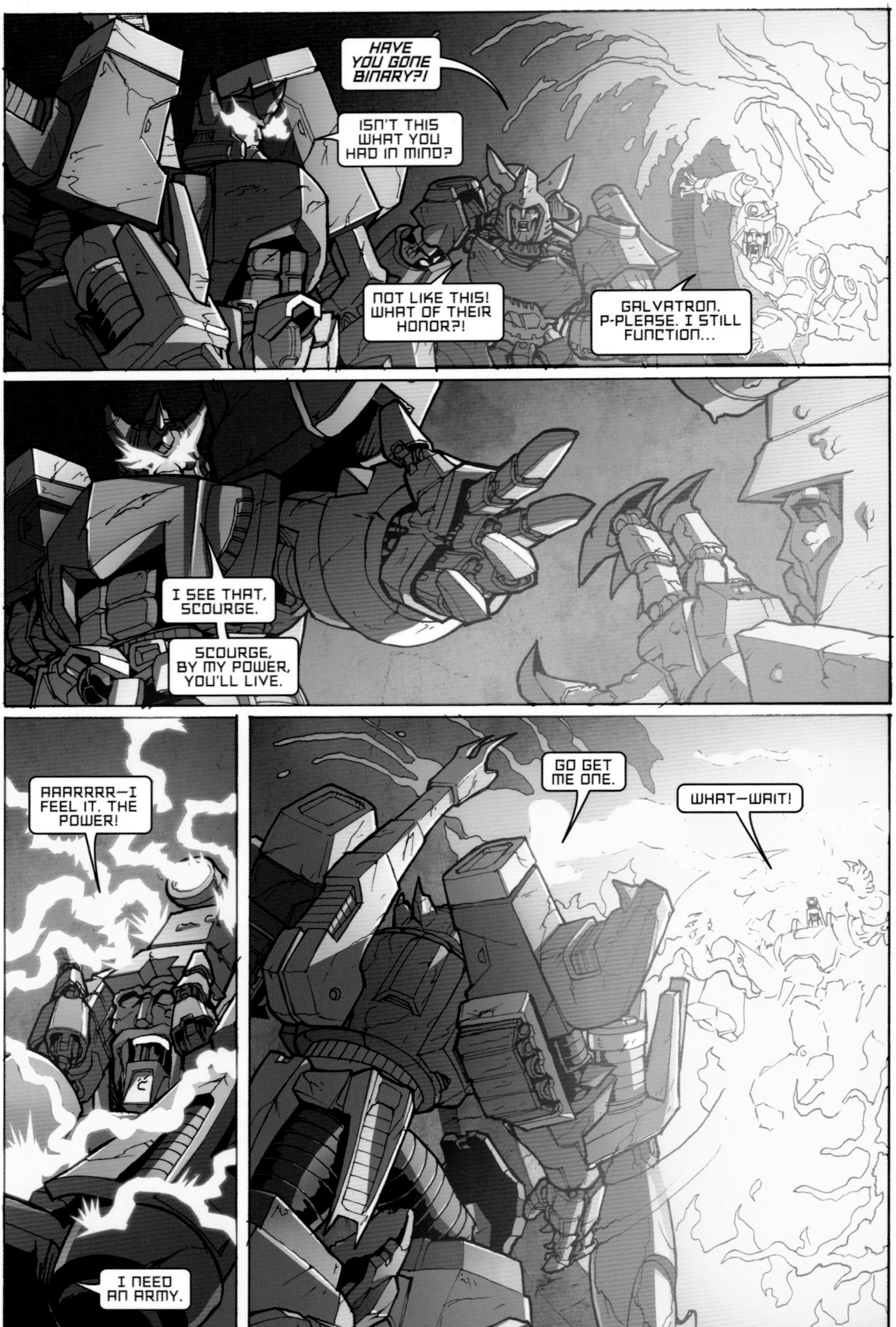

HAVE YOU GONE BINARY?!
ISN'T THIS WHAT YOU HAD IN MIND?
NOT LIKE THIS! WHAT OF THEIR HONOR?!
GALVATRON. P-PLEASE. I STILL FUNCTION...
I SEE THAT, SCOURGE.
SCOURGE, BY MY POWER, YOU'LL LIVE.
AAARRRR—I FEEL IT. THE POWER!
I NEED AN ARMY.
GO GET ME ONE.
WHAT—WAIT!

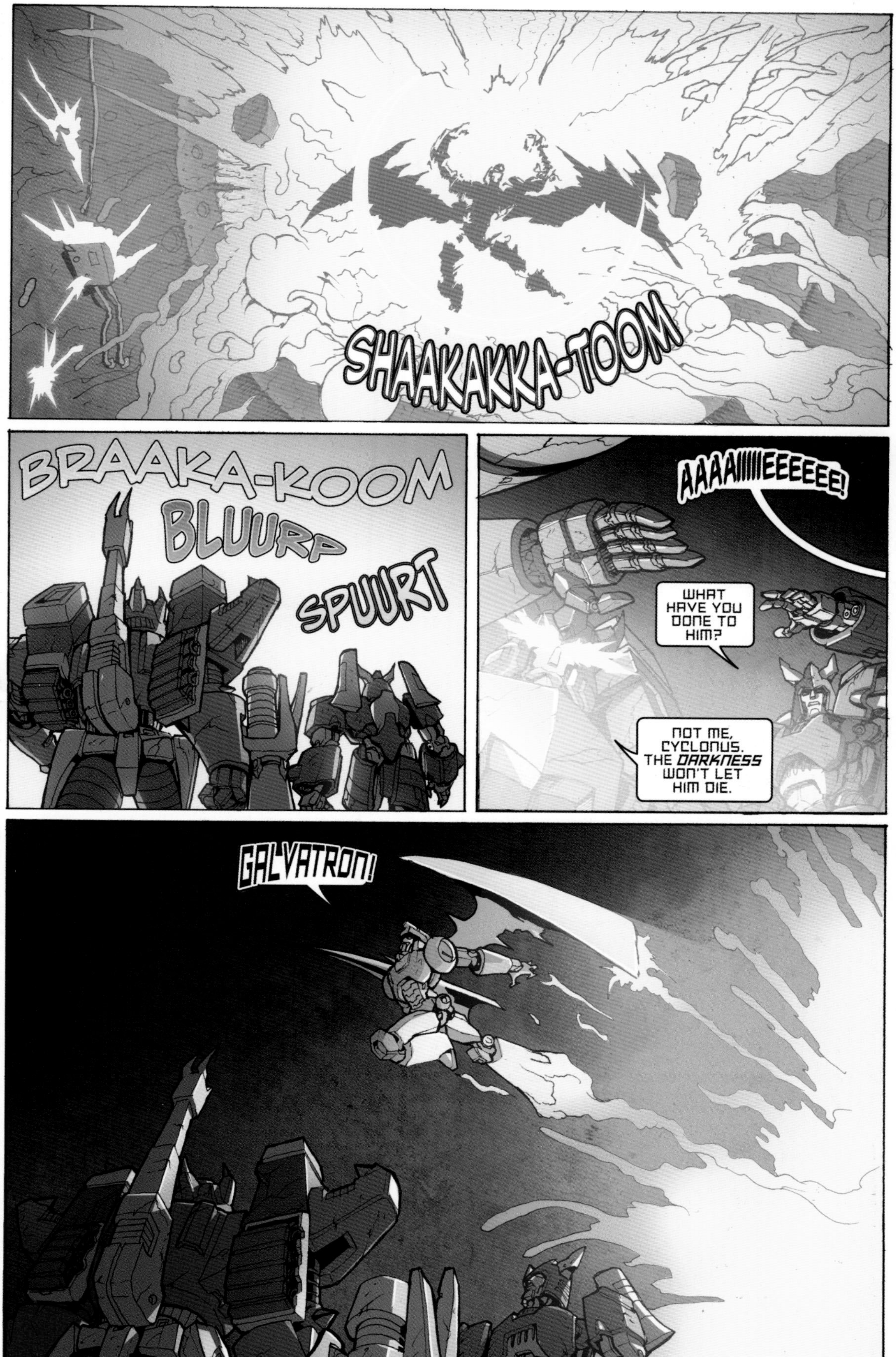
SHAAKAKKA-TOOM
BRAAKA-KOOM
BLUURP
SPUURT
AAAIIIIIIEEEEEE!
WHAT HAVE YOU DONE TO HIM?
NOT ME, CYCLONUS. THE *DARKNESS* WON'T LET HIM DIE.
GALVATRON!

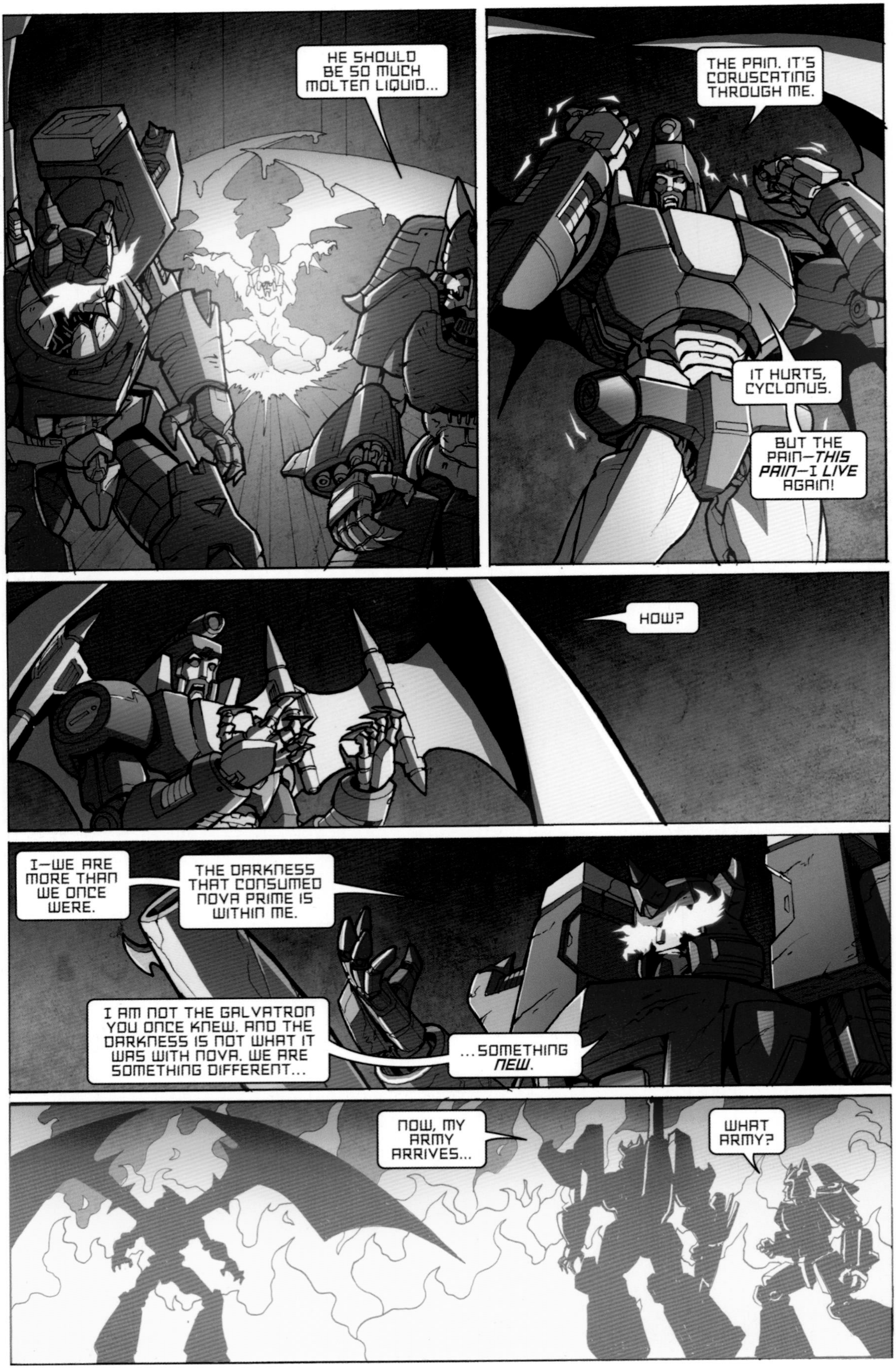
HE SHOULD BE SO MUCH MOLTEN LIQUID...
THE PAIN. IT'S CORUSCATING THROUGH ME.
IT HURTS, CYCLONUS.
BUT THE PAIN—*THIS PAIN*—I *LIVE* AGAIN!
HOW?
I—WE ARE MORE THAN WE ONCE WERE.
THE DARKNESS THAT CONSUMED NOVA PRIME IS WITHIN ME.
I AM NOT THE GALVATRON YOU ONCE KNEW. AND THE DARKNESS IS NOT WHAT IT WAS WITH NOVA. WE ARE SOMETHING DIFFERENT...
...SOMETHING *NEW*.
NOW, MY ARMY ARRIVES...
WHAT ARMY?

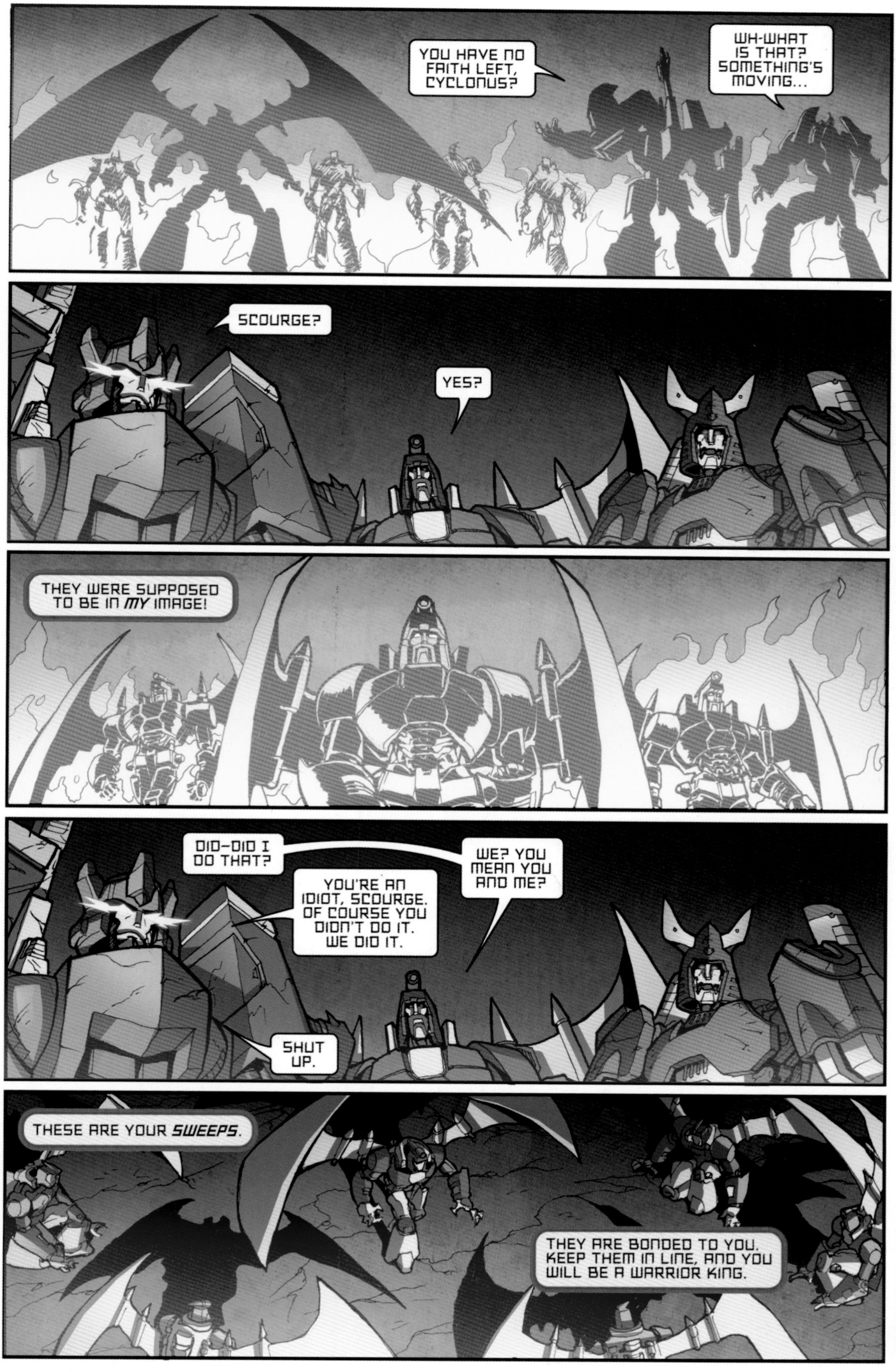
YOU HAVE NO FAITH LEFT, CYCLONUS?
WH-WHAT IS THAT? SOMETHING'S MOVING...
SCOURGE?
YES?
THEY WERE SUPPOSED TO BE IN *MY* IMAGE!
DID-DID I DO THAT?
YOU'RE AN IDIOT, SCOURGE. OF COURSE YOU DIDN'T DO IT. WE DID IT.
WE? YOU MEAN YOU AND ME?
SHUT UP.
THESE ARE YOUR *SWEEPS*.
THEY ARE BONDED TO YOU. KEEP THEM IN LINE, AND YOU WILL BE A WARRIOR KING.

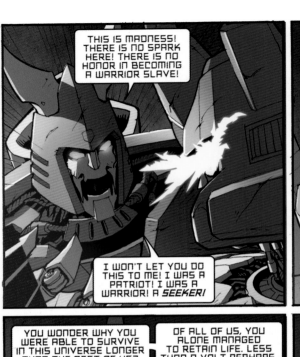

THIS IS MADNESS! THERE IS NO SPARK HERE! THERE IS NO HONOR IN BECOMING A WARRIOR SLAVE!

I WON'T LET YOU DO THIS TO ME! I WAS A PATRIOT! I WAS A WARRIOR! A *SEEKER!*

CALM YOURSELF, CYCLONUS. THAT IS NOT THE FATE WE HAVE IN MIND FOR YOU.

YOUR CUNNING, YOUR SPIRIT. IT REFUSES TO DIE. YOU ARE NOBLE— INCORRUPTIBLE.

YOU WONDER WHY YOU WERE ABLE TO SURVIVE IN THIS UNIVERSE LONGER THAN THE REST OF US?

OF ALL OF US, YOU ALONE MANAGED TO RETAIN LIFE. LESS THAN A VOLT PERHAPS, BUT IT WAS ENOUGH TO ALLOW YOU TO CROSS BETWEEN BOTH UNIVERSES.

YOU WERE NEVER GOING TO SUCCUMB TO THE SAME FATE AS THE REST OF US.

TRUST ME.

JOIN ME.

SEEK FOR ME.

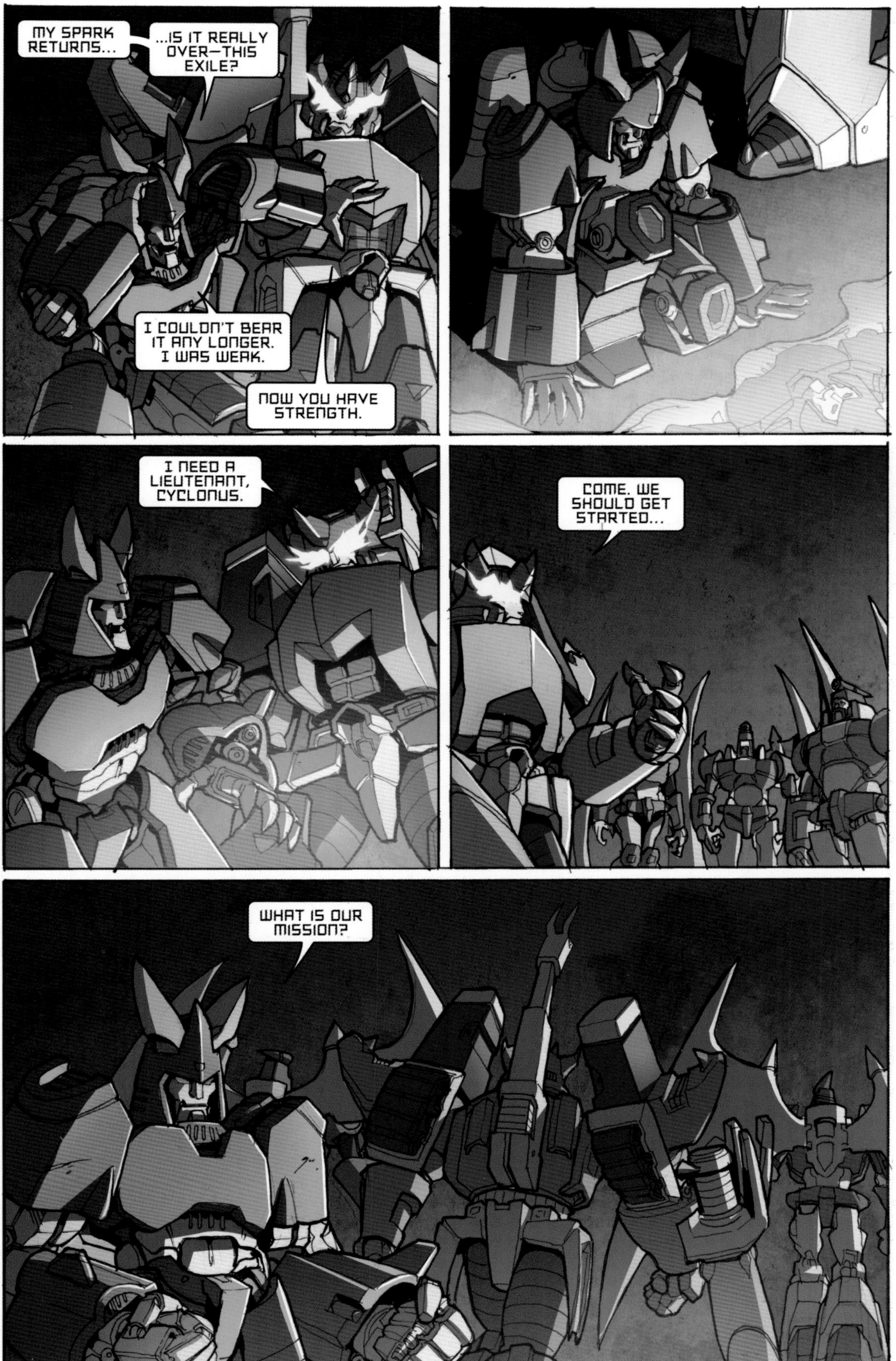
MY SPARK RETURNS...
...IS IT REALLY OVER—THIS EXILE?
I COULDN'T BEAR IT ANY LONGER. I WAS WEAK.
NOW YOU HAVE STRENGTH.
I NEED A LIEUTENANT, CYCLONUS.
COME. WE SHOULD GET STARTED...
WHAT IS OUR MISSION?

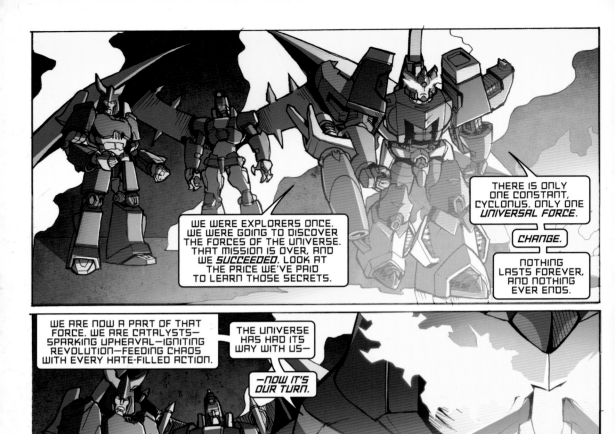

WE WERE EXPLORERS ONCE. WE WERE GOING TO DISCOVER THE FORCES OF THE UNIVERSE. THAT MISSION IS OVER, AND WE *SUCCEEDED*. LOOK AT THE PRICE WE'VE PAID TO LEARN THOSE SECRETS.

THERE IS ONLY ONE CONSTANT, CYCLONUS. ONLY ONE *UNIVERSAL FORCE*.

CHANGE.

NOTHING LASTS FOREVER, AND NOTHING EVER ENDS.

WE ARE NOW A PART OF THAT FORCE. WE ARE CATALYSTS— SPARKING UPHEAVAL—IGNITING REVOLUTION—FEEDING CHAOS WITH EVERY HATE-FILLED ACTION.

THE UNIVERSE HAS HAD ITS WAY WITH US—

—NOW IT'S OUR TURN.

WHAT DOES THAT MEAN?

I HAVE NO IDEA.

SO WHAT DO WE DO?

OUR FUNCTION IS TO SEEK, SCOURGE...

...WE FOLLOW HIM.

THE END.

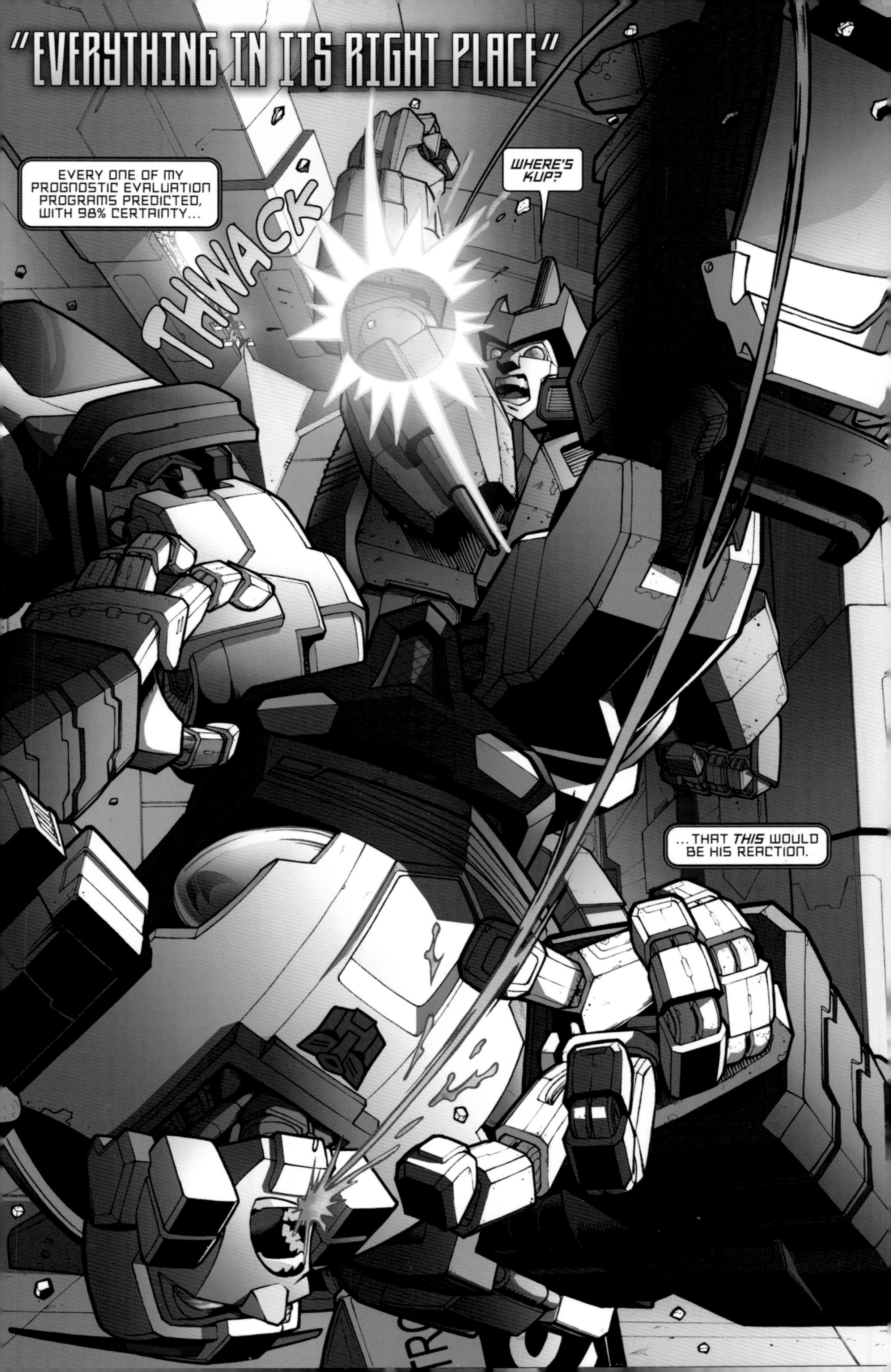
"EVERYTHING IN ITS RIGHT PLACE"
EVERY ONE OF MY PROGNOSTIC EVALUATION PROGRAMS PREDICTED, WITH 98% CERTAINTY...
WHERE'S KUP?
THWACK
...THAT THIS WOULD BE HIS REACTION.

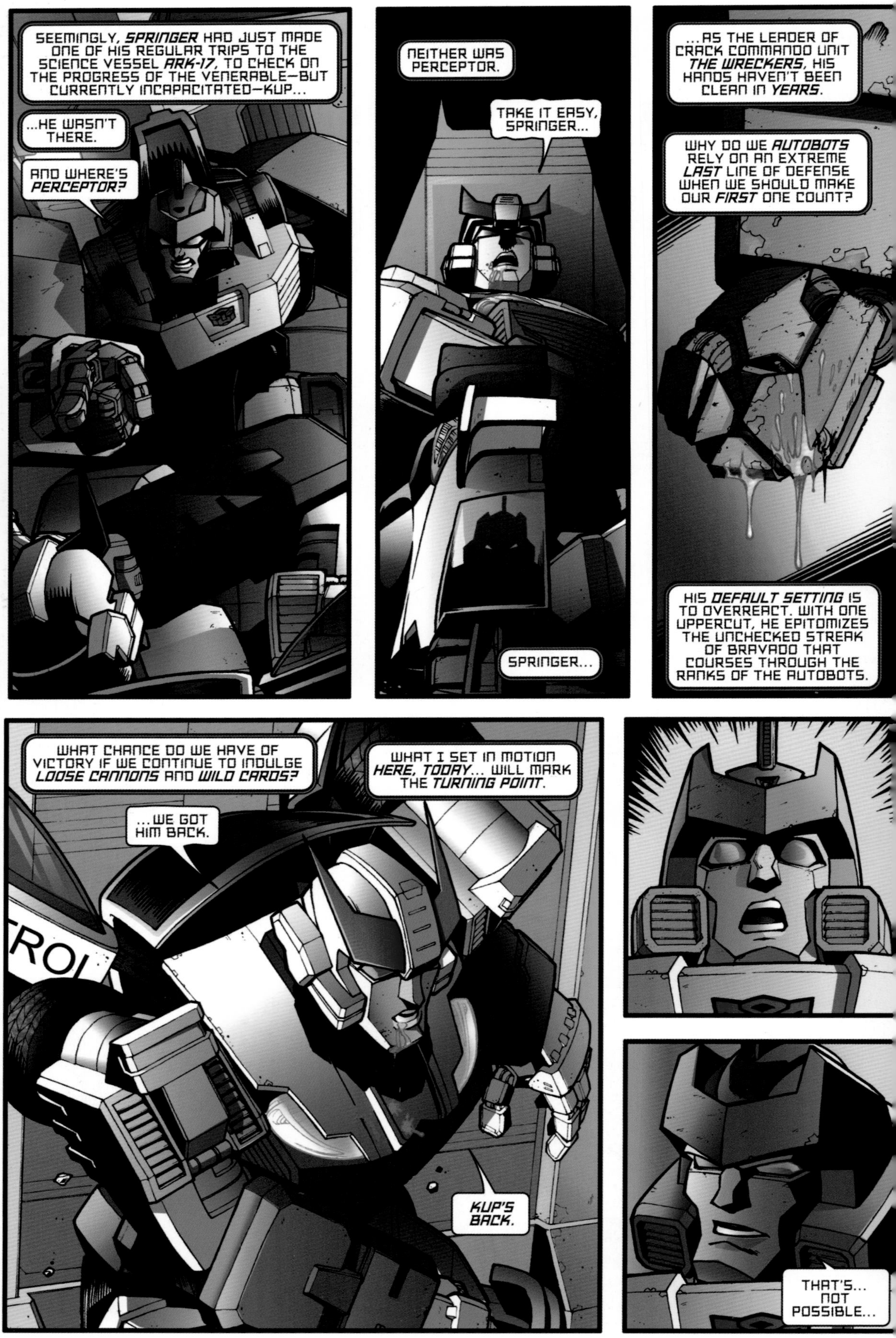
SEEMINGLY, SPRINGER HAD JUST MADE ONE OF HIS REGULAR TRIPS TO THE SCIENCE VESSEL ARK-17, TO CHECK ON THE PROGRESS OF THE VENERABLE—BUT CURRENTLY INCAPACITATED—KUP...
...HE WASN'T THERE.
AND WHERE'S PERCEPTOR?
NEITHER WAS PERCEPTOR.
TAKE IT EASY, SPRINGER...
SPRINGER...
...AS THE LEADER OF CRACK COMMANDO UNIT THE WRECKERS, HIS HANDS HAVEN'T BEEN CLEAN IN YEARS.
WHY DO WE AUTOBOTS RELY ON AN EXTREME LAST LINE OF DEFENSE WHEN WE SHOULD MAKE OUR FIRST ONE COUNT?
HIS DEFAULT SETTING IS TO OVERREACT. WITH ONE UPPERCUT, HE EPITOMIZES THE UNCHECKED STREAK OF BRAVADO THAT COURSES THROUGH THE RANKS OF THE AUTOBOTS.
WHAT CHANCE DO WE HAVE OF VICTORY IF WE CONTINUE TO INDULGE LOOSE CANNONS AND WILD CARDS?
...WE GOT HIM BACK.
WHAT I SET IN MOTION HERE, TODAY... WILL MARK THE TURNING POINT.
TROL
KUP'S BACK.
THAT'S... NOT POSSIBLE...

"*YOU* DIDN'T SEE WHAT HE WAS LIKE WHEN WE FOUND HIM. HE WAS *SICK*, HIS MIND FRIED FROM THE CRYSTALS HE BECAME ADDICTED TO ON THAT PLANET."

"DAMMIT, HIS NEURO-CORE WAS SO CHEWED UP BY RADIATION, HE THOUGHT HE WAS DEFENDING HIMSELF FROM NIGHT-TERRORS AND *GHOSTS*"

"BUT INSTEAD..."

"... HE WAS MANIFOLD-DEEP IN THE FUEL OF THE AUTOBOTS *I'D* SENT TO RESCUE HIM—AUTOBOTS HE SLAUGHTERED WITH HIS *BARE SERVOS*.

"PERCEPTOR SAID HE WAS TOO FAR GONE, PHYSICALLY AND MENTALLY; THAT THERE WAS *NOTHING*–"

YES. AND THAT'S EXACTLY *WHY* I HAD PERCEPTOR BRING KUP HERE...

"...TO THE *KIMIA* FACILITY. YOU KNOW WHAT THEY'RE CAPABLE OF HERE, RIGHT?"

"THIS IS *HIGH-END* STUFF WE'RE TALKING ABOUT: LIQUID SHRAPNEL, FOLD-SPACE, IMPORTED MEMORY..."

"...SCIENCE THAT EXISTS ALMOST ON A PURELY THEORETICAL LEVEL.

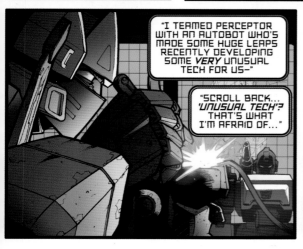

"I TEAMED PERCEPTOR WITH AN AUTOBOT WHO'S MADE SOME HUGE LEAPS RECENTLY DEVELOPING SOME *VERY* UNUSUAL TECH FOR US–"

"SCROLL BACK... *'UNUSUAL TECH'*? THAT'S WHAT I'M AFRAID OF..."

...I KNOW *ALL* ABOUT THIS PLACE, PROWL. DO YOU HAVE ANY IDEA HOW MANY FREAKY GRAVITON BLASTERS AND CHRONAL-DISPLACEMENT GRENADES THE WRECKERS HAVE TESTED OUT FOR KIMIA? THE STUFF THESE GUYS COOK UP...

...WAIT A CYC'...

...TELL ME YOU DIDN'T JUST DRAG KUP HERE TO REVERSE-ENGINEER SOME KIND OF WEAPON THAT CAN INFLICT THAT SORT OF RADIATION DAMAGE ON A DECEPTICON?

NO, SPRINGER—

BUT DON'T THINK I DIDN'T CONSIDER IT.

—I HAD KUP BROUGHT HERE BECAUSE *THIS* WAS WHERE BREAKTHROUGHS WERE BEING MADE... WITH THE *PRETENDER PROCESS*.

OVER-REACTION PREDICTED WITH 89% ACCURACY.

WAIT—*THE PRETENDER PROCESS*?!

THE *SAME* PRETENDER PROCESS THAT 'CON ZEALOT *BLUDGEON* HOME-BREWED? THE *SAME* ONE THAT LED TO THE WHOLE *THUNDERWING* MESS, WHICH MEANS *WE* DON'T GET TO LIVE ON *CYBERTRON* ANYMORE?

NICE PLAY, PROWL. THIS SCHEME MAKES KUP'S RESCUE MISSION LOOK AS SMOOTH AS A GEAR CHANGE FROM *BLURR*.

I HAVE HEARD THIS EXACT *SPRINGERISM* PRECISELY *76* TIMES OVER THE LAST THREE-DOZEN DECA-CYCLES. THERE IS NOTHING ABOUT HIM I CANNOT PREDICT.

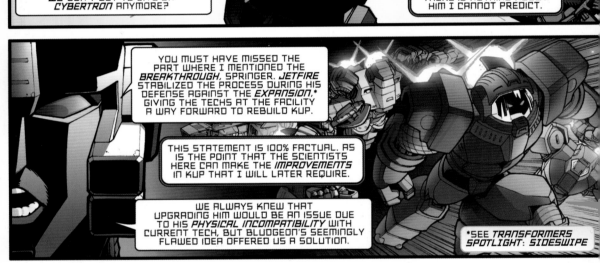

YOU MUST HAVE MISSED THE PART WHERE I MENTIONED THE *BREAKTHROUGH*, SPRINGER. *JETFIRE* STABILIZED THE PROCESS DURING HIS DEFENSE AGAINST THE *EXPANSION*,* GIVING THE TECHS AT THE FACILITY A WAY FORWARD TO REBUILD KUP.

THIS STATEMENT IS 100% FACTUAL. AS IS THE POINT THAT THE SCIENTISTS HERE CAN MAKE THE *IMPROVEMENTS* IN KUP THAT I WILL LATER REQUIRE.

WE ALWAYS KNEW THAT UPGRADING HIM WOULD BE AN ISSUE DUE TO HIS *PHYSICAL INCOMPATIBILITY* WITH CURRENT TECH, BUT BLUDGEON'S SEEMINGLY FLAWED IDEA OFFERED US A SOLUTION.

*SEE TRANSFORMERS SPOTLIGHT: SIDESWIPE

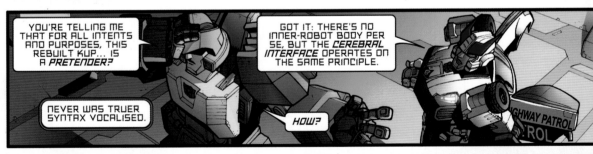

YOU'RE TELLING ME THAT FOR ALL INTENTS AND PURPOSES, THIS REBUILT KUP... IS A *PRETENDER*?

GOT IT: THERE'S NO INNER-ROBOT BODY PER SE, BUT THE *CEREBRAL INTERFACE* OPERATES ON THE SAME PRINCIPLE.

NEVER WAS TRUER SYNTAX VOCALISED.

HOW?

HOW CAN YOU *HAVE* A CEREBRAL INTERFACE WHEN HE BARELY HAS A CEREBRO-CORTEX LEFT TO INTERFACE WITH?

I DON'T HAVE TO RUN PROJECTED PERSONALITY SIMULATIONS TO KNOW THAT GUILT, WORRY, AND A REFUSAL TO MOVE ON ARE FUELLING HIS DISBELIEF. BUT HE CAN BE SO TIRING...

THE SCIENTISTS MADE A BREAKTHROUGH, SPRINGER. THAT'S THEIR JOB. DON'T YOU GET IT? THIS IS REAL. KUP'S *BACK*. WATCH.

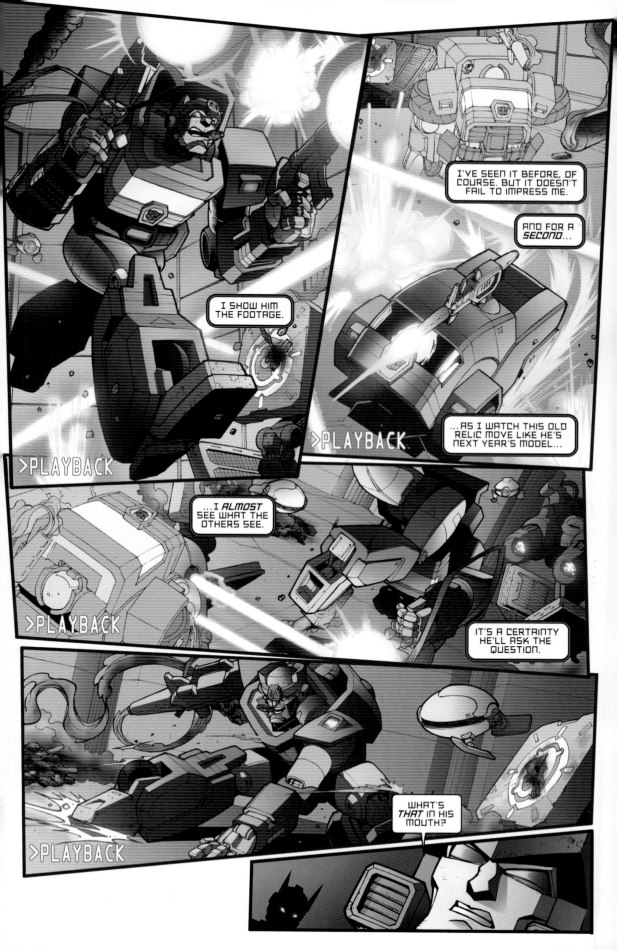

I SHOW HIM THE FOOTAGE.

>PLAYBACK

I'VE SEEN IT BEFORE, OF COURSE. BUT IT DOESN'T FAIL TO IMPRESS ME.

AND FOR A *SECOND*...

>PLAYBACK

...AS I WATCH THIS OLD RELIC MOVE LIKE HE'S NEXT YEAR'S MODEL...

...I *ALMOST* SEE WHAT THE OTHERS SEE.

>PLAYBACK

IT'S A CERTAINTY HE'LL ASK THE QUESTION.

>PLAYBACK

WHAT'S *THAT* IN HIS MOUTH?

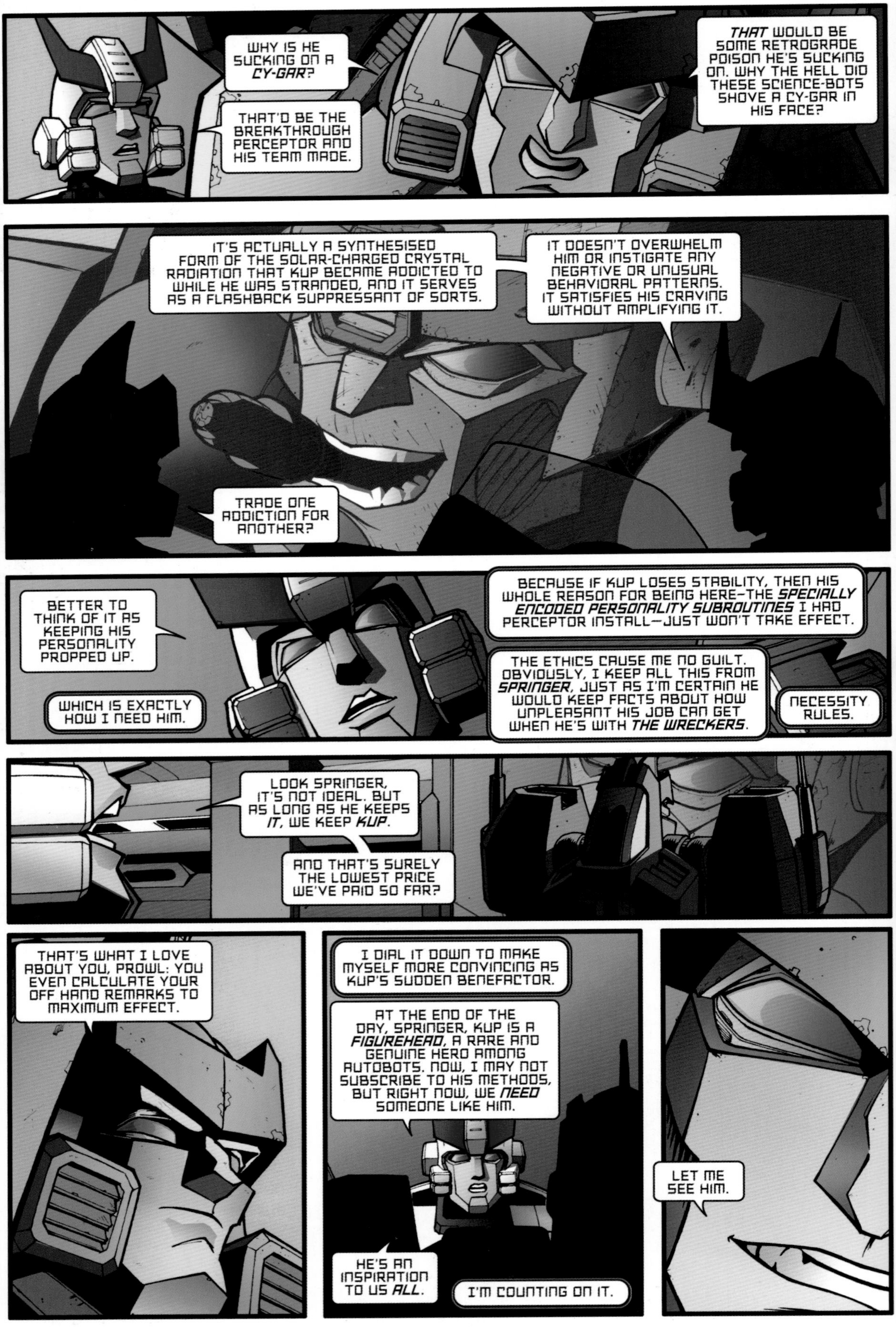
WHY IS HE SUCKING ON A *CY-GAR*?
THAT'D BE THE BREAKTHROUGH PERCEPTOR AND HIS TEAM MADE.
THAT WOULD BE SOME RETROGRADE POISON HE'S SUCKING ON. WHY THE HELL DID THESE SCIENCE-BOTS SHOVE A CY-GAR IN HIS FACE?
IT'S ACTUALLY A SYNTHESISED FORM OF THE SOLAR-CHARGED CRYSTAL RADIATION THAT KUP BECAME ADDICTED TO WHILE HE WAS STRANDED, AND IT SERVES AS A FLASHBACK SUPPRESSANT OF SORTS.
IT DOESN'T OVERWHELM HIM OR INSTIGATE ANY NEGATIVE OR UNUSUAL BEHAVIORAL PATTERNS. IT SATISFIES HIS CRAVING WITHOUT AMPLIFYING IT.
TRADE ONE ADDICTION FOR ANOTHER?
BETTER TO THINK OF IT AS KEEPING HIS PERSONALITY PROPPED UP.
WHICH IS EXACTLY HOW I NEED HIM.
BECAUSE IF KUP LOSES STABILITY, THEN HIS WHOLE REASON FOR BEING HERE—THE *SPECIALLY ENCODED PERSONALITY SUBROUTINES* I HAD PERCEPTOR INSTALL—JUST WON'T TAKE EFFECT.
THE ETHICS CAUSE ME NO GUILT. OBVIOUSLY, I KEEP ALL THIS FROM *SPRINGER*, JUST AS I'M CERTAIN HE WOULD KEEP FACTS ABOUT HOW UNPLEASANT HIS JOB CAN GET WHEN HE'S WITH *THE WRECKERS*.
NECESSITY RULES.
LOOK SPRINGER, IT'S NOT IDEAL. BUT AS LONG AS HE KEEPS *IT*, WE KEEP *KUP*.
AND THAT'S SURELY THE LOWEST PRICE WE'VE PAID SO FAR?
THAT'S WHAT I LOVE ABOUT YOU, PROWL: YOU EVEN CALCULATE YOUR OFF HAND REMARKS TO MAXIMUM EFFECT.
I DIAL IT DOWN TO MAKE MYSELF MORE CONVINCING AS KUP'S SUDDEN BENEFACTOR.
AT THE END OF THE DAY, SPRINGER, KUP IS A *FIGUREHEAD*, A RARE AND GENUINE HERO AMONG AUTOBOTS. NOW, I MAY NOT SUBSCRIBE TO HIS METHODS, BUT RIGHT NOW, WE *NEED* SOMEONE LIKE HIM.
HE'S AN INSPIRATION TO US *ALL*.
I'M COUNTING ON IT.
LET ME SEE HIM.

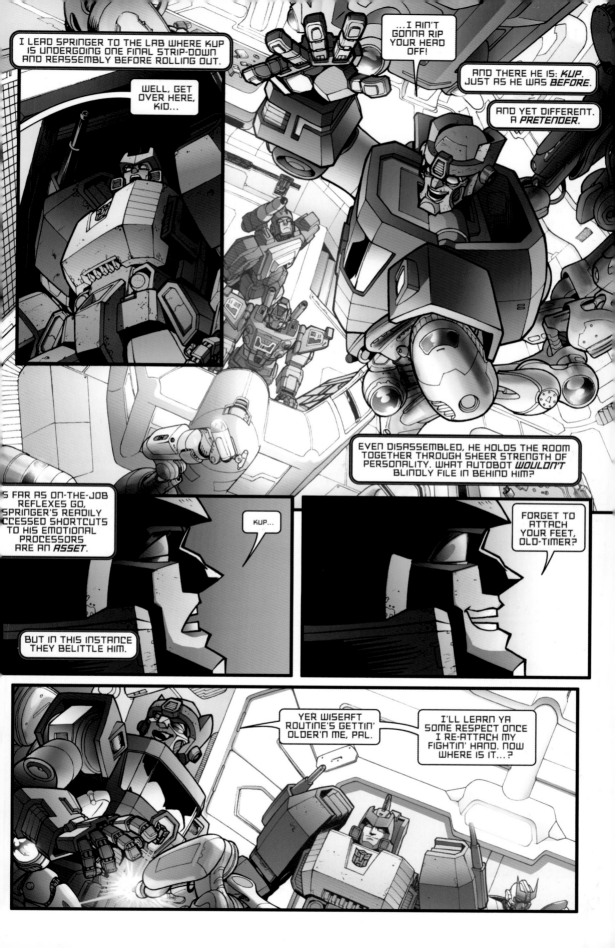

I LEAD SPRINGER TO THE LAB WHERE KUP IS UNDERGOING ONE FINAL STRIP-DOWN AND REASSEMBLY BEFORE ROLLING OUT.

WELL, GET OVER HERE, KID...

...I AIN'T GONNA RIP YOUR HEAD OFF!

AND THERE HE IS: *KUP*. JUST AS HE WAS *BEFORE*.

AND YET DIFFERENT. A *PRETENDER*.

EVEN DISASSEMBLED, HE HOLDS THE ROOM TOGETHER THROUGH SHEER STRENGTH OF PERSONALITY. WHAT AUTOBOT *WOULDN'T* BLINDLY FILE IN BEHIND HIM?

S FAR AS ON-THE-JOB REFLEXES GO, SPRINGER'S READILY CCESSED SHORTCUTS TO HIS EMOTIONAL PROCESSORS ARE AN *ASSET*.

KUP...

FORGET TO ATTACH YOUR FEET, OLD-TIMER?

BUT IN THIS INSTANCE THEY BELITTLE HIM.

YER WISEAFT ROUTINE'S GETTIN' OLDER'N ME, PAL.

I'LL LEARN YA SOME RESPECT ONCE I RE-ATTACH MY FIGHTIN' HAND. NOW WHERE IS IT...?

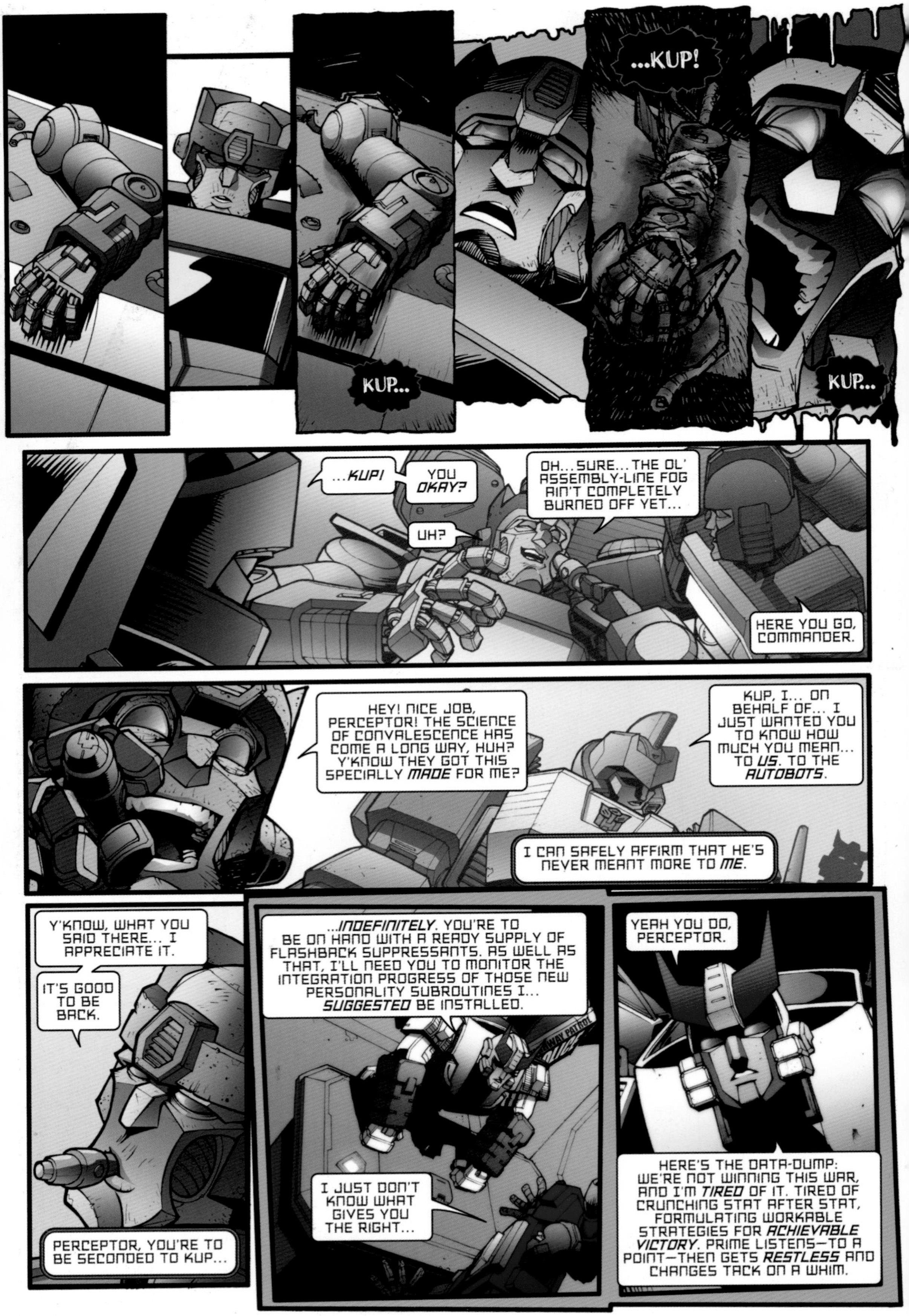

KUP...
...KUP!
KUP...
...KUP!
YOU OKAY?
UH?
OH... SURE... THE OL' ASSEMBLY-LINE FOG AIN'T COMPLETELY BURNED OFF YET...
HERE YOU GO, COMMANDER.
HEY! NICE JOB, PERCEPTOR! THE SCIENCE OF CONVALESCENCE HAS COME A LONG WAY, HUH? Y'KNOW THEY GOT THIS SPECIALLY MADE FOR ME?
KUP, I... ON BEHALF OF... I JUST WANTED YOU TO KNOW HOW MUCH YOU MEAN... TO US. TO THE AUTOBOTS.
I CAN SAFELY AFFIRM THAT HE'S NEVER MEANT MORE TO ME.
Y'KNOW, WHAT YOU SAID THERE... I APPRECIATE IT.
IT'S GOOD TO BE BACK.
PERCEPTOR, YOU'RE TO BE SECONDED TO KUP...
...INDEFINITELY. YOU'RE TO BE ON HAND WITH A READY SUPPLY OF FLASHBACK SUPPRESSANTS. AS WELL AS THAT, I'LL NEED YOU TO MONITOR THE INTEGRATION PROGRESS OF THOSE NEW PERSONALITY SUBROUTINES I... SUGGESTED BE INSTALLED.
I JUST DON'T KNOW WHAT GIVES YOU THE RIGHT...
YEAH YOU DO, PERCEPTOR.
HERE'S THE DATA-DUMP: WE'RE NOT WINNING THIS WAR, AND I'M TIRED OF IT. TIRED OF CRUNCHING STAT AFTER STAT, FORMULATING WORKABLE STRATEGIES FOR ACHIEVABLE VICTORY. PRIME LISTENS—TO A POINT—THEN GETS RESTLESS AND CHANGES TACK ON A WHIM.

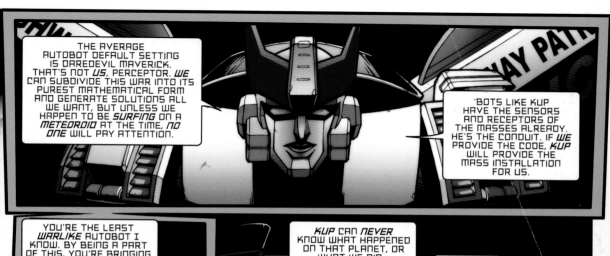

THE AVERAGE AUTOBOT DEFAULT SETTING IS DAREDEVIL MAVERICK. THAT'S NOT *US*, PERCEPTOR. *WE* CAN SUBDIVIDE THIS WAR INTO ITS PUREST MATHEMATICAL FORM AND GENERATE SOLUTIONS ALL WE WANT, BUT UNLESS WE HAPPEN TO BE *SURFING* ON A *METEOROID* AT THE TIME, *NO ONE* WILL PAY ATTENTION.

'BOTS LIKE KUP HAVE THE SENSORS AND RECEPTORS OF THE MASSES ALREADY. HE'S THE CONDUIT. IF *WE* PROVIDE THE CODE, *KUP* WILL PROVIDE THE MASS INSTALLATION FOR US.

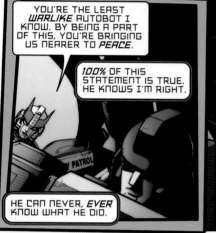

YOU'RE THE LEAST *WARLIKE* AUTOBOT I KNOW. BY BEING A PART OF THIS, YOU'RE BRINGING US NEARER TO *PEACE*.

100% OF THIS STATEMENT IS TRUE. HE KNOWS I'M RIGHT.

HE CAN NEVER, *EVER* KNOW WHAT HE DID.

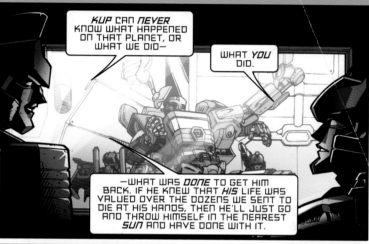

KUP CAN *NEVER* KNOW WHAT HAPPENED ON THAT PLANET, OR WHAT WE DID—

WHAT *YOU* DID.

—WHAT WAS *DONE* TO GET HIM BACK. IF HE KNEW THAT *HIS* LIFE WAS VALUED OVER THE DOZENS WE SENT TO DIE AT HIS HANDS, THEN HE'LL JUST GO AND THROW HIMSELF IN THE NEAREST *SUN* AND HAVE DONE WITH IT.

PERCEPTOR, TRAILBREAKER, SIREN, SIZZLE, AND ANYONE ELSE FROM ARK-17 WHO KNEW WHAT HAPPENED CAN NEVER SPEAK OF THIS TO *ANYONE*.

THE DEAFENING CLATTER OF *SOLIDIFIED OBVIOUSNESS* REVERBERATES AROUND MY AUDIO RECEPTORS.

IT'S BEEN TAKEN CARE OF, SPRINGER.

AS IF I *HADN'T* COVERED THIS. AND EVEN IF I HADN'T, THEIR COLLECTIVE BLIND LOYALTY TO SPRINGER WOULD HAVE ENSURED THEIR SILENCE.

OF COURSE IT HAS. IF THERE WERE SOME ANGLE WHERE YOU COULD SCORE POINTS WITH PRIME FOR THIS, YOU'D HAVE IT COVERED.

CORRECT.

THOUGH IT'S FAIR TO SAY OPTIMUS PRIME WOULD BE ATTRACTED TO THE ROMANTIC NOTION OF RISKING ALL FOR A FALLEN COMRADE.

EVEN WHEN—COMPARED TO THE NUMBERS *LOST* IN RETRIEVING HIM—THAT COMRADE IS OF NEGLIGIBLE STATISTICAL IMPORTANCE. OPTIMUS WOULDN'T *BE* OPTIMUS WITHOUT HIS WILLINGNESS TO GAMBLE ALL FOR NOTHING.

IT'S NOT THAT I DON'T UNDERSTAND IT. AS TRANSFORMERS, IT'S IN OUR NATURE TO ADAPT AND CHANGE ACCORDING TO THE GIVEN SITUATION.

BUT THIS OVERPOWERING SENTIMENTALISM AND ACCEPTANCE OF THE REBEL ELEMENT HOLDS US BACK FROM VICTORY.

I CAN SEE THE CRACKS STARTING TO SHOW. INTEL ON THE CURRENT DECEPTICON SITUATION DRIES UP.

STILL NOTHING, PRIME.

..."STILL NOTHING"...

STATISTICALLY, IT'S A CERTAINTY THAT HIS NEED TO BE ACTIVE WILL BE *SEVERELY* COUNTERPRODUCTIVE.

MY PROJECTIONS AND STRATEGIZING ALL SAY THE SAME THING: DO *NOTHING*.

WAIT.

PRIME TRUSTS MY ADVICE. HE LISTENS TO ME.

BUT SOON, PRIME WON'T BE ABLE TO HEAR ME ANYMORE, MY VOICE JUST A CONDUIT FOR FACTS AND FIGURES. IT DOESN'T SPEAK TO THE *WARRIOR* INSIDE.

NOT LIKE *IRONHIDE* DOES...

YOU KNOW WHAT *I* THINK...

BUT WE ALLOW RATCHET, HOT ROD, GRIMLOCK, AND SPRINGER—SANCTIONING UNTRAINED AUTOBOTS TO RESCUE A DERANGED VETERAN—TO BUCK THE SYSTEM.

ING RANK BORDINATION *UNAUTHORISED ALIEN CONTACT*

REPEATED LOSS OF LIVES UNDER HIS COMMAND WHILE ON NON-ESSENTIAL MISSIONS *FAILURE TO COMPLY WITH PLANET-EVACUATION ORDER*

SEE FILES G001 THROUGH G113 *CO-OPTS AUTOBOT RESOURCES FOR PRIVATE VENDETTAS* *IGNORES DISGUISE/C PROTOCOLS*

SPRINGER

*SANCTIONED SCIENCE TEAM TO ENTER COMBAT SITUATI

AND THEN *CELEBRATE* THEM.

COMPARE THESE EXAMPLES WITH THE DECEPTICONS. OF COURSE, THEY HAVE THEIR OWN ROGUE ELEMENTS—THE *SCORPONOKS*, *BLUDGEONS*, AND *THUNDERWINGS*—BUT FOR THE MOST PART, THEY ACT AS *ONE*.

THEY MAY HAVE SINISTER GOALS, BUT THERE'S NOTHING EVIL ABOUT REASON, ANALYSIS, DISCIPLINE... *LOGIC*.

WHY CAN'T THESE BE THE *TOOLS* OF THE *AUTOBOTS*?

I'M JUST NOT THE FIGUREHEAD AUTOBOTS SEEM TO *NEED*. BUT THEN, I DON'T *WANT* TO BE. I DON'T *THRIVE* ON ATTENTION. IT'S THE BADGE ON MY CHEST THAT MATTERS, NOT MY FACE.

SO FROM NOW ON, *KUP'S* MY FACE.

OR ONE OF THEM.

HE WAS ALREADY A LIVING LEGEND. NOW HE'S BACK ONLINE, HE'LL BE IN THE SPOTLIGHT EVEN MORE, ALL OPTICS LOCKED ON *HIM*. GOOD.

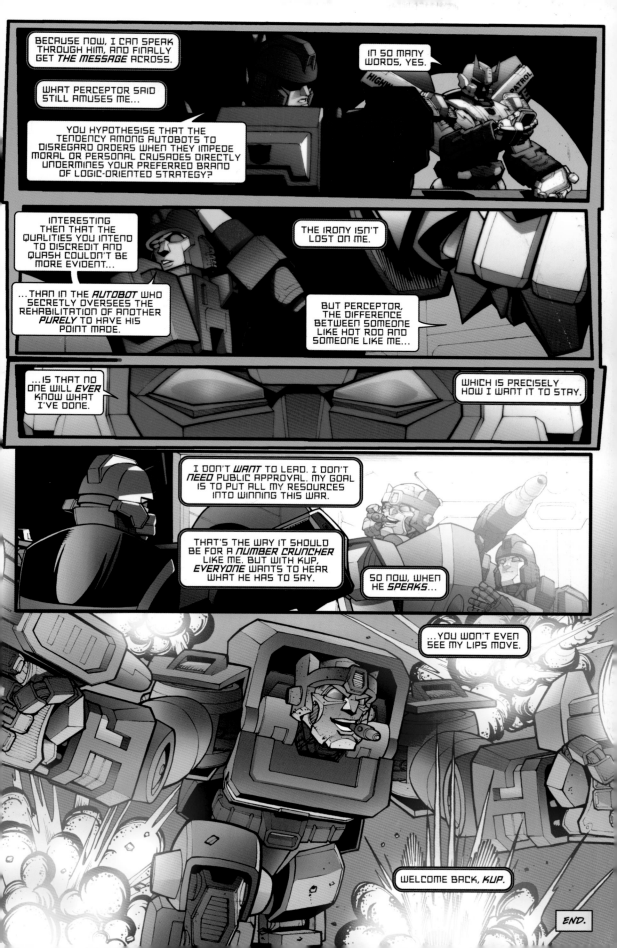

BECAUSE NOW, I CAN SPEAK THROUGH HIM, AND FINALLY GET *THE MESSAGE* ACROSS.

IN SO MANY WORDS, YES.

WHAT PERCEPTOR SAID STILL AMUSES ME...

YOU HYPOTHESISE THAT THE TENDENCY AMONG AUTOBOTS TO DISREGARD ORDERS WHEN THEY IMPEDE MORAL OR PERSONAL CRUSADES DIRECTLY UNDERMINES YOUR PREFERRED BRAND OF LOGIC-ORIENTED STRATEGY?

INTERESTING THEN THAT THE QUALITIES YOU INTEND TO DISCREDIT AND QUASH COULDN'T BE MORE EVIDENT...

THE IRONY ISN'T LOST ON ME.

...THAN IN THE *AUTOBOT* WHO SECRETLY OVERSEES THE REHABILITATION OF ANOTHER *PURELY* TO HAVE HIS POINT MADE.

BUT PERCEPTOR, THE DIFFERENCE BETWEEN SOMEONE LIKE HOT ROD AND SOMEONE LIKE ME...

...IS THAT NO ONE WILL *EVER* KNOW WHAT I'VE DONE.

WHICH IS PRECISELY HOW I WANT IT TO STAY.

I DON'T *WANT* TO LEAD. I DON'T *NEED* PUBLIC APPROVAL. MY GOAL IS TO PUT ALL MY RESOURCES INTO WINNING THIS WAR.

THAT'S THE WAY IT SHOULD BE FOR A *NUMBER CRUNCHER* LIKE ME. BUT WITH KUP, *EVERYONE* WANTS TO HEAR WHAT HE HAS TO SAY.

SO NOW, WHEN HE *SPEAKS*...

...YOU WON'T EVEN SEE MY LIPS MOVE.

WELCOME BACK, *KUP*.

END.

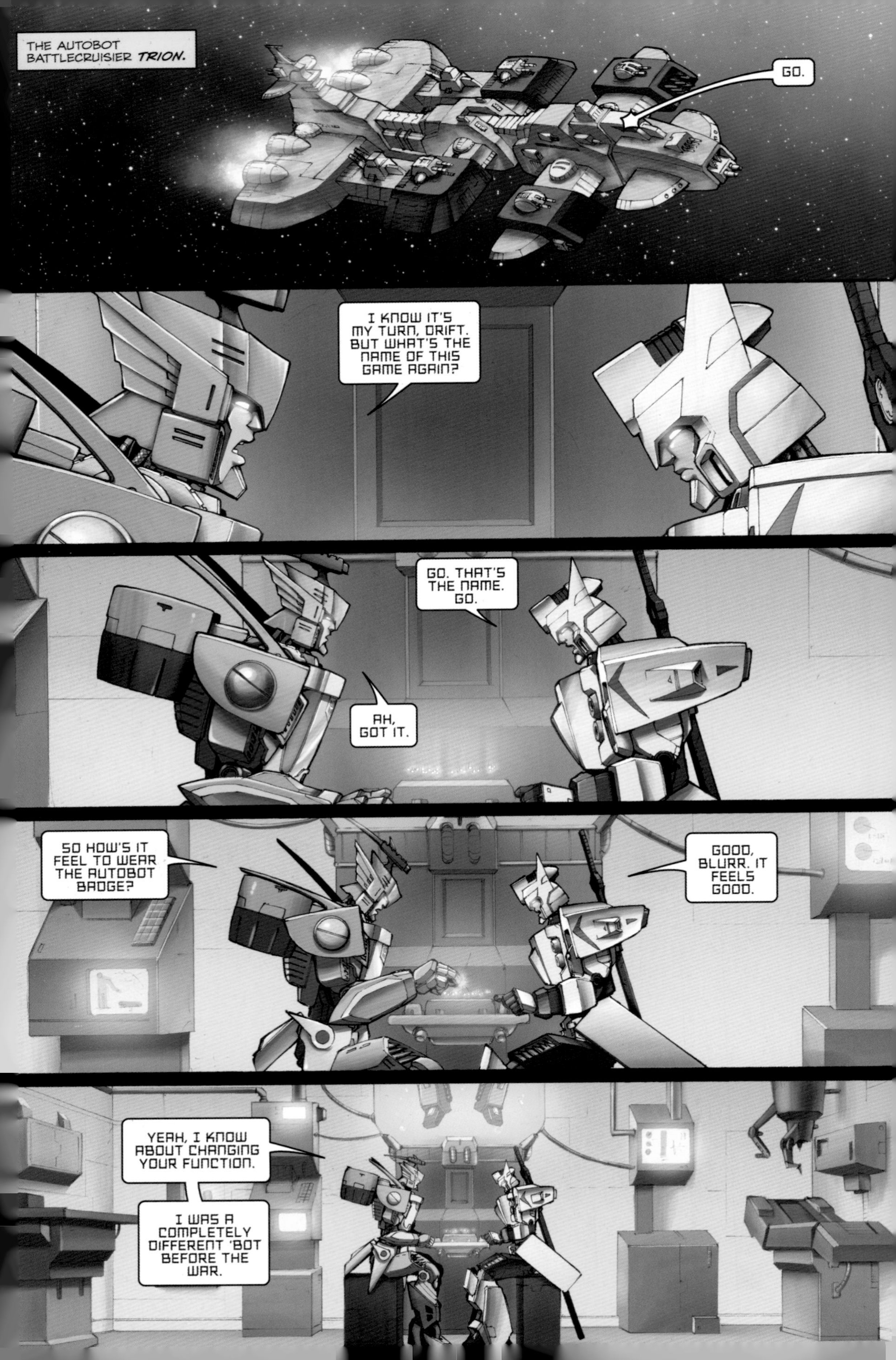
THE AUTOBOT BATTLECRUISIER TRION.
GO.
I KNOW IT'S MY TURN, DRIFT. BUT WHAT'S THE NAME OF THIS GAME AGAIN?
GO. THAT'S THE NAME. GO.
AH, GOT IT.
SO HOW'S IT FEEL TO WEAR THE AUTOBOT BADGE?
GOOD, BLURR. IT FEELS GOOD.
YEAH, I KNOW ABOUT CHANGING YOUR FUNCTION.
I WAS A COMPLETELY DIFFERENT 'BOT BEFORE THE WAR.

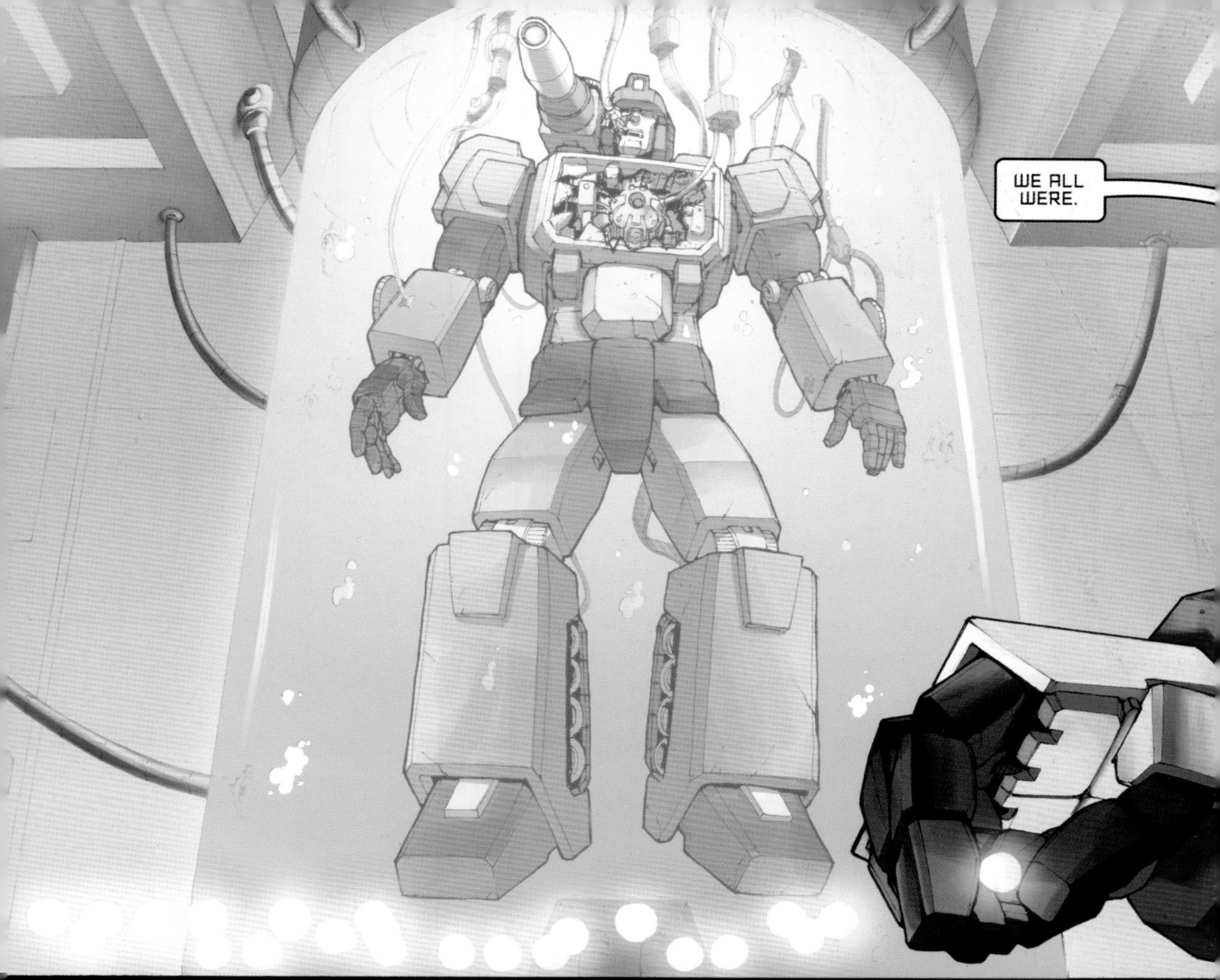
WE ALL WERE.

"LOST & FOUND"

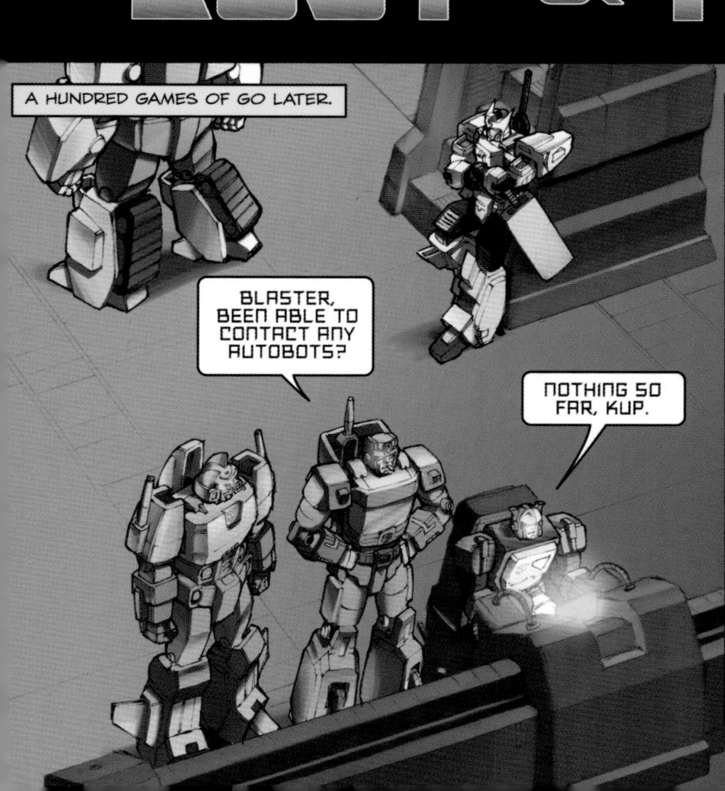
A HUNDRED GAMES OF GO LATER.
BLASTER, BEEN ABLE TO CONTACT ANY AUTOBOTS?
NOTHING SO FAR, KUP.

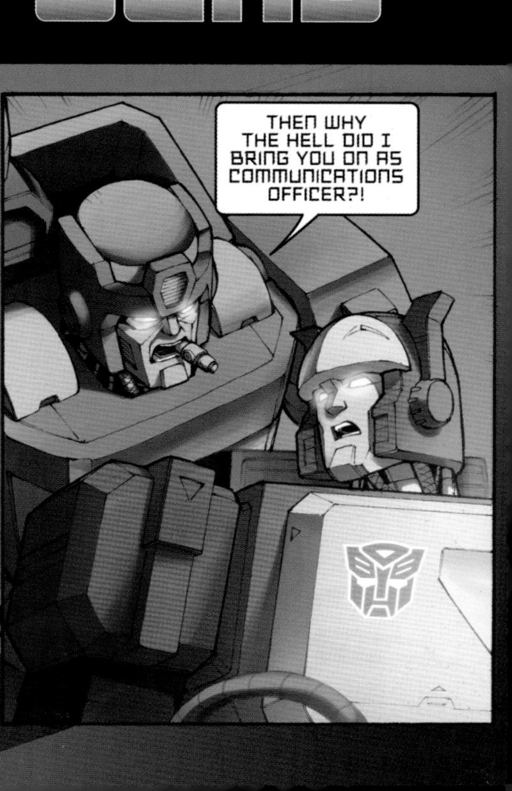
THEN WHY THE HELL DID I BRING YOU ON AS COMMUNICATIONS OFFICER?!

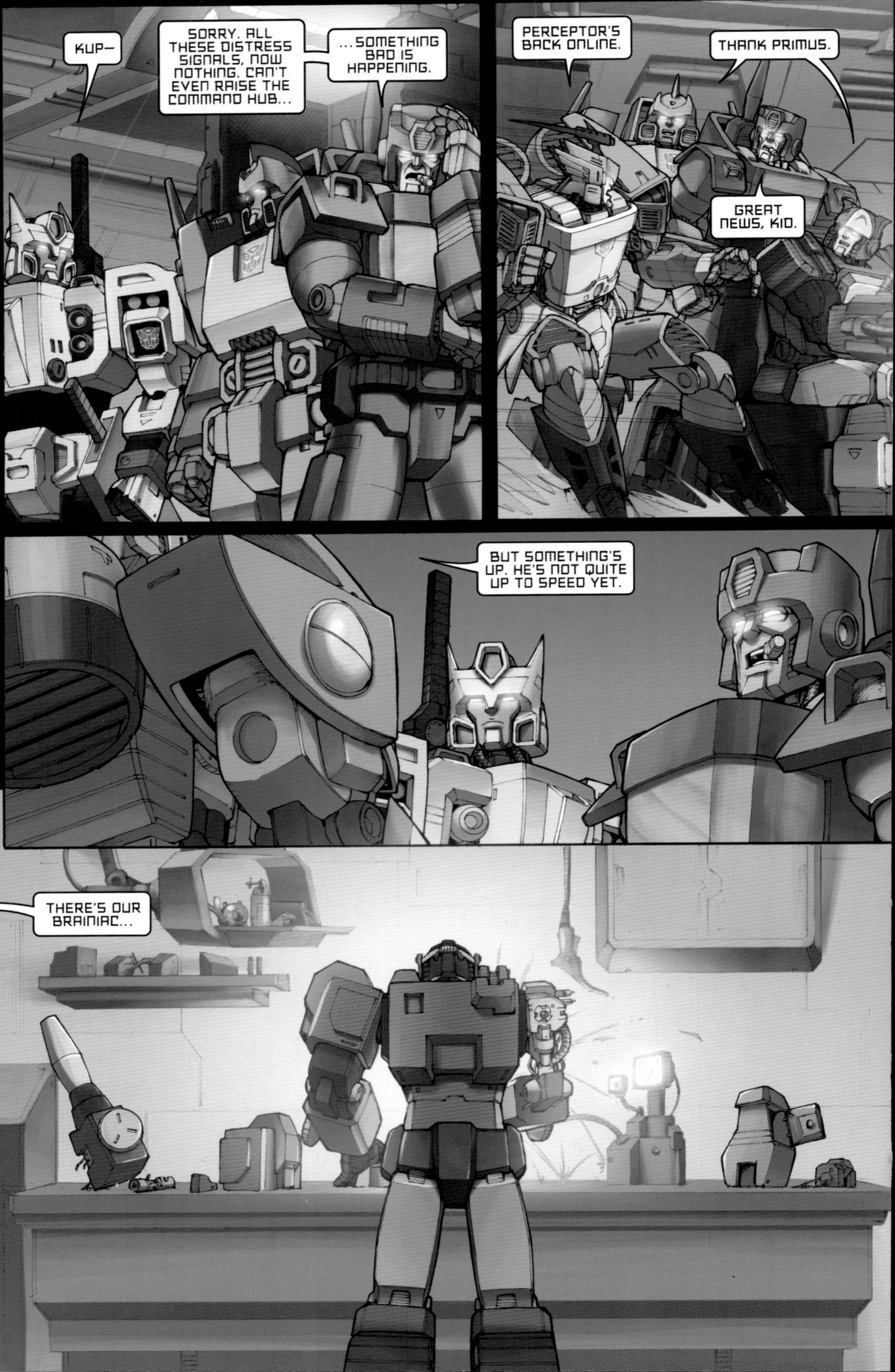
KUP—
SORRY. ALL THESE DISTRESS SIGNALS, NOW NOTHING. CAN'T EVEN RAISE THE COMMAND HUB...
...SOMETHING BAD IS HAPPENING.
PERCEPTOR'S BACK ONLINE.
THANK PRIMUS.
GREAT NEWS, KID.
BUT SOMETHING'S UP. HE'S NOT QUITE UP TO SPEED YET.
THERE'S OUR BRAINIAC...

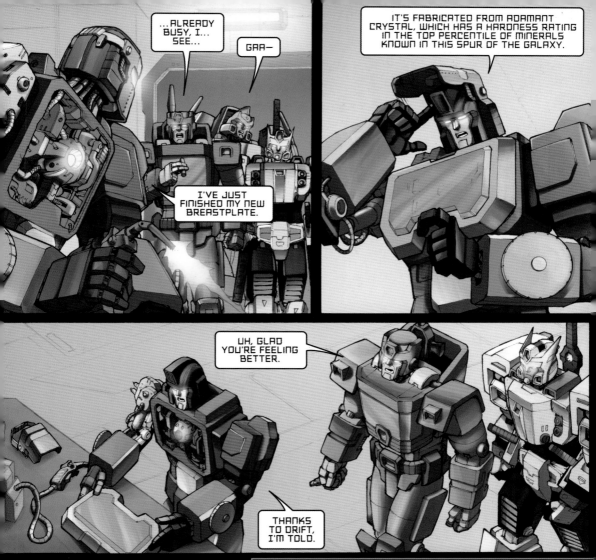

...ALREADY BUSY, I... SEE...

GAA—

I'VE JUST FINISHED MY NEW BREASTPLATE.

IT'S FABRICATED FROM ADAMANT CRYSTAL, WHICH HAS A HARDNESS RATING IN THE TOP PERCENTILE OF MINERALS KNOWN IN THIS SPUR OF THE GALAXY.

UH, GLAD YOU'RE FEELING BETTER.

THANKS TO DRIFT, I'M TOLD.

MUCH OBLIGED.

BUT LYING THERE HELPLESS WITH A MASSIVE APERTURE IN MY CHEST...

...I WON'T LET THAT HAPPEN AGAIN.

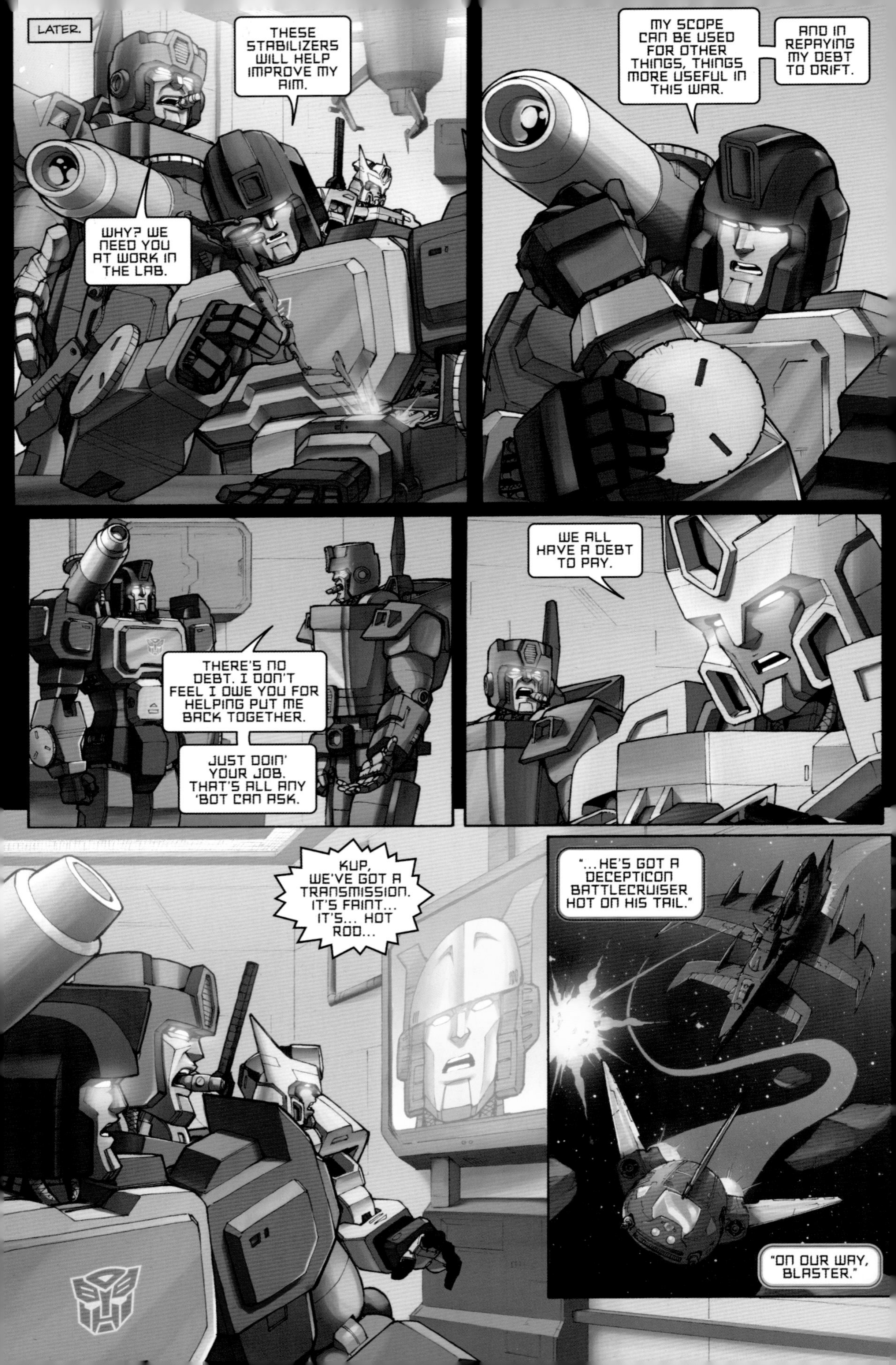
LATER.
THESE STABILIZERS WILL HELP IMPROVE MY AIM.
WHY? WE NEED YOU AT WORK IN THE LAB.
MY SCOPE CAN BE USED FOR OTHER THINGS, THINGS MORE USEFUL IN THIS WAR.
AND IN REPAYING MY DEBT TO DRIFT.
THERE'S NO DEBT. I DON'T FEEL I OWE YOU FOR HELPING PUT ME BACK TOGETHER.
JUST DOIN' YOUR JOB. THAT'S ALL ANY 'BOT CAN ASK.
WE ALL HAVE A DEBT TO PAY.
KUP, WE'VE GOT A TRANSMISSION. IT'S FAINT... IT'S... HOT ROD...
"...HE'S GOT A DECEPTICON BATTLECRUISER HOT ON HIS TAIL."
"ON OUR WAY, BLASTER."

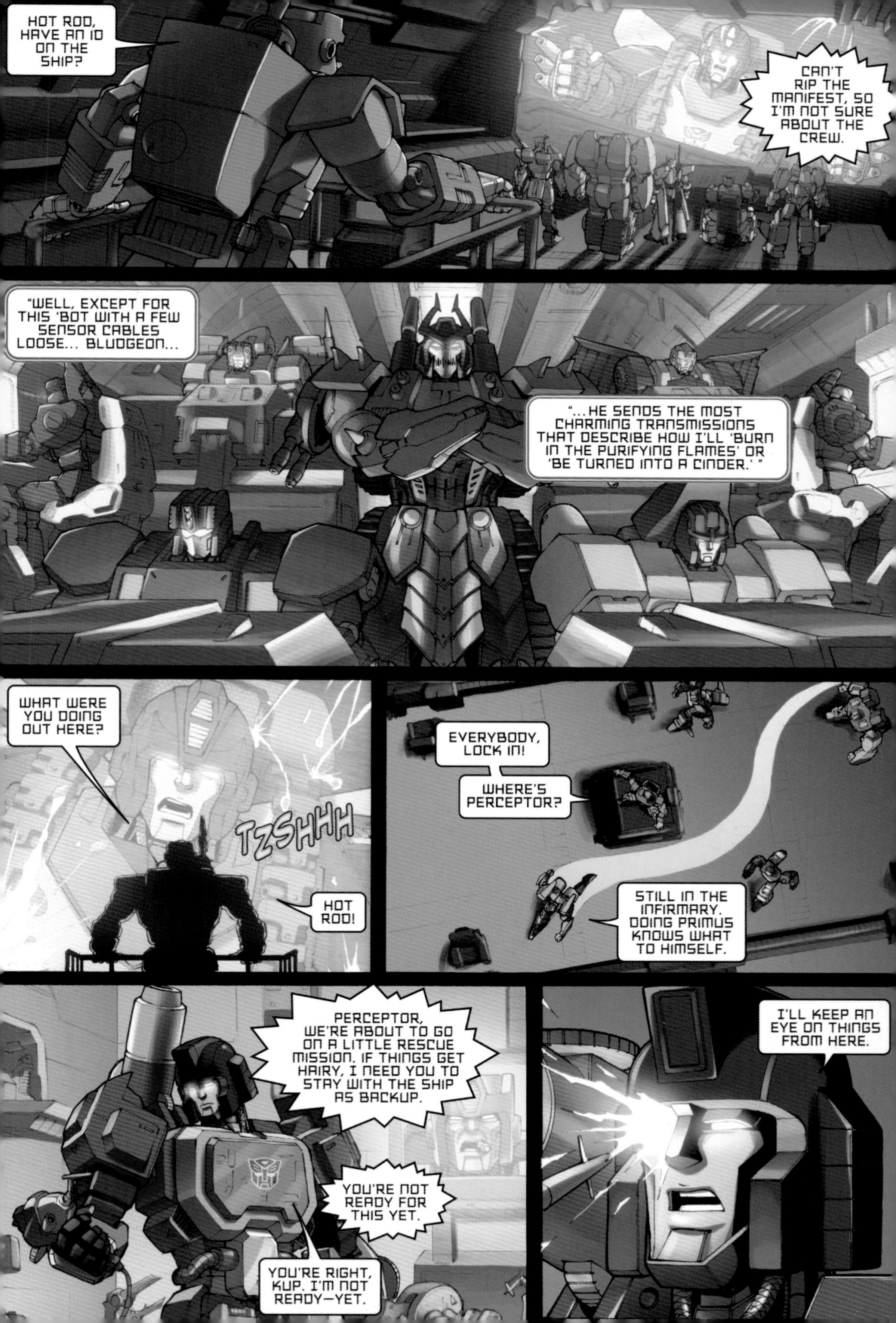
HOT ROD, HAVE AN ID ON THE SHIP?
CAN'T RIP THE MANIFEST, SO I'M NOT SURE ABOUT THE CREW.
"WELL, EXCEPT FOR THIS 'BOT WITH A FEW SENSOR CABLES LOOSE... BLUDGEON...
"...HE SENDS THE MOST CHARMING TRANSMISSIONS THAT DESCRIBE HOW I'LL 'BURN IN THE PURIFYING FLAMES' OR 'BE TURNED INTO A CINDER.' "
WHAT WERE YOU DOING OUT HERE?
TZSHHH
HOT ROD!
EVERYBODY, LOCK IN!
WHERE'S PERCEPTOR?
STILL IN THE INFIRMARY. DOING PRIMUS KNOWS WHAT TO HIMSELF.
PERCEPTOR, WE'RE ABOUT TO GO ON A LITTLE RESCUE MISSION. IF THINGS GET HAIRY, I NEED YOU TO STAY WITH THE SHIP AS BACKUP.
YOU'RE NOT READY FOR THIS YET.
YOU'RE RIGHT, KUP. I'M NOT READY—YET.
I'LL KEEP AN EYE ON THINGS FROM HERE.

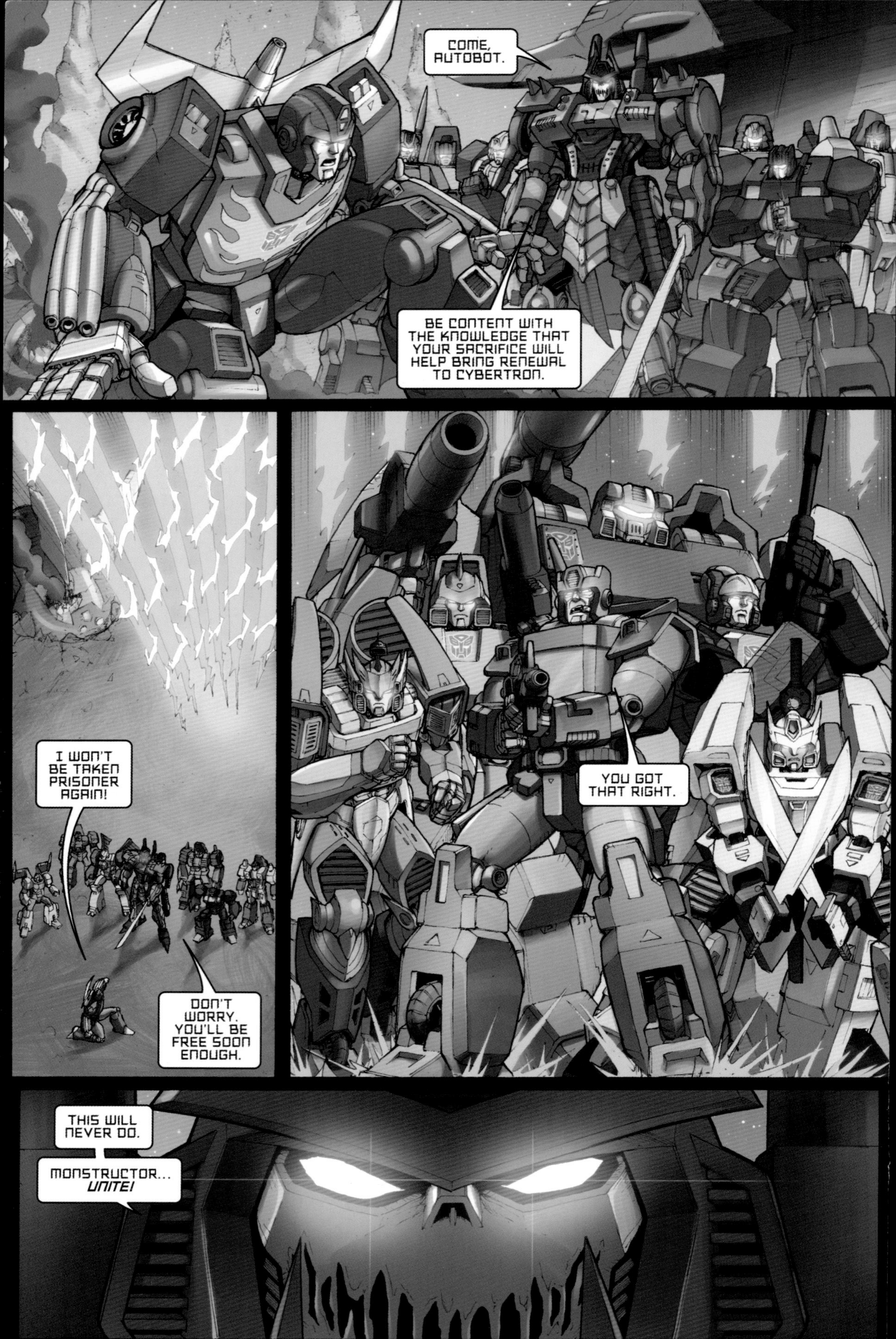
COME, AUTOBOT.
BE CONTENT WITH THE KNOWLEDGE THAT YOUR SACRIFICE WILL HELP BRING RENEWAL TO CYBERTRON.
I WON'T BE TAKEN PRISONER AGAIN!
DON'T WORRY. YOU'LL BE FREE SOON ENOUGH.
YOU GOT THAT RIGHT.
THIS WILL NEVER DO.
MONSTRUCTOR... UNITE!

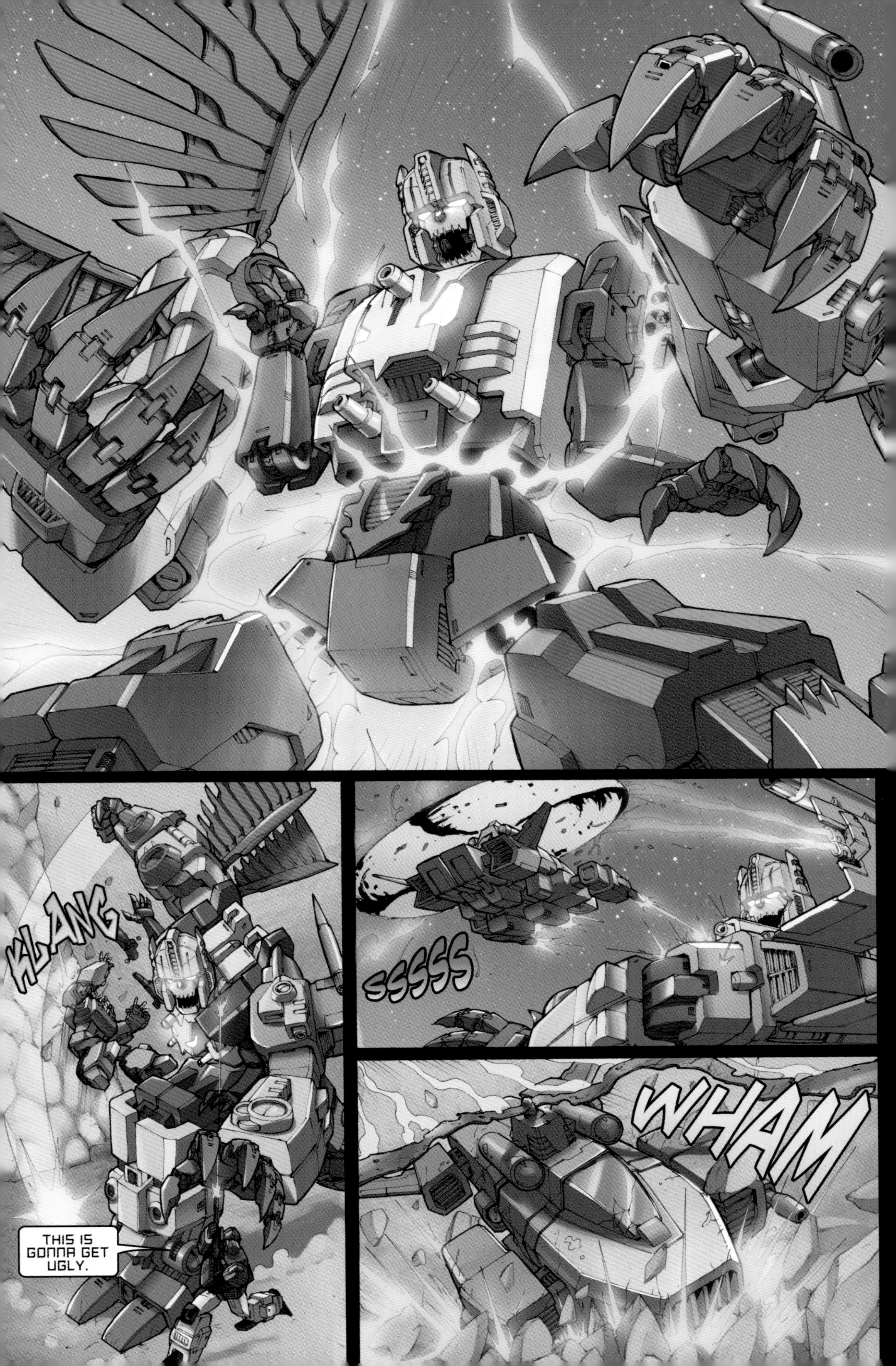
KLANG
THIS IS GONNA GET UGLY.
SSSSS
WHAM

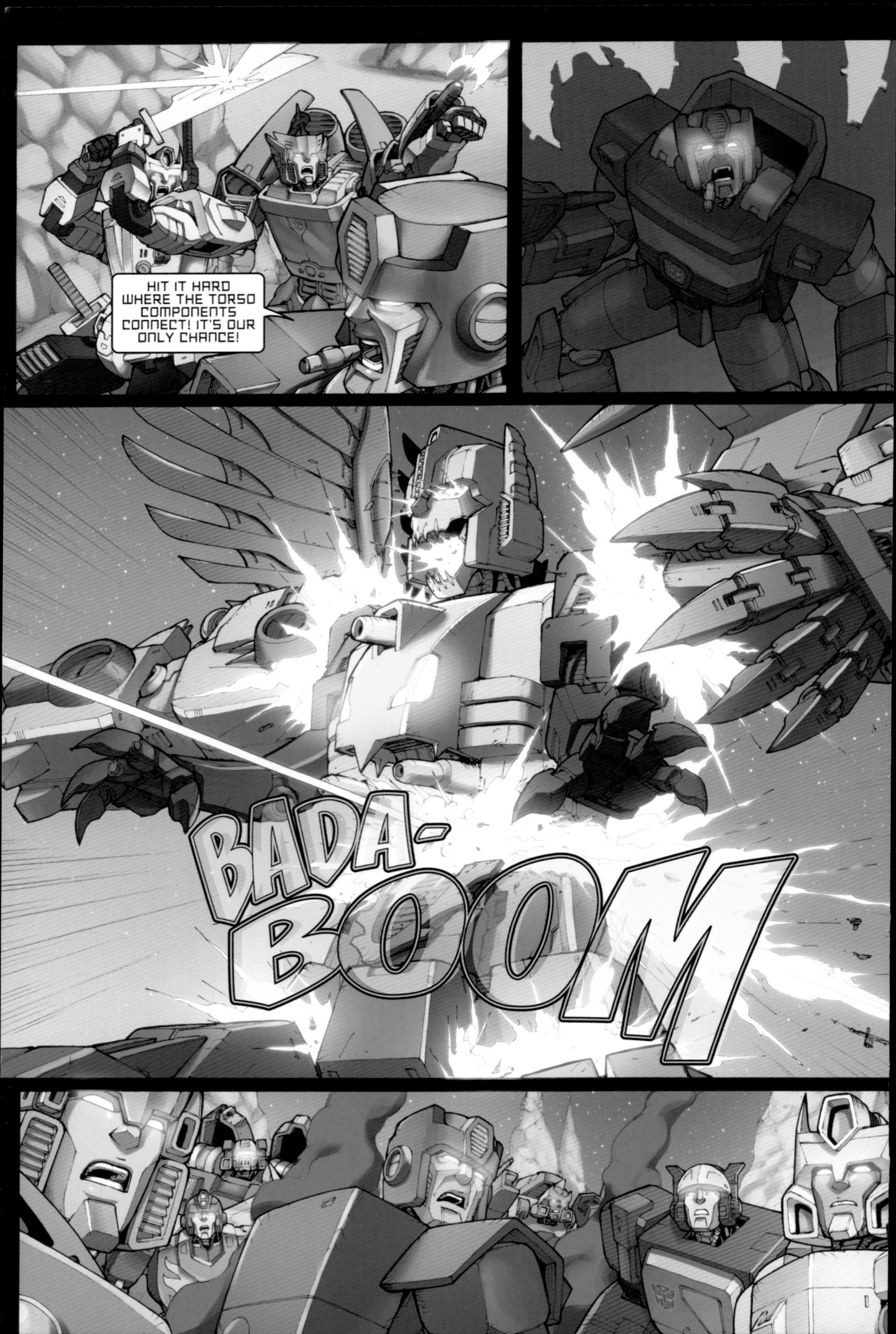

HIT IT HARD WHERE THE TORSO COMPONENTS CONNECT! IT'S OUR ONLY CHANCE!
BADA-BOOM

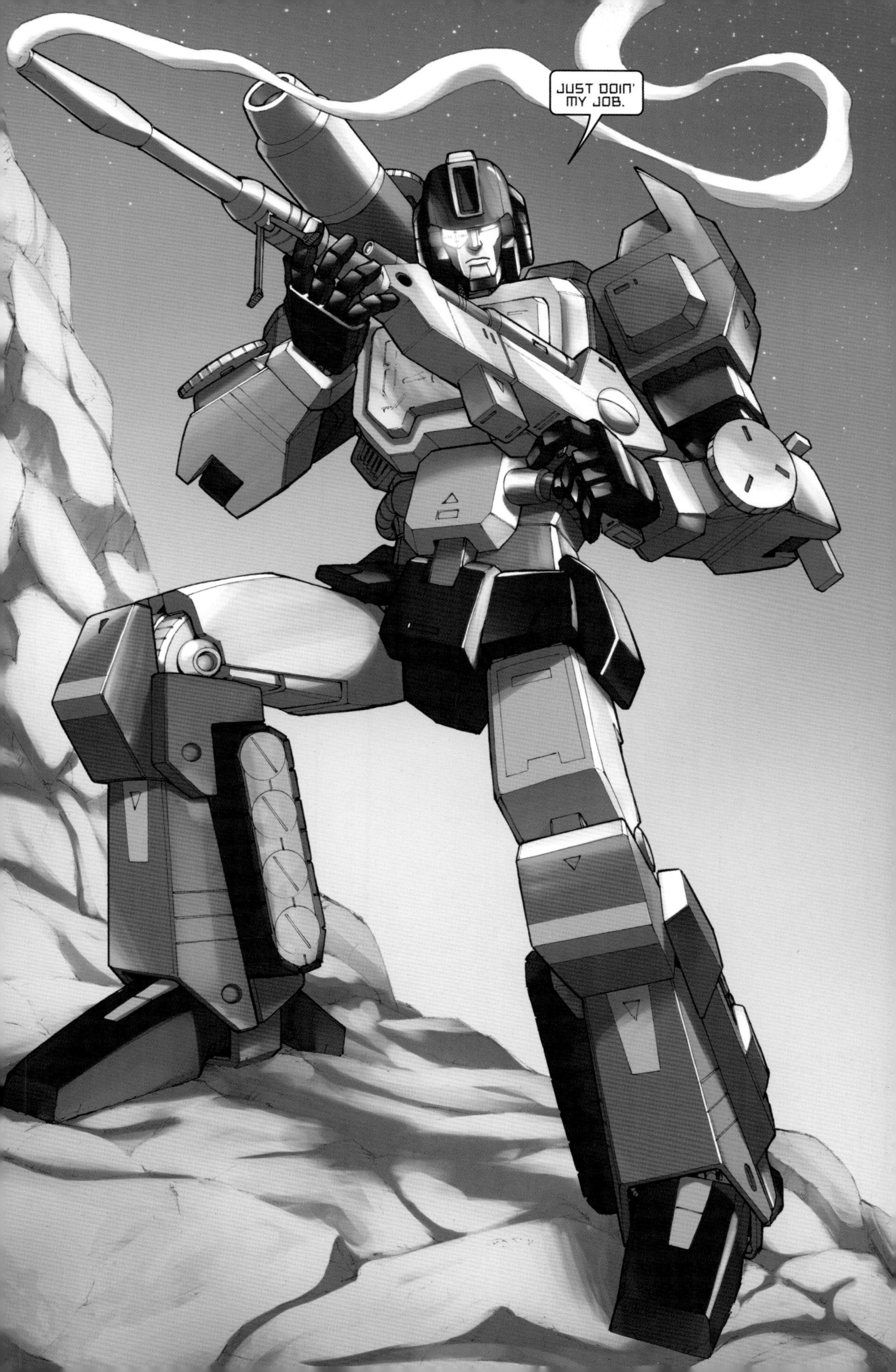
JUST DOIN' MY JOB.

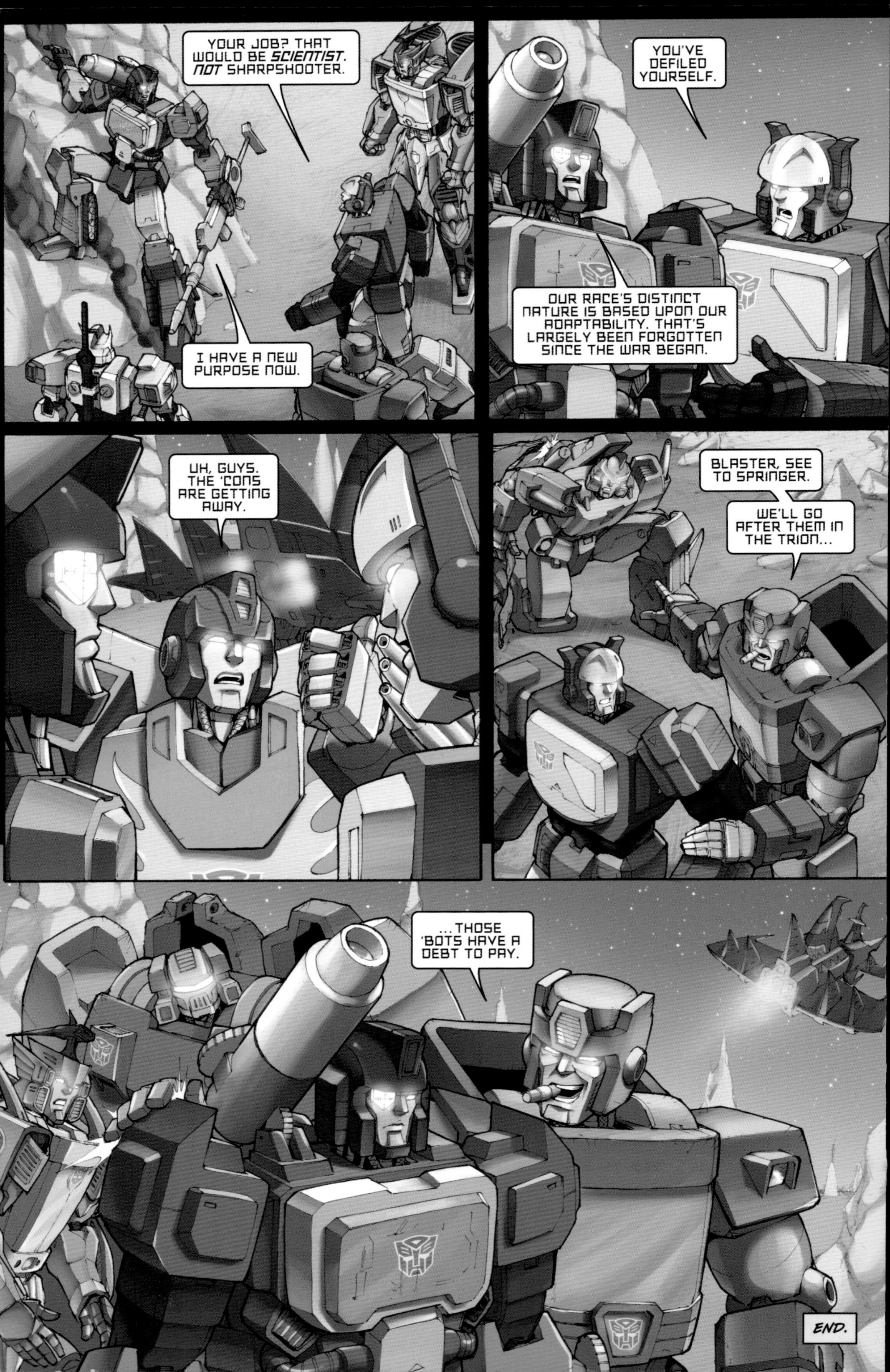

YOUR JOB? THAT WOULD BE *SCIENTIST*. *NOT* SHARPSHOOTER.
I HAVE A NEW PURPOSE NOW.
YOU'VE DEFILED YOURSELF.
OUR RACE'S DISTINCT NATURE IS BASED UPON OUR ADAPTABILITY. THAT'S LARGELY BEEN FORGOTTEN SINCE THE WAR BEGAN.
UH, GUYS. THE 'CONS ARE GETTING AWAY.
BLASTER, SEE TO SPRINGER.
WE'LL GO AFTER THEM IN THE TRION...
...THOSE 'BOTS HAVE A DEBT TO PAY.
END.

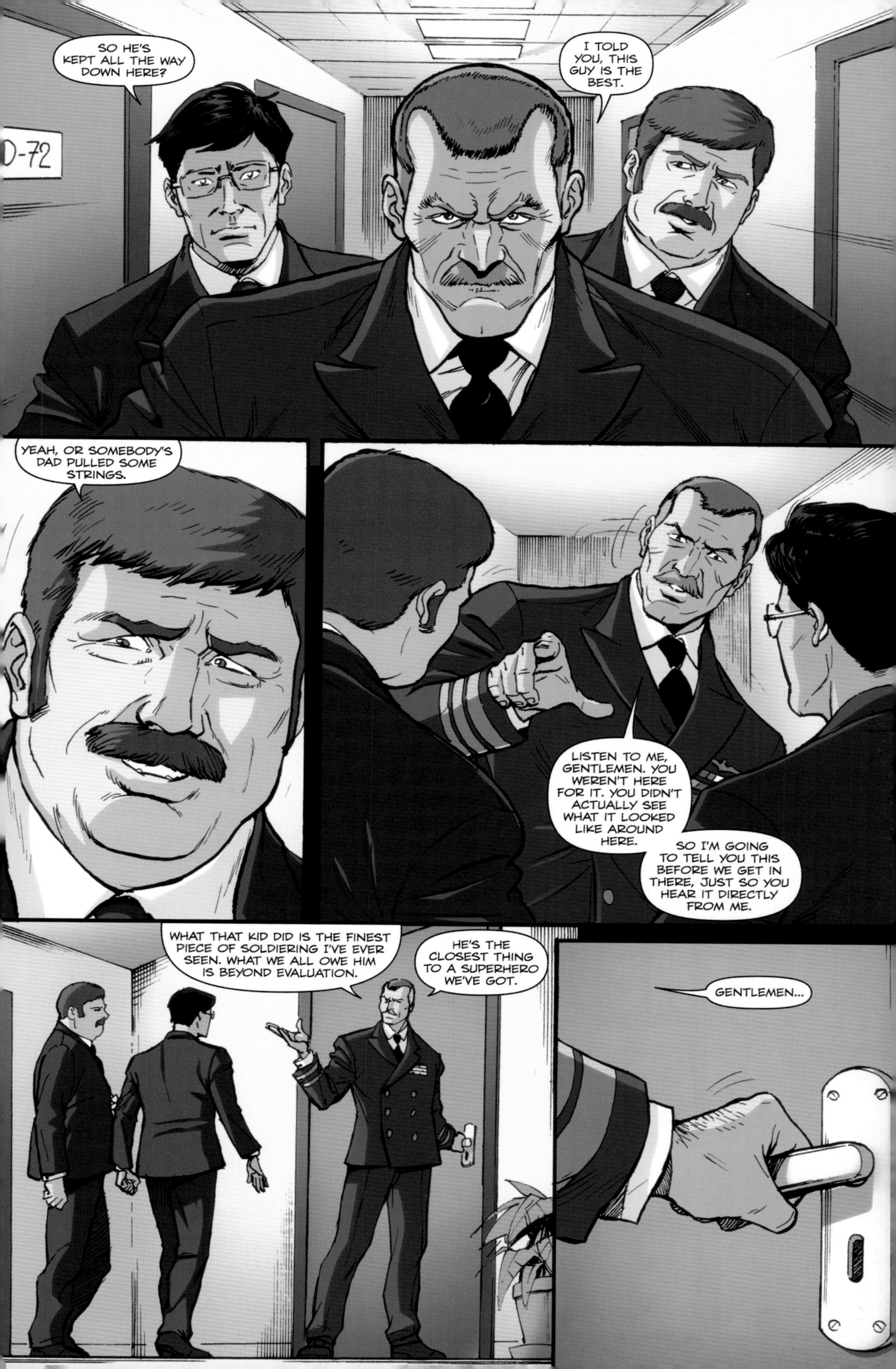
D-72
SO HE'S KEPT ALL THE WAY DOWN HERE?
I TOLD YOU, THIS GUY IS THE BEST.
YEAH, OR SOMEBODY'S DAD PULLED SOME STRINGS.
LISTEN TO ME, GENTLEMEN. YOU WEREN'T HERE FOR IT. YOU DIDN'T ACTUALLY SEE WHAT IT LOOKED LIKE AROUND HERE.
SO I'M GOING TO TELL YOU THIS BEFORE WE GET IN THERE, JUST SO YOU HEAR IT DIRECTLY FROM ME.
WHAT THAT KID DID IS THE FINEST PIECE OF SOLDIERING I'VE EVER SEEN. WHAT WE ALL OWE HIM IS BEYOND EVALUATION.
HE'S THE CLOSEST THING TO A SUPERHERO WE'VE GOT.
GENTLEMEN...

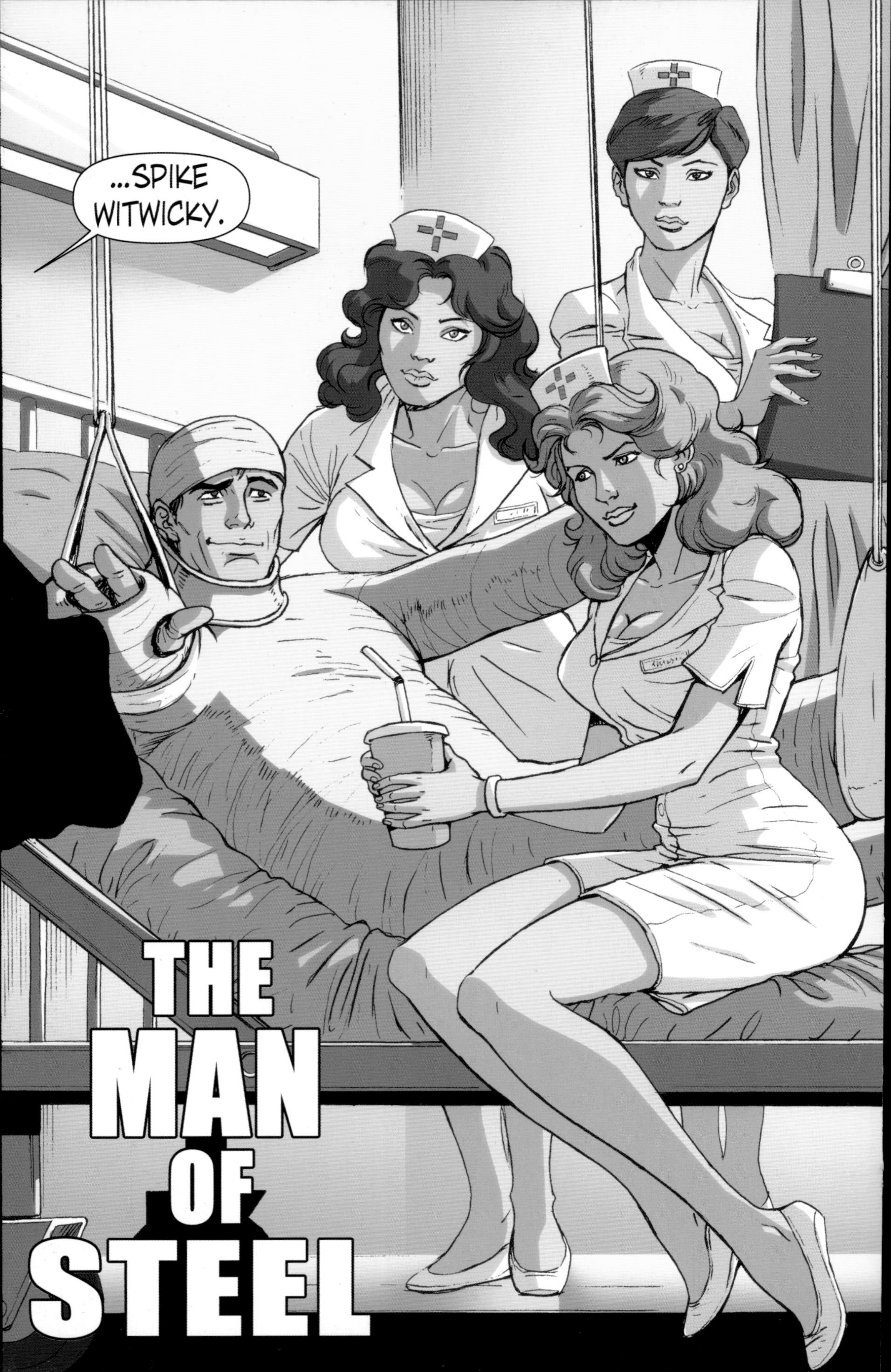
...SPIKE WITWICKY.
THE MAN OF STEEL

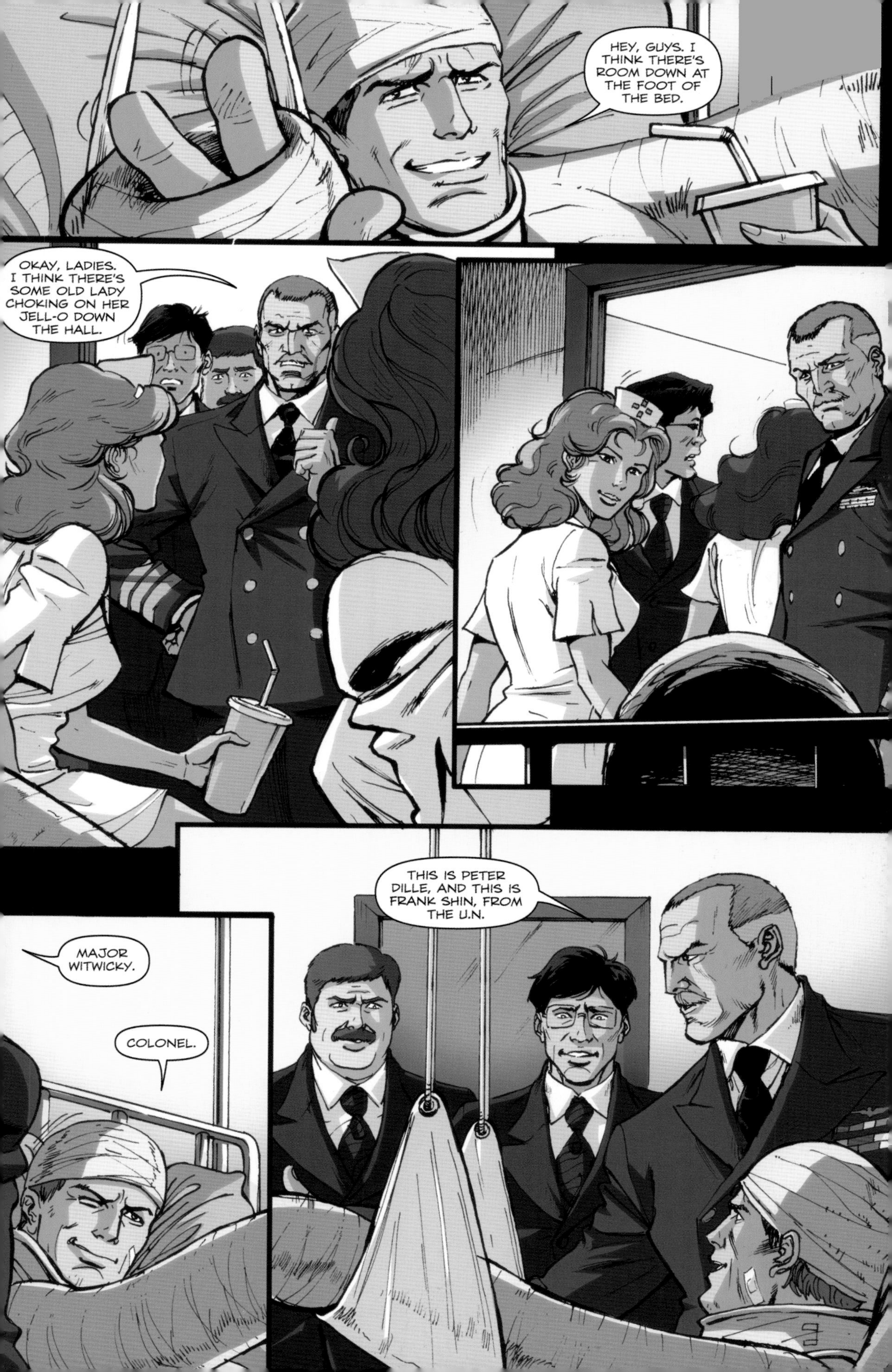
HEY, GUYS. I THINK THERE'S ROOM DOWN AT THE FOOT OF THE BED.
OKAY, LADIES. I THINK THERE'S SOME OLD LADY CHOKING ON HER JELL-O DOWN THE HALL.
MAJOR WITWICKY.
COLONEL.
THIS IS PETER DILLE, AND THIS IS FRANK SHIN, FROM THE U.N.

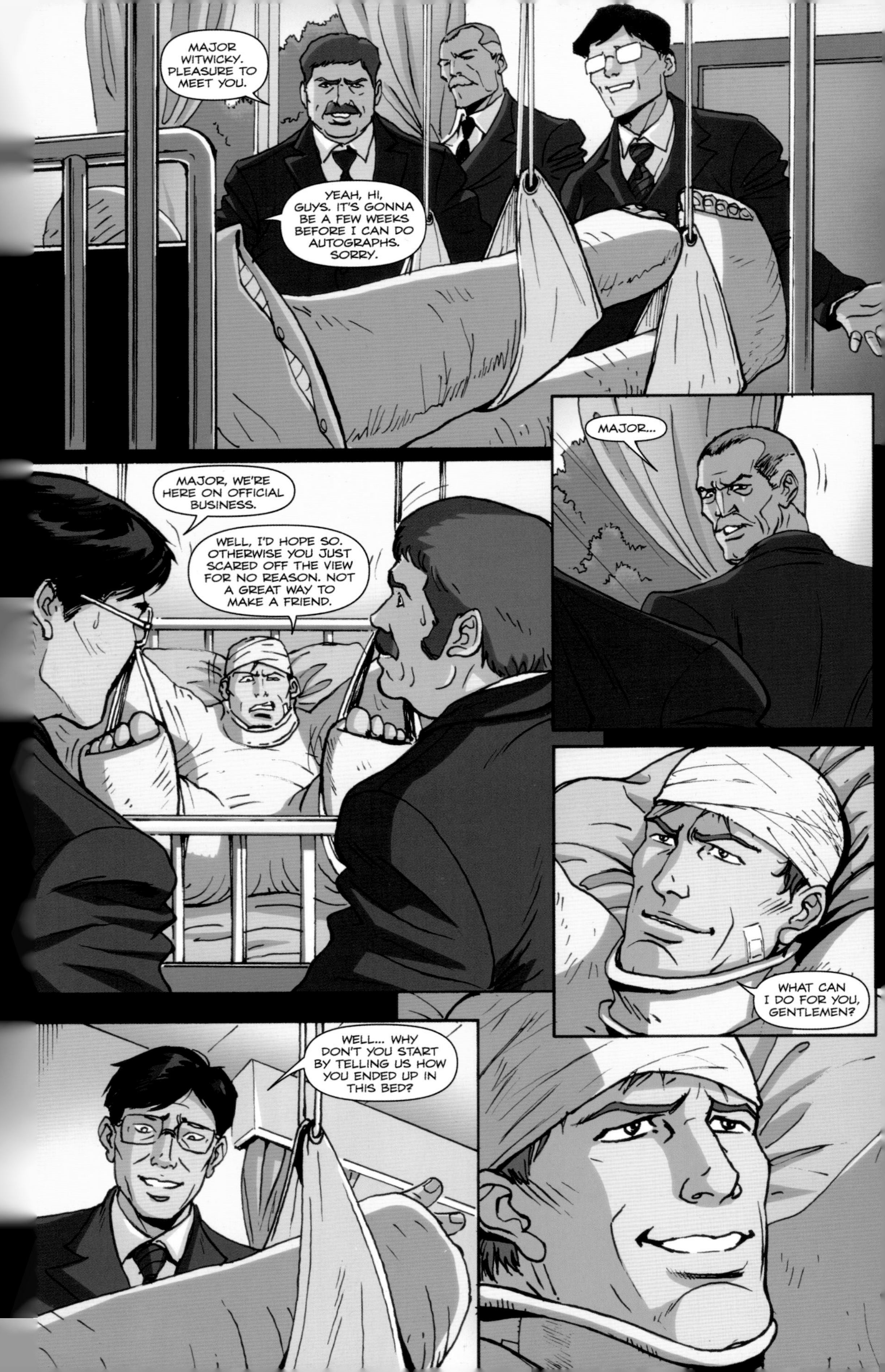
MAJOR WITWICKY. PLEASURE TO MEET YOU.
YEAH, HI, GUYS. IT'S GONNA BE A FEW WEEKS BEFORE I CAN DO AUTOGRAPHS. SORRY.
MAJOR, WE'RE HERE ON OFFICIAL BUSINESS.
WELL, I'D HOPE SO. OTHERWISE YOU JUST SCARED OFF THE VIEW FOR NO REASON. NOT A GREAT WAY TO MAKE A FRIEND.
MAJOR...
WHAT CAN I DO FOR YOU, GENTLEMEN?
WELL... WHY DON'T YOU START BY TELLING US HOW YOU ENDED UP IN THIS BED?

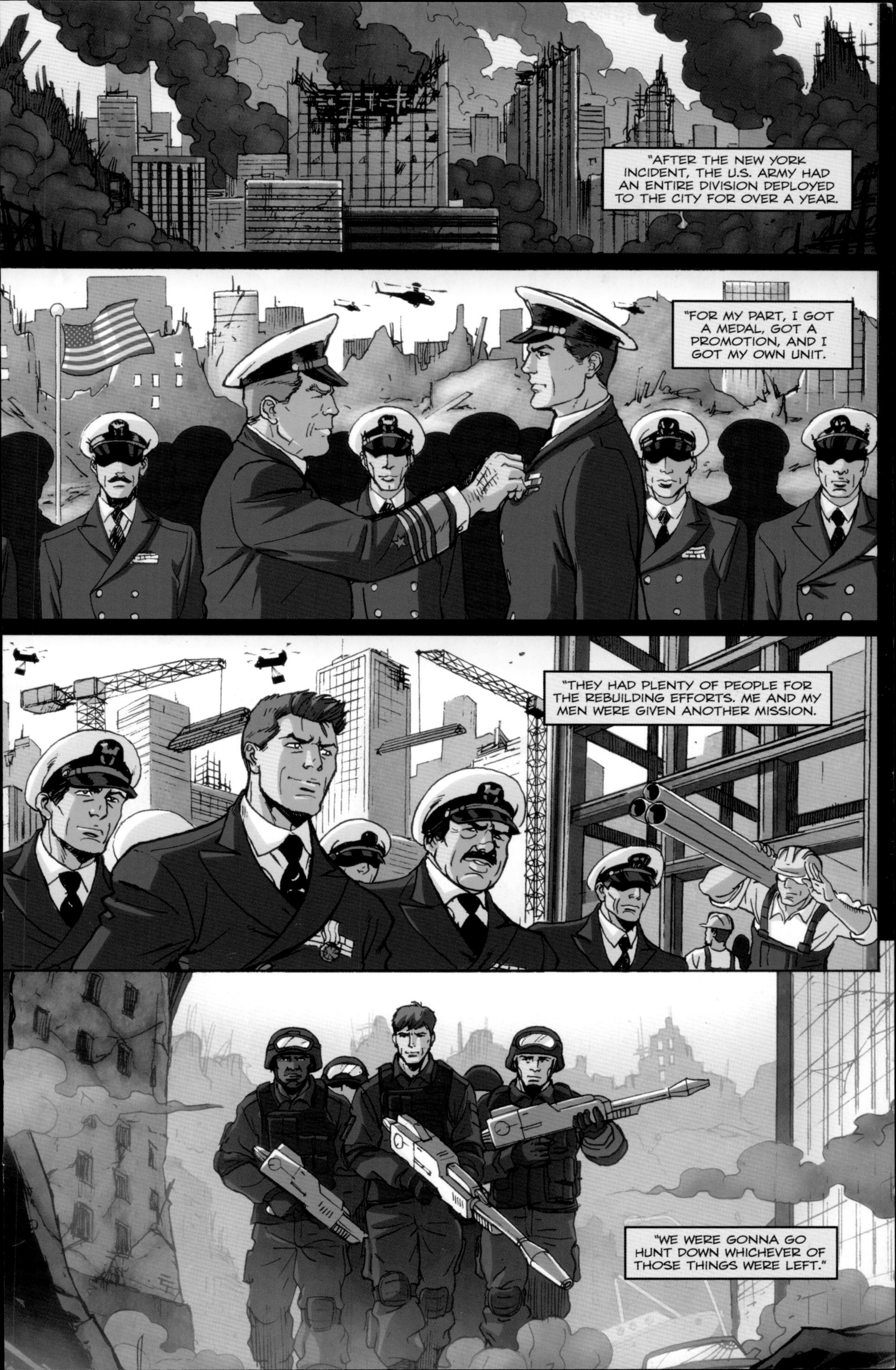
"AFTER THE NEW YORK INCIDENT, THE U.S. ARMY HAD AN ENTIRE DIVISION DEPLOYED TO THE CITY FOR OVER A YEAR.
"FOR MY PART, I GOT A MEDAL, GOT A PROMOTION, AND I GOT MY OWN UNIT.
"THEY HAD PLENTY OF PEOPLE FOR THE REBUILDING EFFORTS. ME AND MY MEN WERE GIVEN ANOTHER MISSION.
"WE WERE GONNA GO HUNT DOWN WHICHEVER OF THOSE THINGS WERE LEFT."

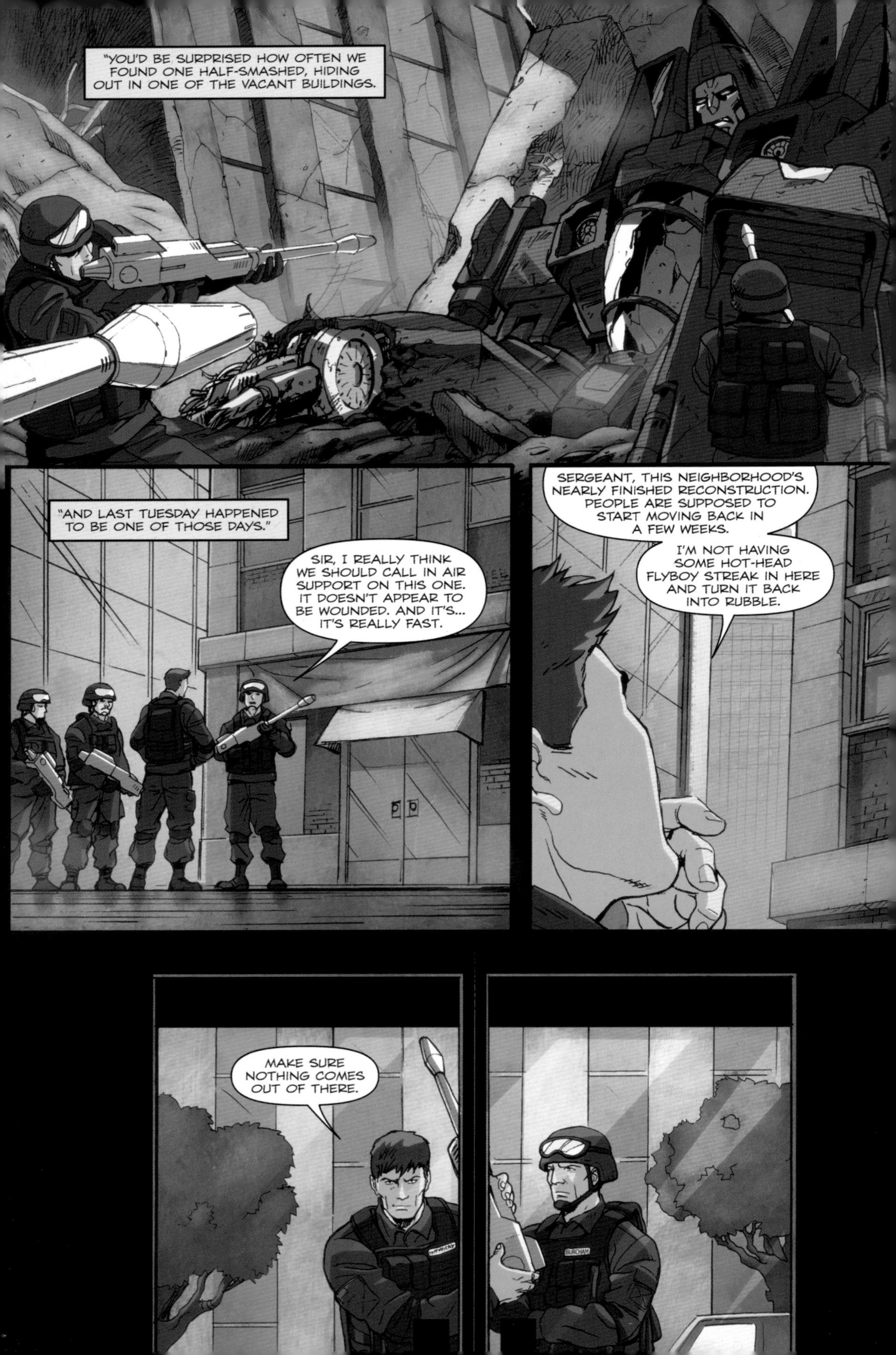
"YOU'D BE SURPRISED HOW OFTEN WE FOUND ONE HALF-SMASHED, HIDING OUT IN ONE OF THE VACANT BUILDINGS.
"AND LAST TUESDAY HAPPENED TO BE ONE OF THOSE DAYS."
SIR, I REALLY THINK WE SHOULD CALL IN AIR SUPPORT ON THIS ONE. IT DOESN'T APPEAR TO BE WOUNDED. AND IT'S... IT'S REALLY FAST.
SERGEANT, THIS NEIGHBORHOOD'S NEARLY FINISHED RECONSTRUCTION. PEOPLE ARE SUPPOSED TO START MOVING BACK IN A FEW WEEKS.
I'M NOT HAVING SOME HOT-HEAD FLYBOY STREAK IN HERE AND TURN IT BACK INTO RUBBLE.
MAKE SURE NOTHING COMES OUT OF THERE.

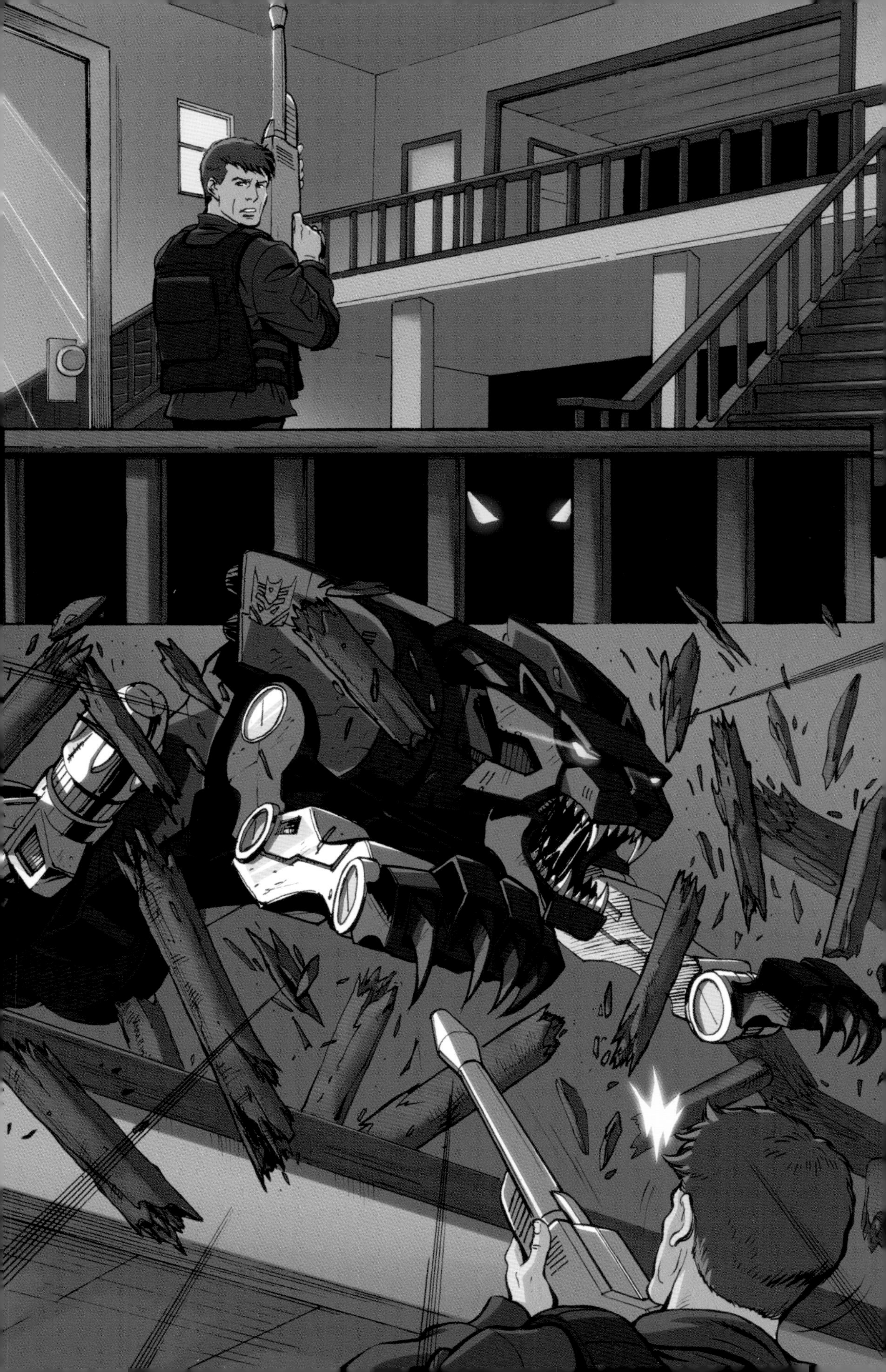

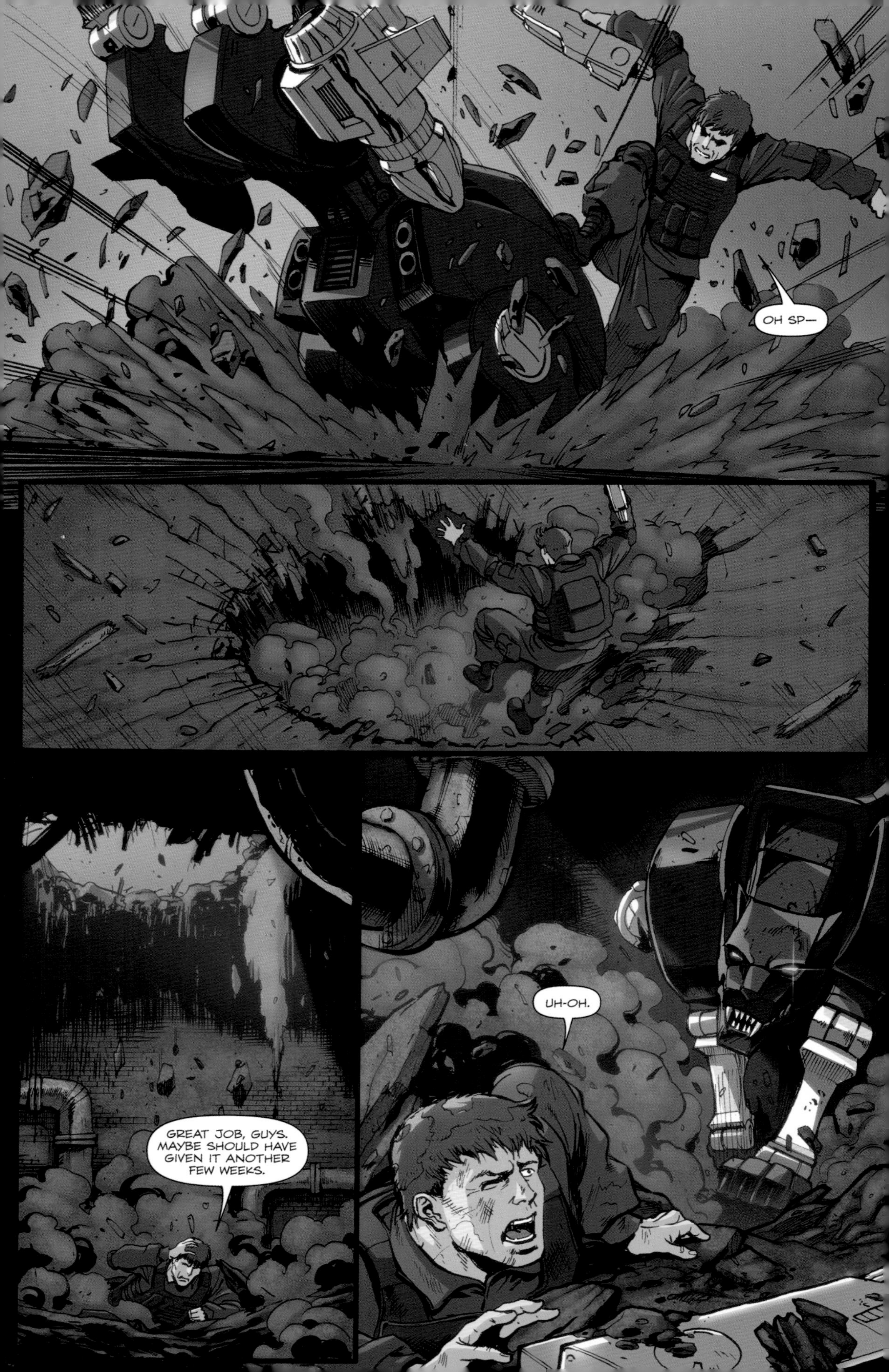
OH SP—
GREAT JOB, GUYS. MAYBE SHOULD HAVE GIVEN IT ANOTHER FEW WEEKS.
UH-OH.

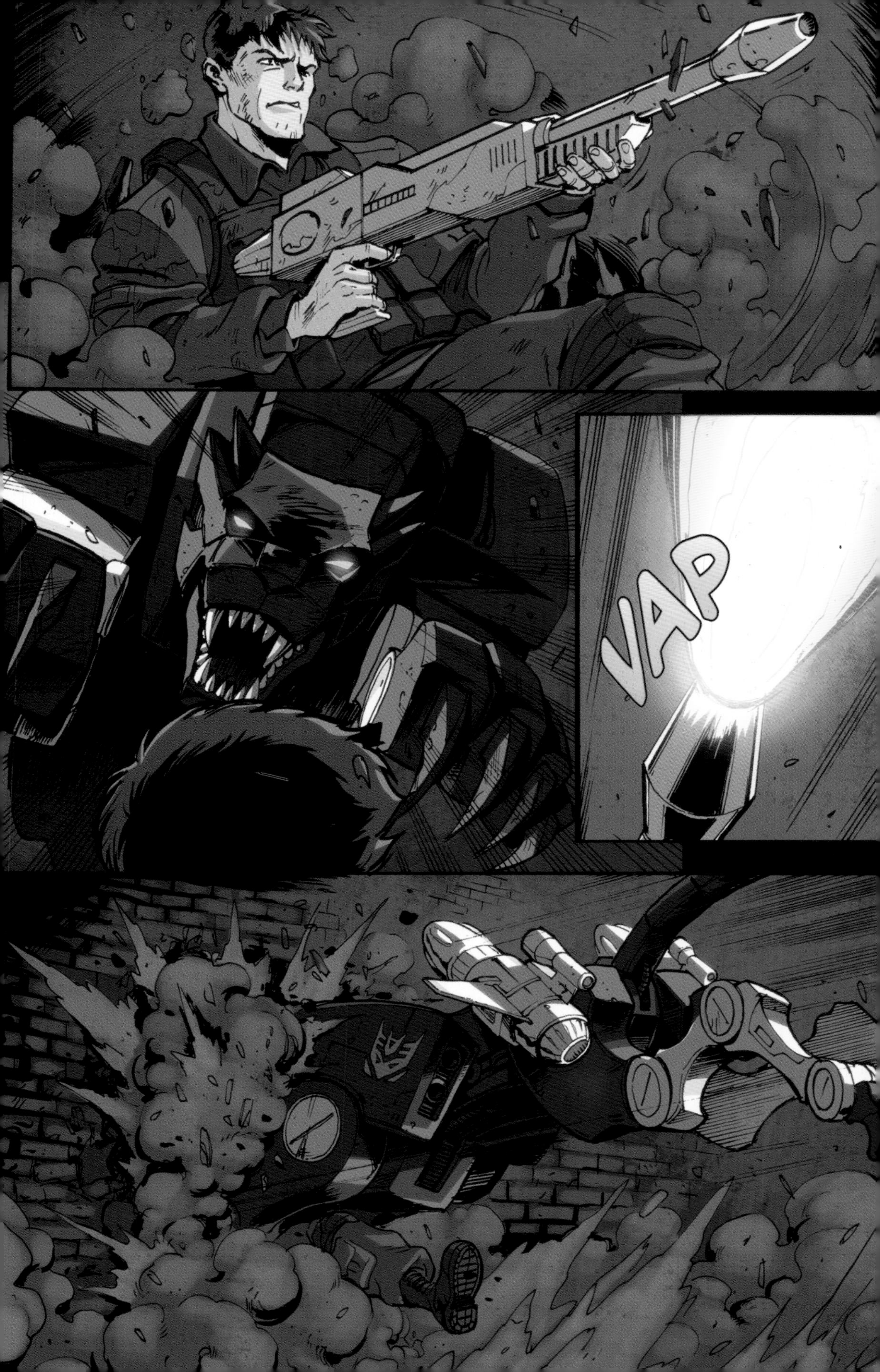
VAP

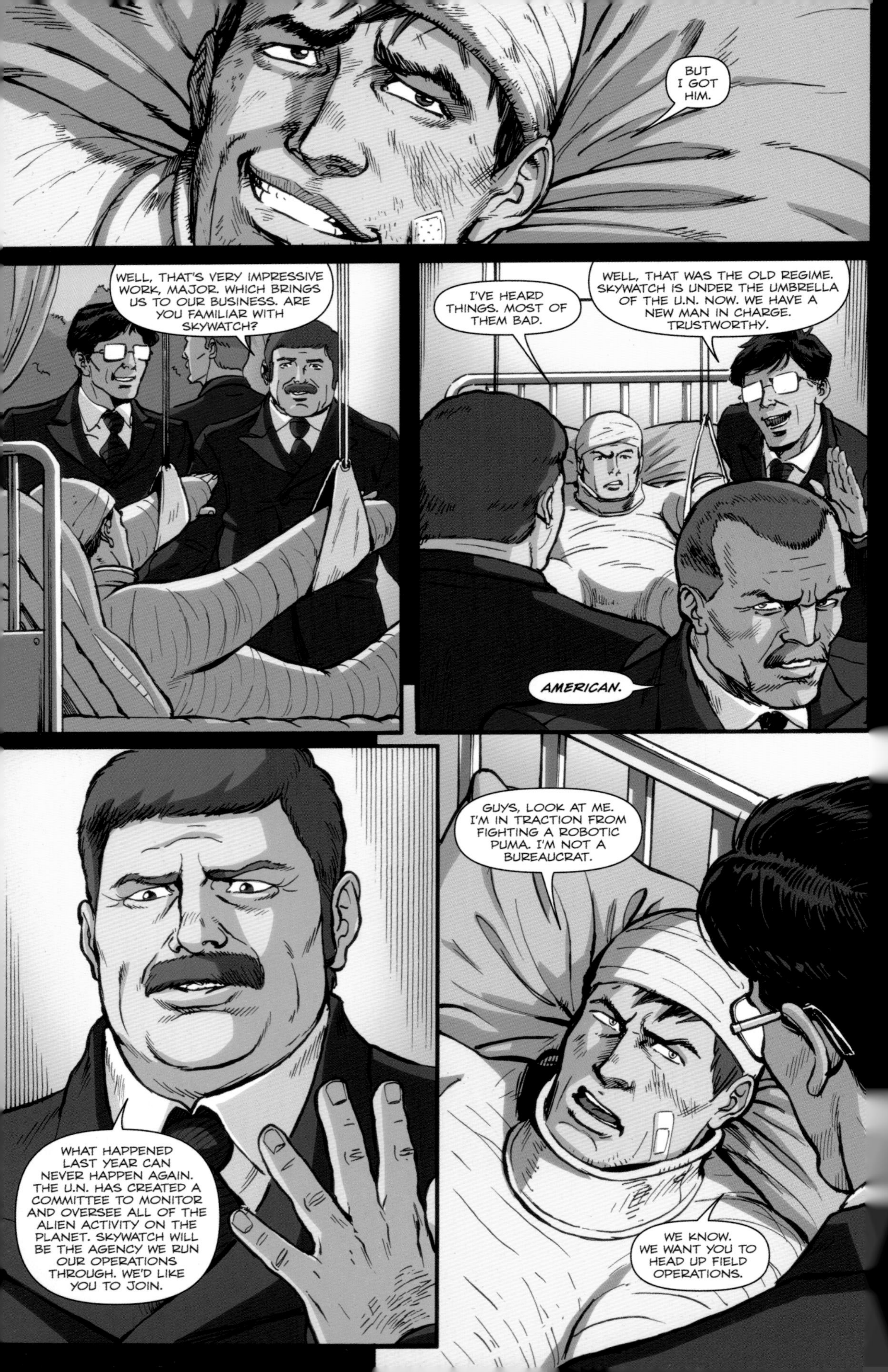
BUT I GOT HIM.
WELL, THAT'S VERY IMPRESSIVE WORK, MAJOR. WHICH BRINGS US TO OUR BUSINESS. ARE YOU FAMILIAR WITH SKYWATCH?
I'VE HEARD THINGS. MOST OF THEM BAD.
WELL, THAT WAS THE OLD REGIME. SKYWATCH IS UNDER THE UMBRELLA OF THE U.N. NOW. WE HAVE A NEW MAN IN CHARGE. TRUSTWORTHY.
AMERICAN.
WHAT HAPPENED LAST YEAR CAN NEVER HAPPEN AGAIN. THE U.N. HAS CREATED A COMMITTEE TO MONITOR AND OVERSEE ALL OF THE ALIEN ACTIVITY ON THE PLANET. SKYWATCH WILL BE THE AGENCY WE RUN OUR OPERATIONS THROUGH. WE'D LIKE YOU TO JOIN.
GUYS, LOOK AT ME. I'M IN TRACTION FROM FIGHTING A ROBOTIC PUMA. I'M NOT A BUREAUCRAT.
WE KNOW. WE WANT YOU TO HEAD UP FIELD OPERATIONS.

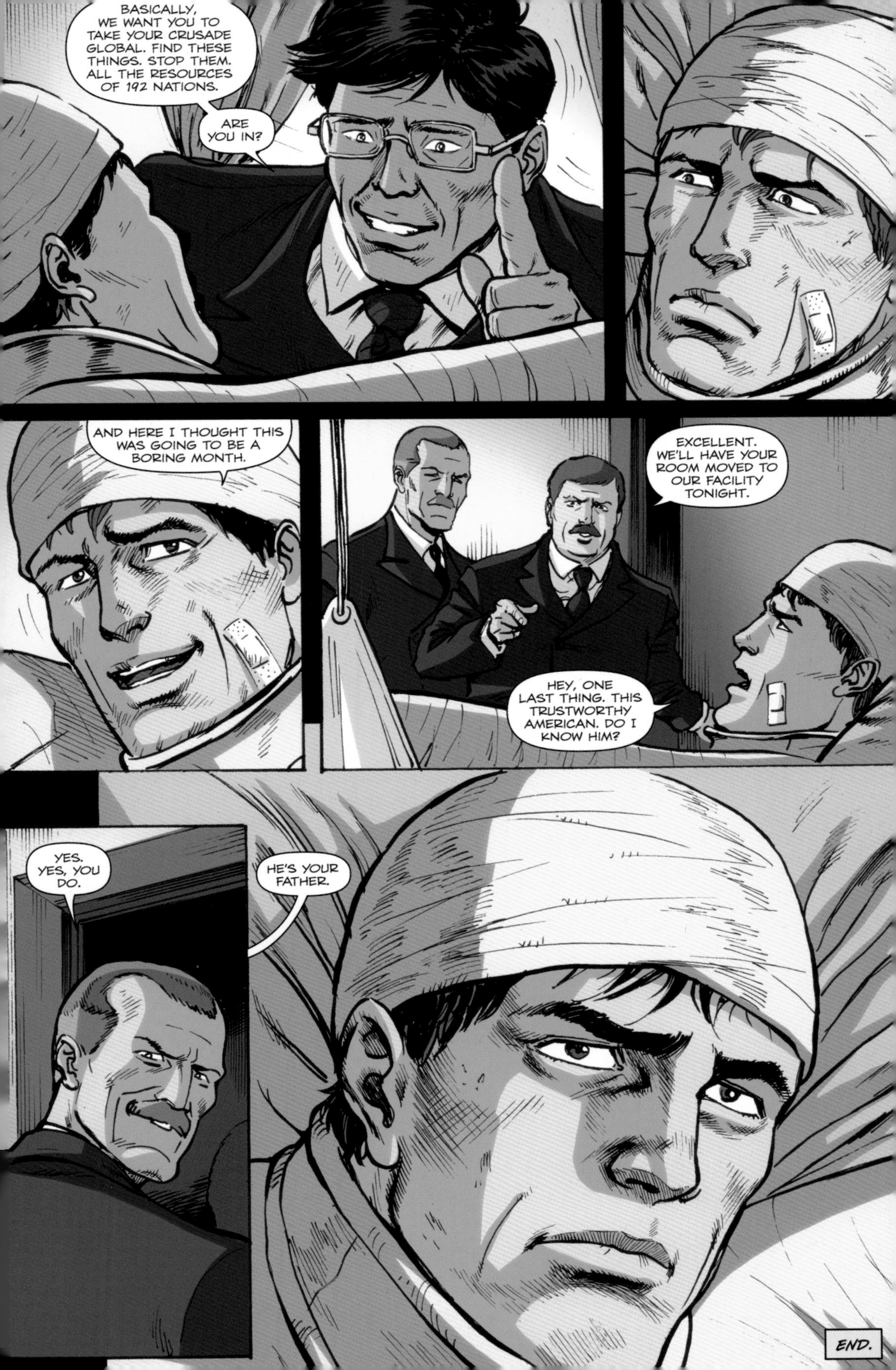
BASICALLY, WE WANT YOU TO TAKE YOUR CRUSADE GLOBAL. FIND THESE THINGS. STOP THEM. ALL THE RESOURCES OF 192 NATIONS.
ARE YOU IN?
AND HERE I THOUGHT THIS WAS GOING TO BE A BORING MONTH.
EXCELLENT. WE'LL HAVE YOUR ROOM MOVED TO OUR FACILITY TONIGHT.
HEY, ONE LAST THING. THIS TRUSTWORTHY AMERICAN. DO I KNOW HIM?
YES. YES, YOU DO.
HE'S YOUR FATHER.
END.

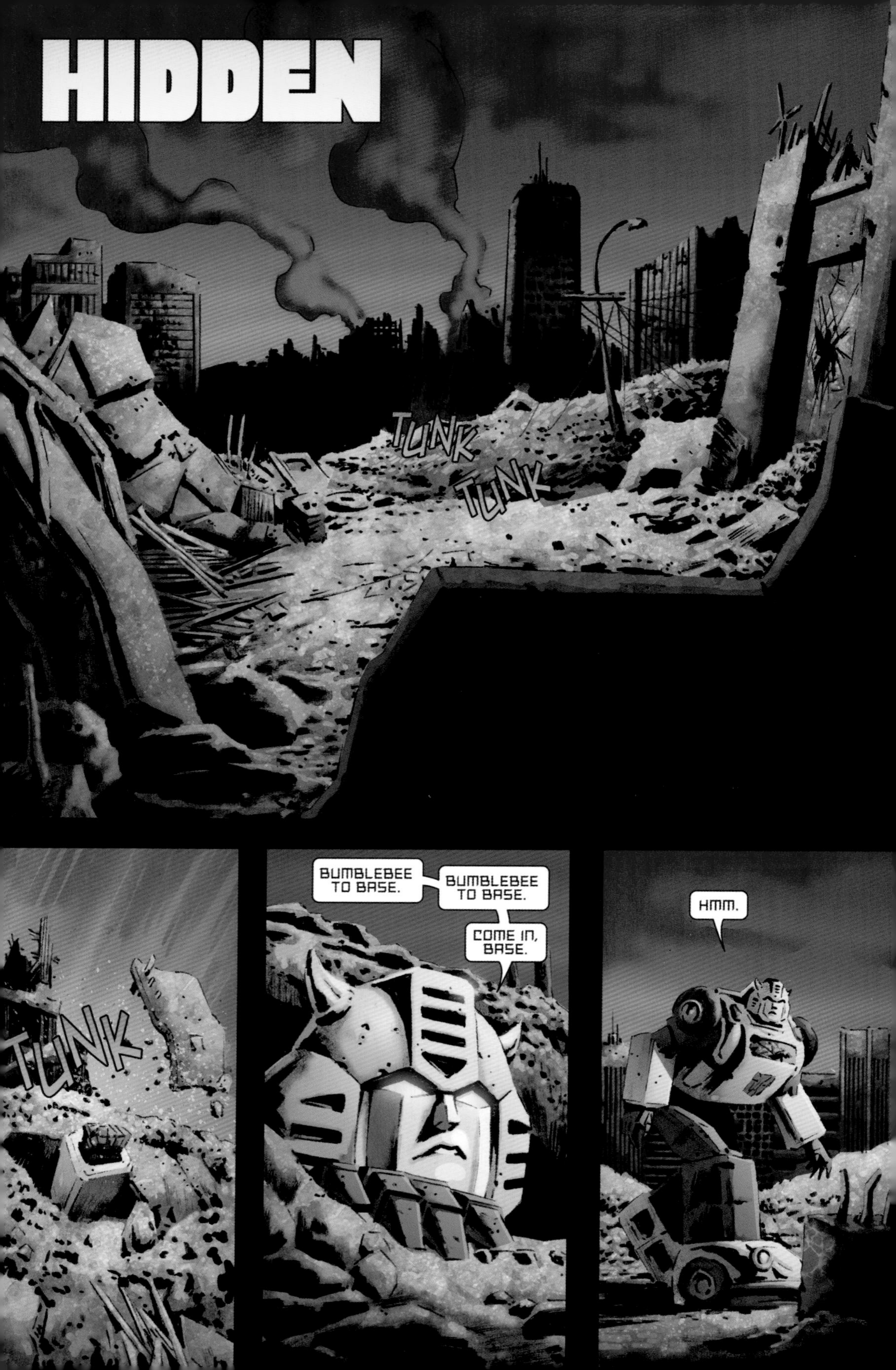
HIDDEN
TUNK
TUNK
TUNK
BUMBLEBEE TO BASE.
BUMBLEBEE TO BASE.
COME IN, BASE.
HMM.

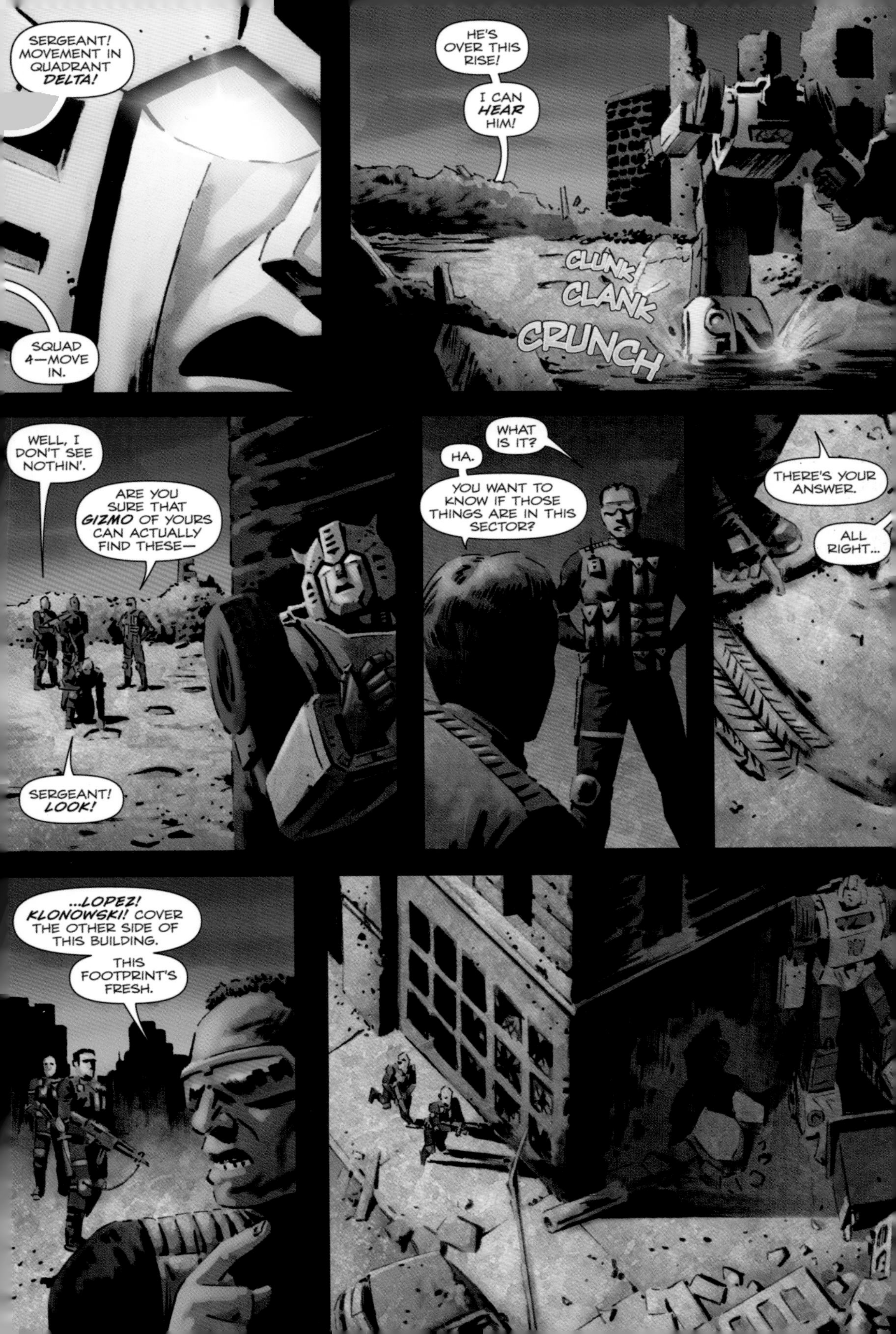
SERGEANT! MOVEMENT IN QUADRANT DELTA!
SQUAD 4—MOVE IN.
HE'S OVER THIS RISE!
I CAN HEAR HIM!
CLUNK
CLANK
CRUNCH
WELL, I DON'T SEE NOTHIN'.
ARE YOU SURE THAT GIZMO OF YOURS CAN ACTUALLY FIND THESE—
SERGEANT! LOOK!
WHAT IS IT?
HA.
YOU WANT TO KNOW IF THOSE THINGS ARE IN THIS SECTOR?
THERE'S YOUR ANSWER.
ALL RIGHT...
...LOPEZ! KLONOWSKI! COVER THE OTHER SIDE OF THIS BUILDING.
THIS FOOTPRINT'S FRESH.

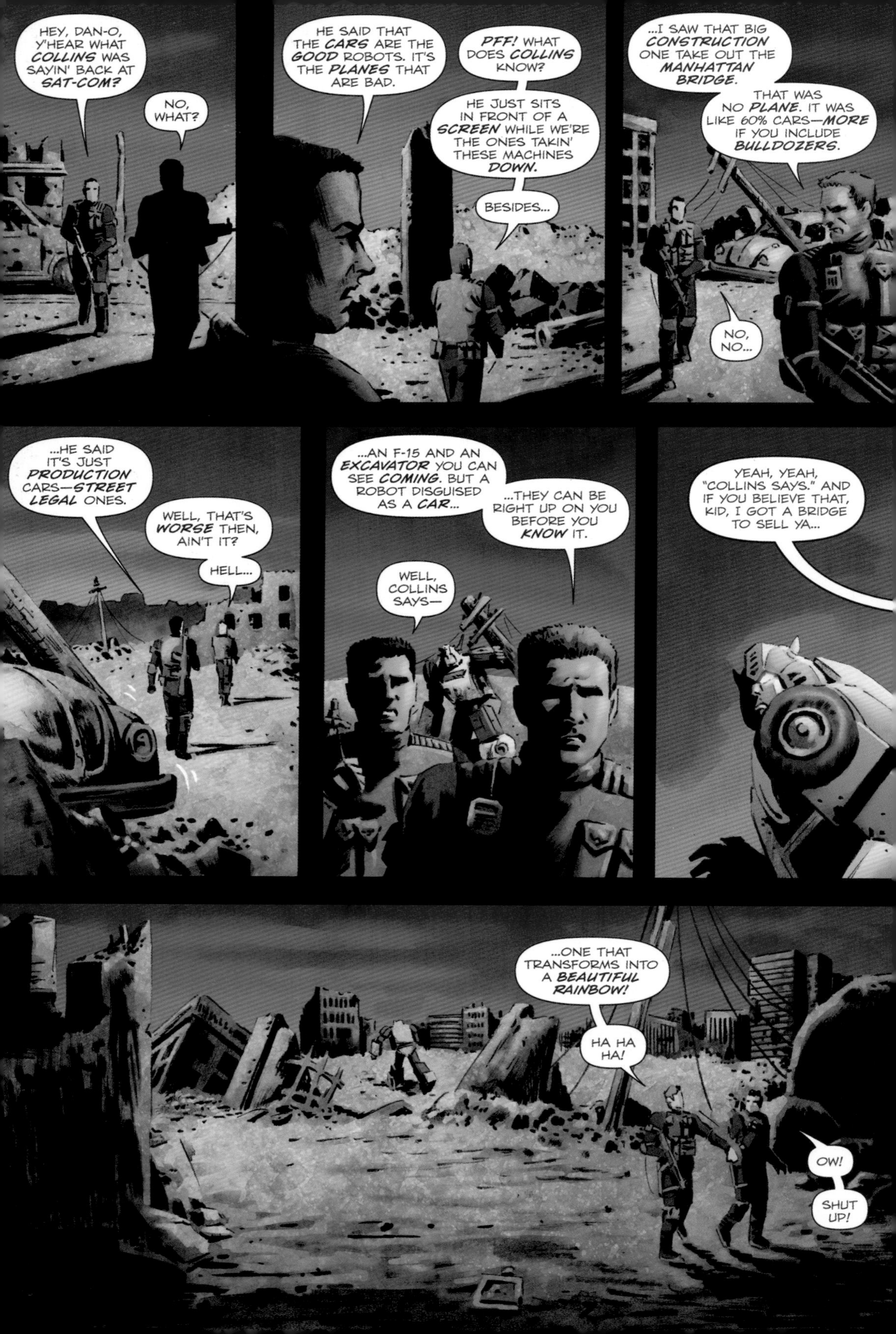
HEY, DAN-O, Y'HEAR WHAT COLLINS WAS SAYIN' BACK AT SAT-COM?
NO, WHAT?
HE SAID THAT THE CARS ARE THE GOOD ROBOTS. IT'S THE PLANES THAT ARE BAD.
PFF! WHAT DOES COLLINS KNOW?
HE JUST SITS IN FRONT OF A SCREEN WHILE WE'RE THE ONES TAKIN' THESE MACHINES DOWN.
BESIDES...
...I SAW THAT BIG CONSTRUCTION ONE TAKE OUT THE MANHATTAN BRIDGE.
THAT WAS NO PLANE. IT WAS LIKE 60% CARS—MORE IF YOU INCLUDE BULLDOZERS.
NO, NO...
...HE SAID IT'S JUST PRODUCTION CARS—STREET LEGAL ONES.
WELL, THAT'S WORSE THEN, AIN'T IT?
HELL...
...AN F-15 AND AN EXCAVATOR YOU CAN SEE COMING. BUT A ROBOT DISGUISED AS A CAR...
...THEY CAN BE RIGHT UP ON YOU BEFORE YOU KNOW IT.
WELL, COLLINS SAYS—
YEAH, YEAH, "COLLINS SAYS." AND IF YOU BELIEVE THAT, KID, I GOT A BRIDGE TO SELL YA...
...ONE THAT TRANSFORMS INTO A BEAUTIFUL RAINBOW!
HA HA HA!
OW!
SHUT UP!

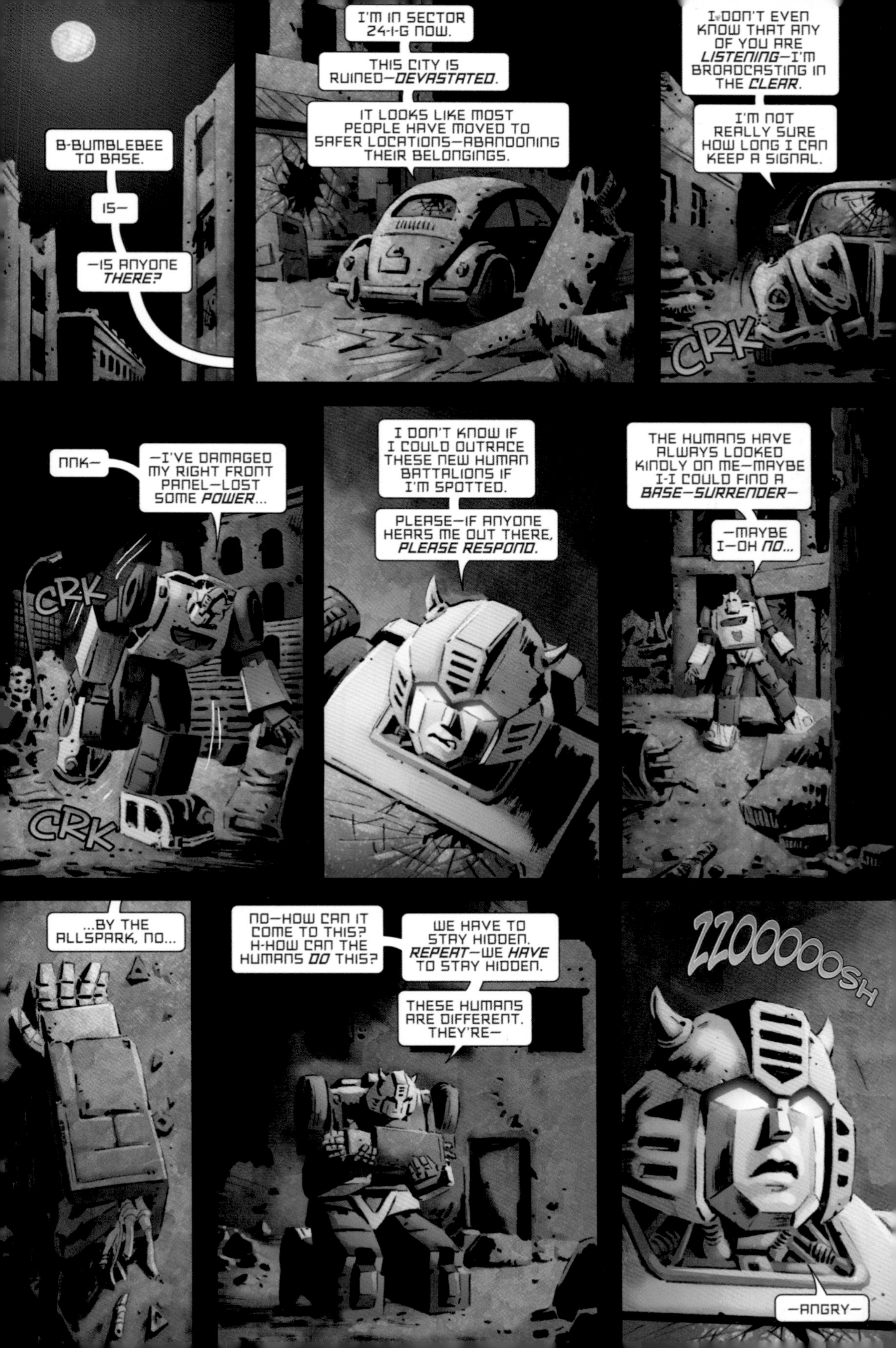
B-BUMBLEBEE TO BASE.
IS—
—IS ANYONE *THERE?*
I'M IN SECTOR 24-I-G NOW.
THIS CITY IS RUINED—*DEVASTATED*.
IT LOOKS LIKE MOST PEOPLE HAVE MOVED TO SAFER LOCATIONS—ABANDONING THEIR BELONGINGS.
I DON'T EVEN KNOW THAT ANY OF YOU ARE *LISTENING*—I'M BROADCASTING IN THE *CLEAR*.
I'M NOT REALLY SURE HOW LONG I CAN KEEP A SIGNAL.
CRK
NNK—
—I'VE DAMAGED MY RIGHT FRONT PANEL—LOST SOME *POWER*...
CRK
CRK
I DON'T KNOW IF I COULD OUTRACE THESE NEW HUMAN BATTALIONS IF I'M SPOTTED.
PLEASE—IF ANYONE HEARS ME OUT THERE, *PLEASE RESPOND.*
THE HUMANS HAVE ALWAYS LOOKED KINDLY ON ME—MAYBE I-I COULD FIND A *BASE—SURRENDER*—
—MAYBE I—OH *NO*...
...BY THE ALLSPARK, NO...
NO—HOW CAN IT COME TO THIS? H-HOW CAN THE HUMANS *DO* THIS?
WE HAVE TO STAY HIDDEN. *REPEAT*—WE *HAVE* TO STAY HIDDEN.
THESE HUMANS ARE DIFFERENT. THEY'RE—
ZZOOOOOOSH
—ANGRY—

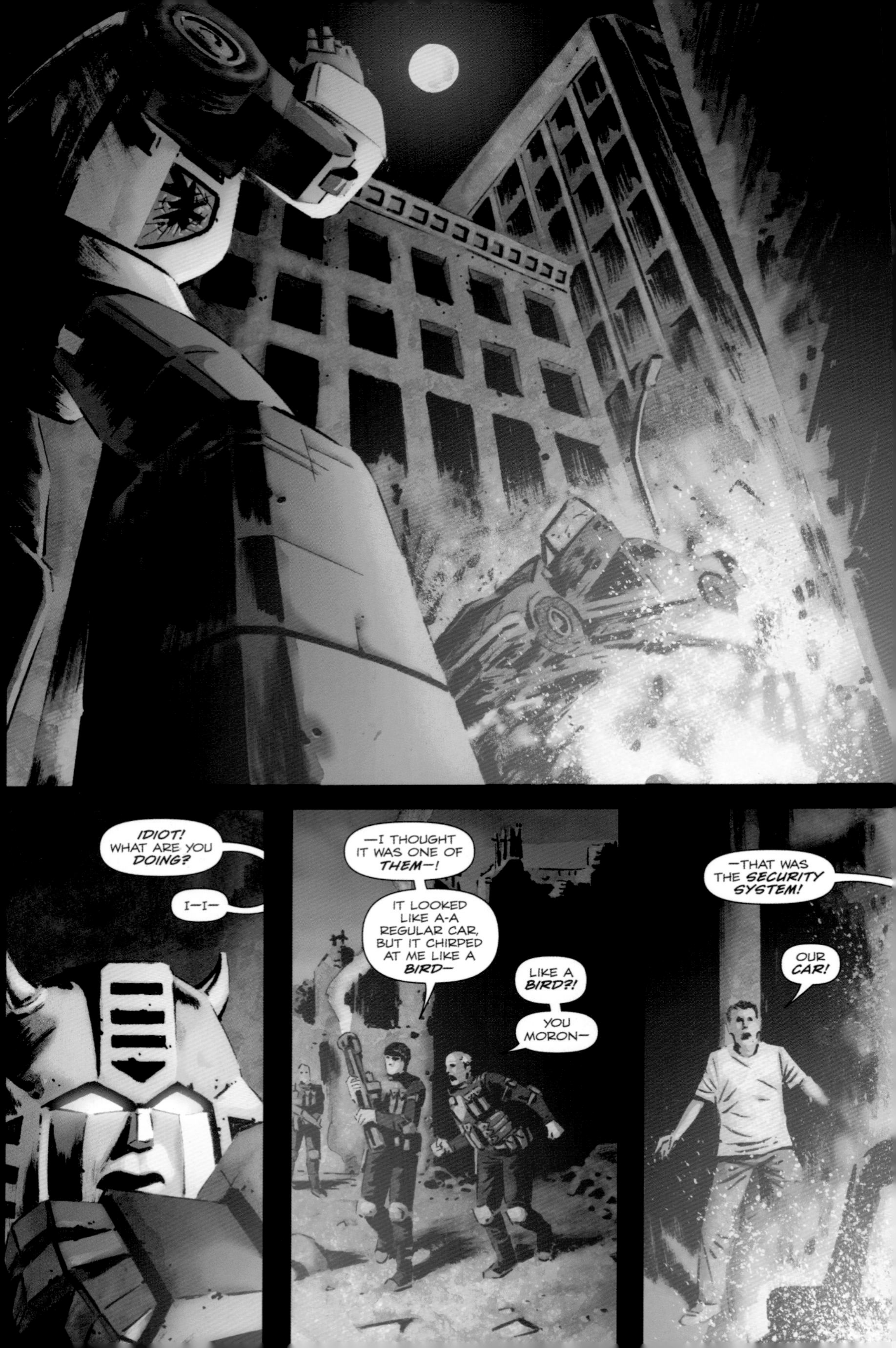
IDIOT! WHAT ARE YOU DOING?
I—I—
—I THOUGHT IT WAS ONE OF THEM—!
IT LOOKED LIKE A-A REGULAR CAR, BUT IT CHIRPED AT ME LIKE A BIRD—
LIKE A BIRD?!
YOU MORON—
—THAT WAS THE SECURITY SYSTEM!
OUR CAR!

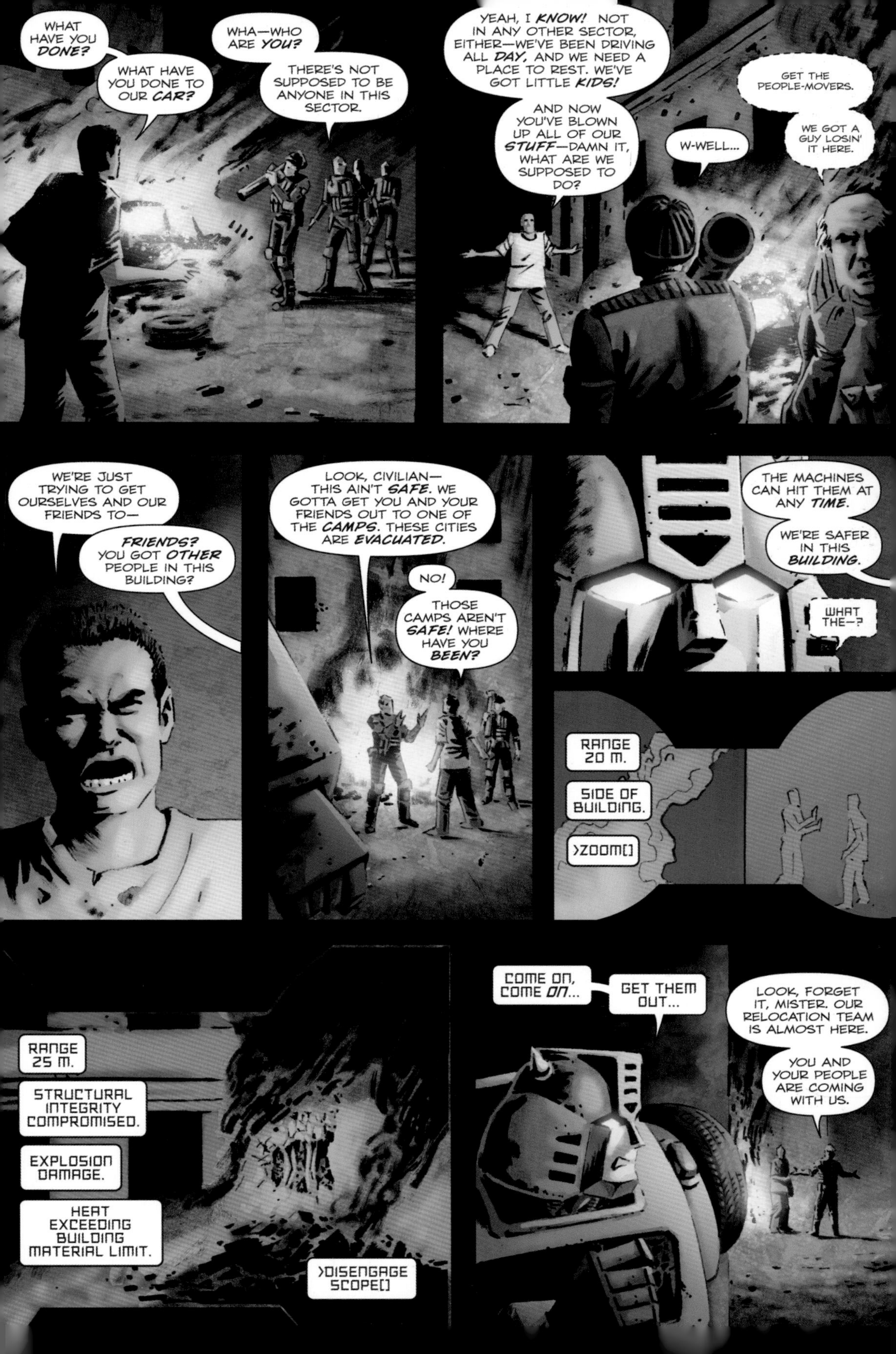
WHAT HAVE YOU DONE?
WHAT HAVE YOU DONE TO OUR CAR?
WHA—WHO ARE YOU?
THERE'S NOT SUPPOSED TO BE ANYONE IN THIS SECTOR.
YEAH, I KNOW! NOT IN ANY OTHER SECTOR, EITHER—WE'VE BEEN DRIVING ALL DAY, AND WE NEED A PLACE TO REST. WE'VE GOT LITTLE KIDS!
AND NOW YOU'VE BLOWN UP ALL OF OUR STUFF—DAMN IT, WHAT ARE WE SUPPOSED TO DO?
W-WELL...
GET THE PEOPLE-MOVERS.
WE GOT A GUY LOSIN' IT HERE.
WE'RE JUST TRYING TO GET OURSELVES AND OUR FRIENDS TO—
FRIENDS? YOU GOT OTHER PEOPLE IN THIS BUILDING?
LOOK, CIVILIAN— THIS AIN'T SAFE. WE GOTTA GET YOU AND YOUR FRIENDS OUT TO ONE OF THE CAMPS. THESE CITIES ARE EVACUATED.
NO!
THOSE CAMPS AREN'T SAFE! WHERE HAVE YOU BEEN?
THE MACHINES CAN HIT THEM AT ANY TIME.
WE'RE SAFER IN THIS BUILDING.
WHAT THE—?
RANGE 20 M.
SIDE OF BUILDING.
>ZOOM[]
RANGE 25 M.
STRUCTURAL INTEGRITY COMPROMISED.
EXPLOSION DAMAGE.
HEAT EXCEEDING BUILDING MATERIAL LIMIT.
>DISENGAGE SCOPE[]
COME ON, COME ON...
GET THEM OUT...
LOOK, FORGET IT, MISTER. OUR RELOCATION TEAM IS ALMOST HERE.
YOU AND YOUR PEOPLE ARE COMING WITH US.

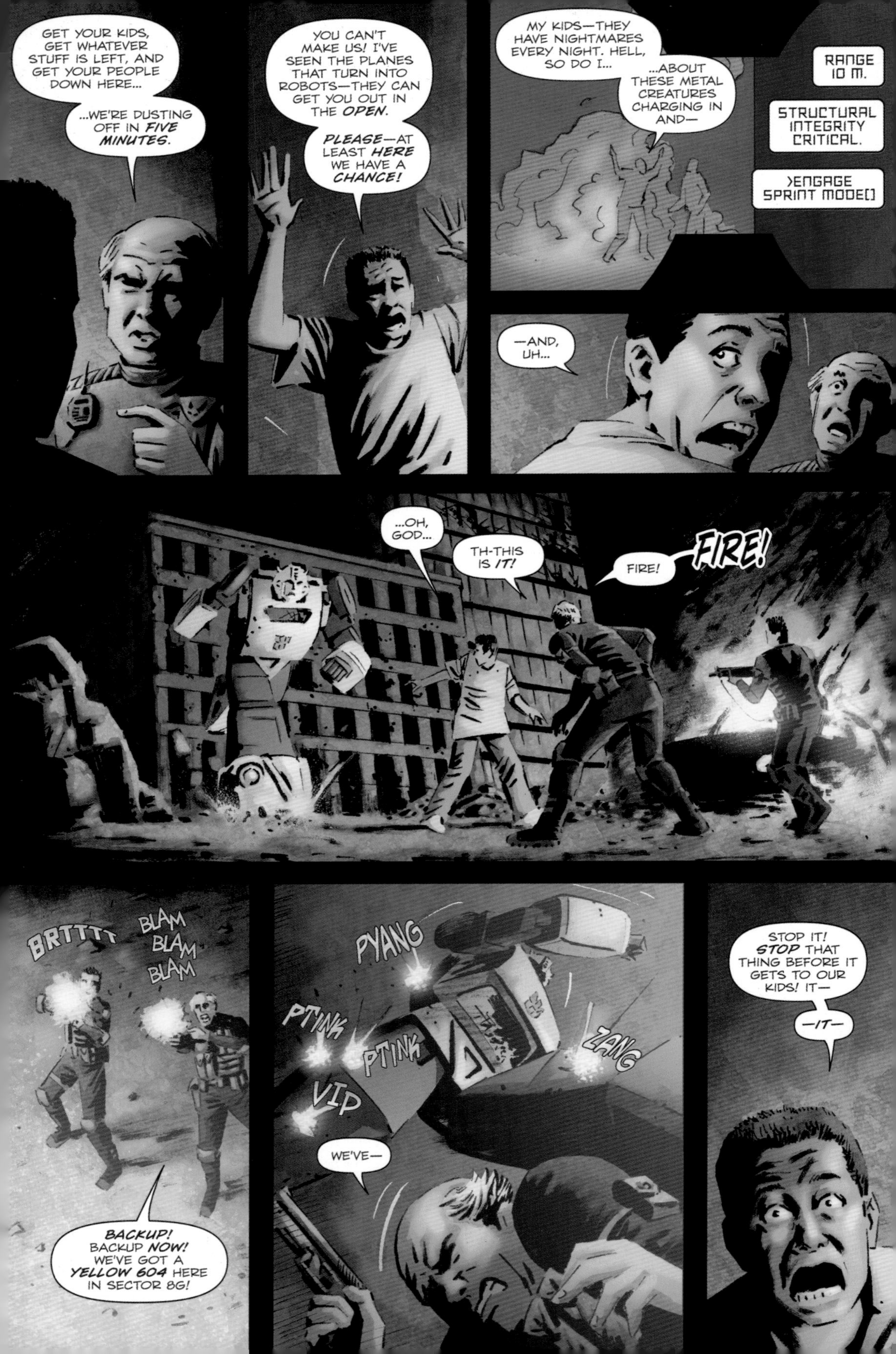
GET YOUR KIDS, GET WHATEVER STUFF IS LEFT, AND GET YOUR PEOPLE DOWN HERE...
...WE'RE DUSTING OFF IN FIVE MINUTES.
YOU CAN'T MAKE US! I'VE SEEN THE PLANES THAT TURN INTO ROBOTS—THEY CAN GET YOU OUT IN THE OPEN.
PLEASE—AT LEAST HERE WE HAVE A CHANCE!
MY KIDS—THEY HAVE NIGHTMARES EVERY NIGHT. HELL, SO DO I...
...ABOUT THESE METAL CREATURES CHARGING IN AND—
RANGE 10 M.
STRUCTURAL INTEGRITY CRITICAL.
>ENGAGE SPRINT MODE[]
—AND, UH...
...OH, GOD...
TH-THIS IS IT!
FIRE!
FIRE!
BRTTTT
BLAM BLAM BLAM
BACKUP! BACKUP NOW! WE'VE GOT A YELLOW 604 HERE IN SECTOR 8G!
PYANG
PTINK
PTINK
ZANG
VIP
WE'VE—
STOP IT! STOP THAT THING BEFORE IT GETS TO OUR KIDS! IT—
—IT—

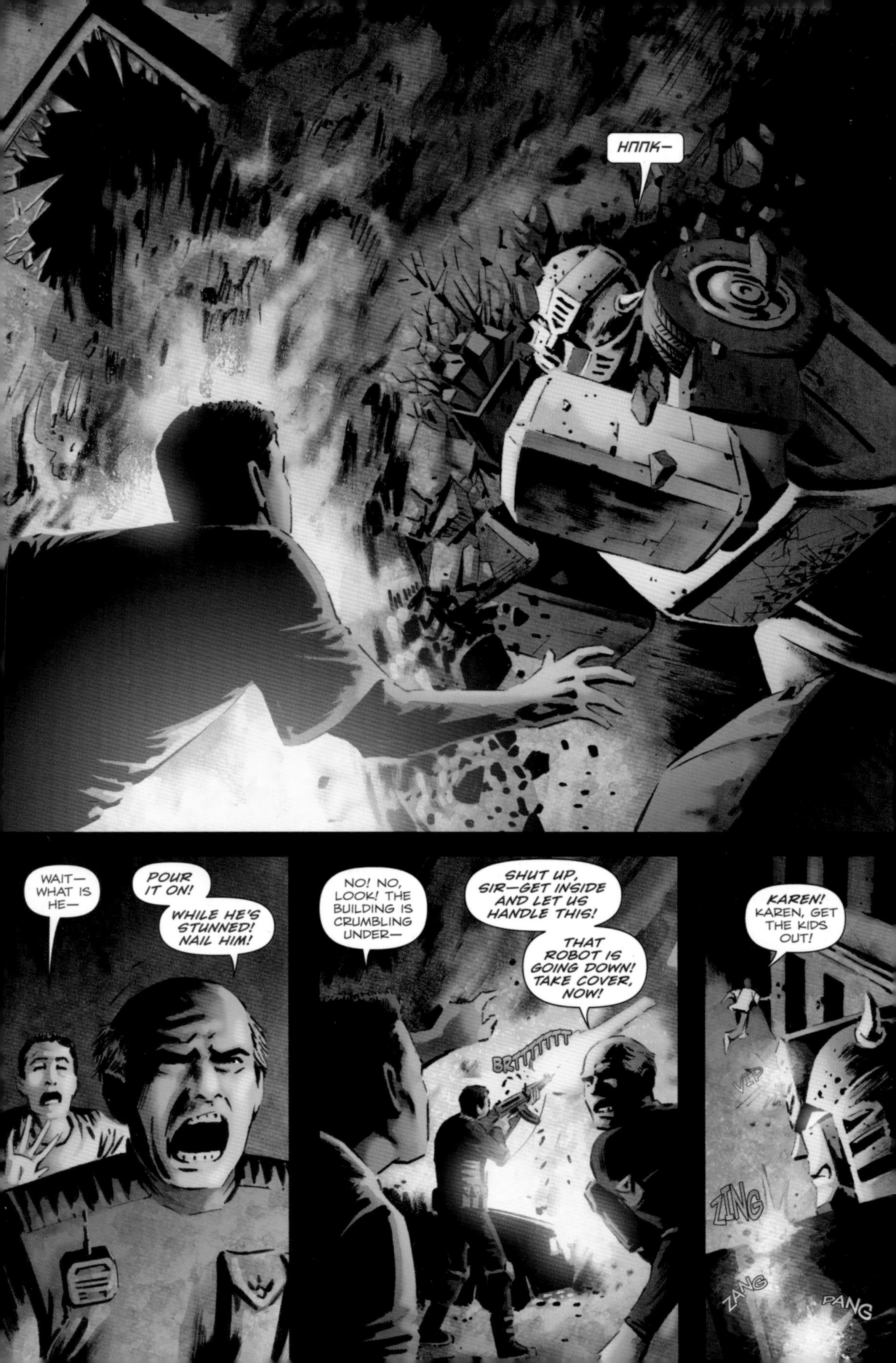
HNNK—
WAIT— WHAT IS HE—
POUR IT ON!
WHILE HE'S STUNNED! NAIL HIM!
NO! NO, LOOK! THE BUILDING IS CRUMBLING UNDER—
SHUT UP, SIR—GET INSIDE AND LET US HANDLE THIS!
THAT ROBOT IS GOING DOWN! TAKE COVER, NOW!
KAREN! KAREN, GET THE KIDS OUT!
VIP
ZING
ZANG
PANG

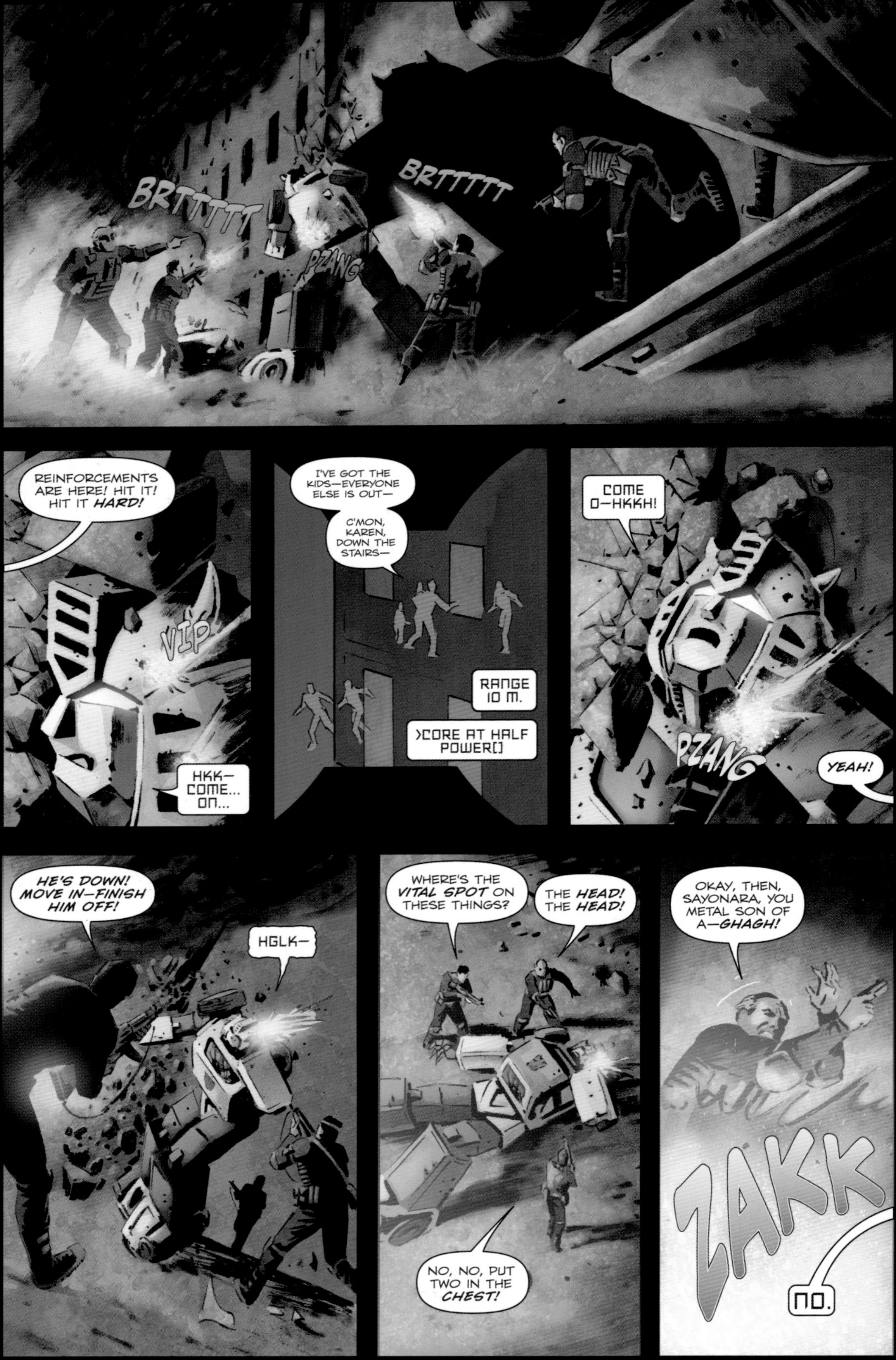
BRTTTTT
BRTTTTT
PZANG
REINFORCEMENTS ARE HERE! HIT IT! HIT IT HARD!
VIP
HKK— COME... ON...
I'VE GOT THE KIDS—EVERYONE ELSE IS OUT—
C'MON, KAREN, DOWN THE STAIRS—
RANGE 10 M.
>CORE AT HALF POWER[]
COME O—HKKH!
PZANG
YEAH!
HE'S DOWN! MOVE IN—FINISH HIM OFF!
HGLK—
WHERE'S THE VITAL SPOT ON THESE THINGS?
THE HEAD! THE HEAD!
NO, NO, PUT TWO IN THE CHEST!
OKAY, THEN, SAYONARA, YOU METAL SON OF A—GHAGH!
ZAKK
NO.

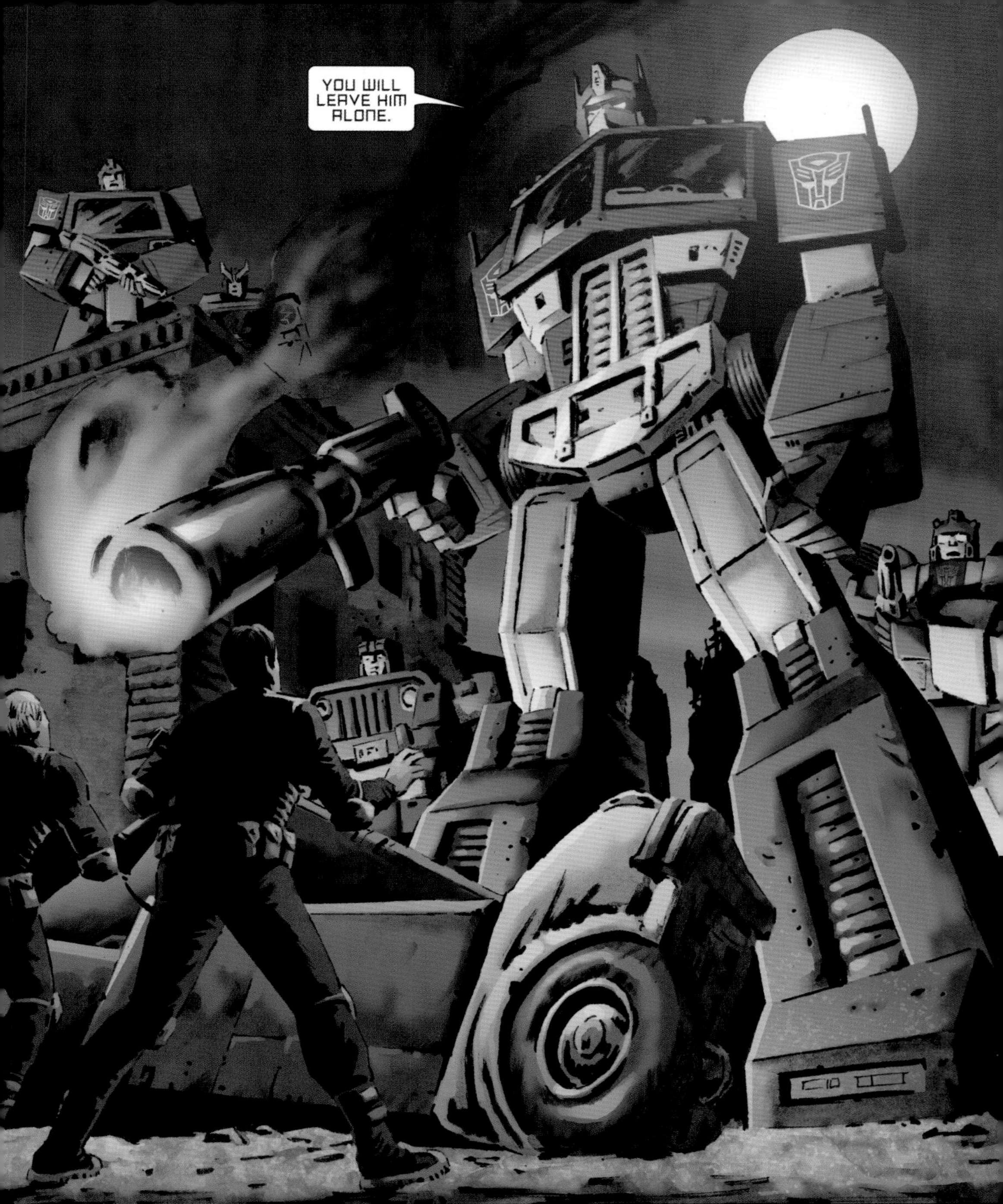
YOU WILL LEAVE HIM ALONE.

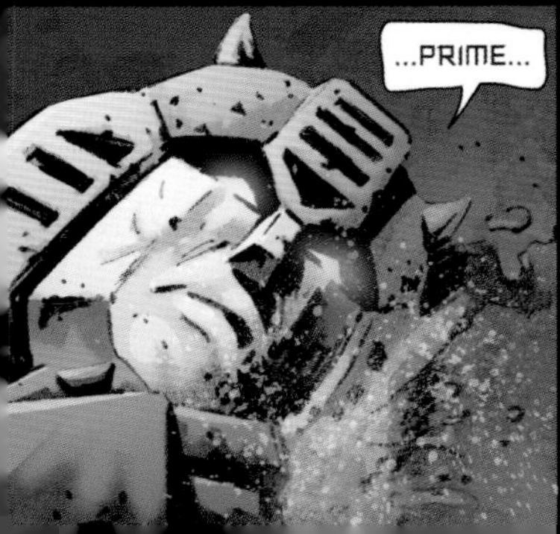
...PRIME...

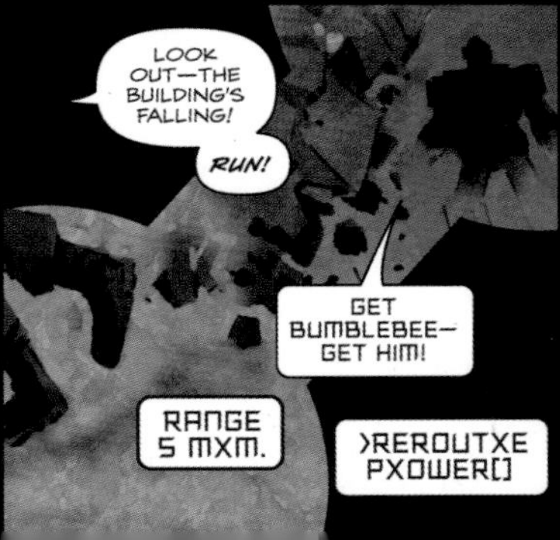
LOOK OUT—THE BUILDING'S FALLING!
RUN!
GET BUMBLEBEE— GET HIM!
RANGE 5 MXM.
>REROUTXE PXOWER[]

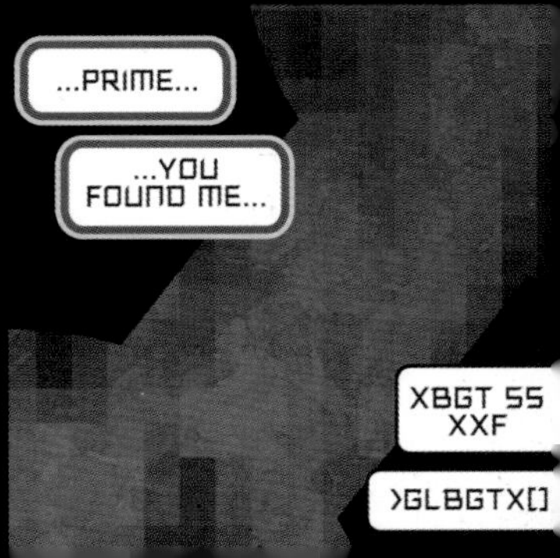
...PRIME...
...YOU FOUND ME...
XBGT 55 XXF
>GLBGTX[]

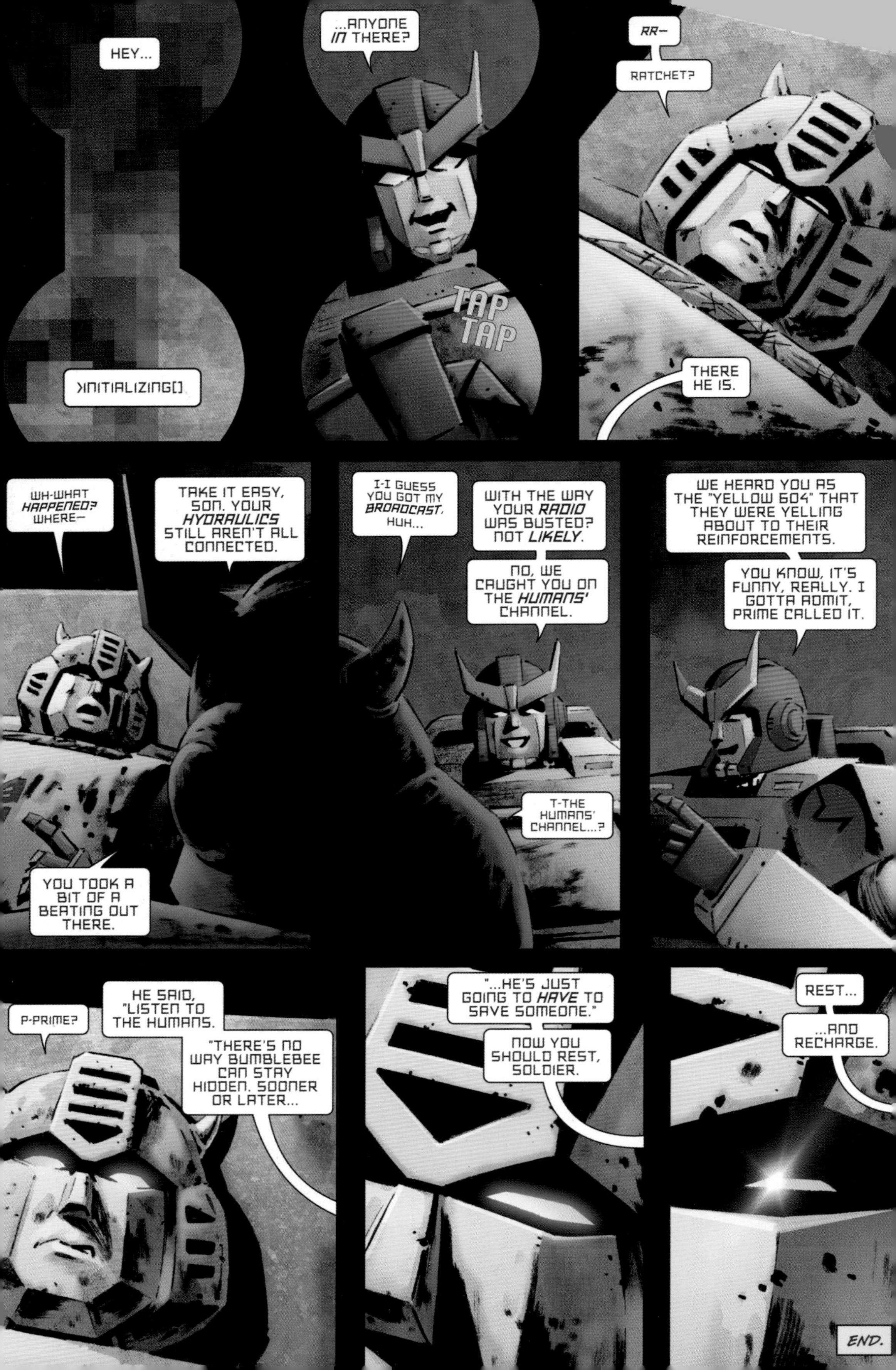
HEY...
>INITIALIZING[]
...ANYONE *IN* THERE?
TAP TAP
RR—
RATCHET?
THERE HE IS.
WH-WHAT *HAPPENED?* WHERE—
TAKE IT EASY, SON. YOUR *HYDRAULICS* STILL AREN'T ALL CONNECTED.
YOU TOOK A BIT OF A BEATING OUT THERE.
I-I GUESS YOU GOT MY *BROADCAST*, HUH...
WITH THE WAY YOUR *RADIO* WAS BUSTED? NOT *LIKELY*.
NO, WE CAUGHT YOU ON THE *HUMANS'* CHANNEL.
T-THE HUMANS' CHANNEL...?
WE HEARD YOU AS THE "YELLOW 604" THAT THEY WERE YELLING ABOUT TO THEIR REINFORCEMENTS.
YOU KNOW, IT'S FUNNY, REALLY. I GOTTA ADMIT, PRIME CALLED IT.
P-PRIME?
HE SAID, "LISTEN TO THE HUMANS.
"THERE'S NO WAY BUMBLEBEE CAN STAY HIDDEN. SOONER OR LATER...
"...HE'S JUST GOING TO *HAVE* TO SAVE SOMEONE."
NOW YOU SHOULD REST, SOLDIER.
REST...
...AND RECHARGE.
END.

ART GALLERY

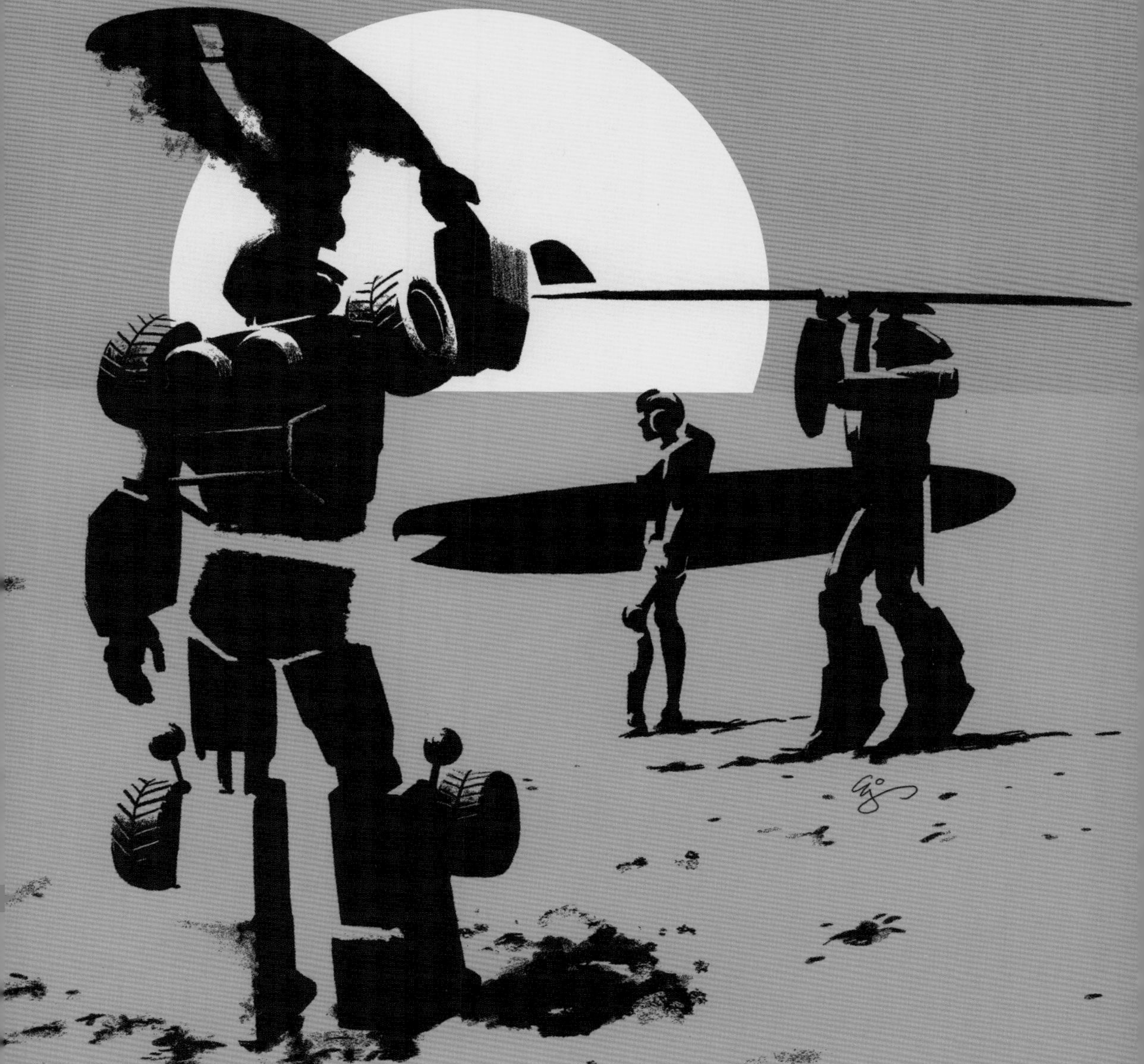

Art and Colors by E.J. Su

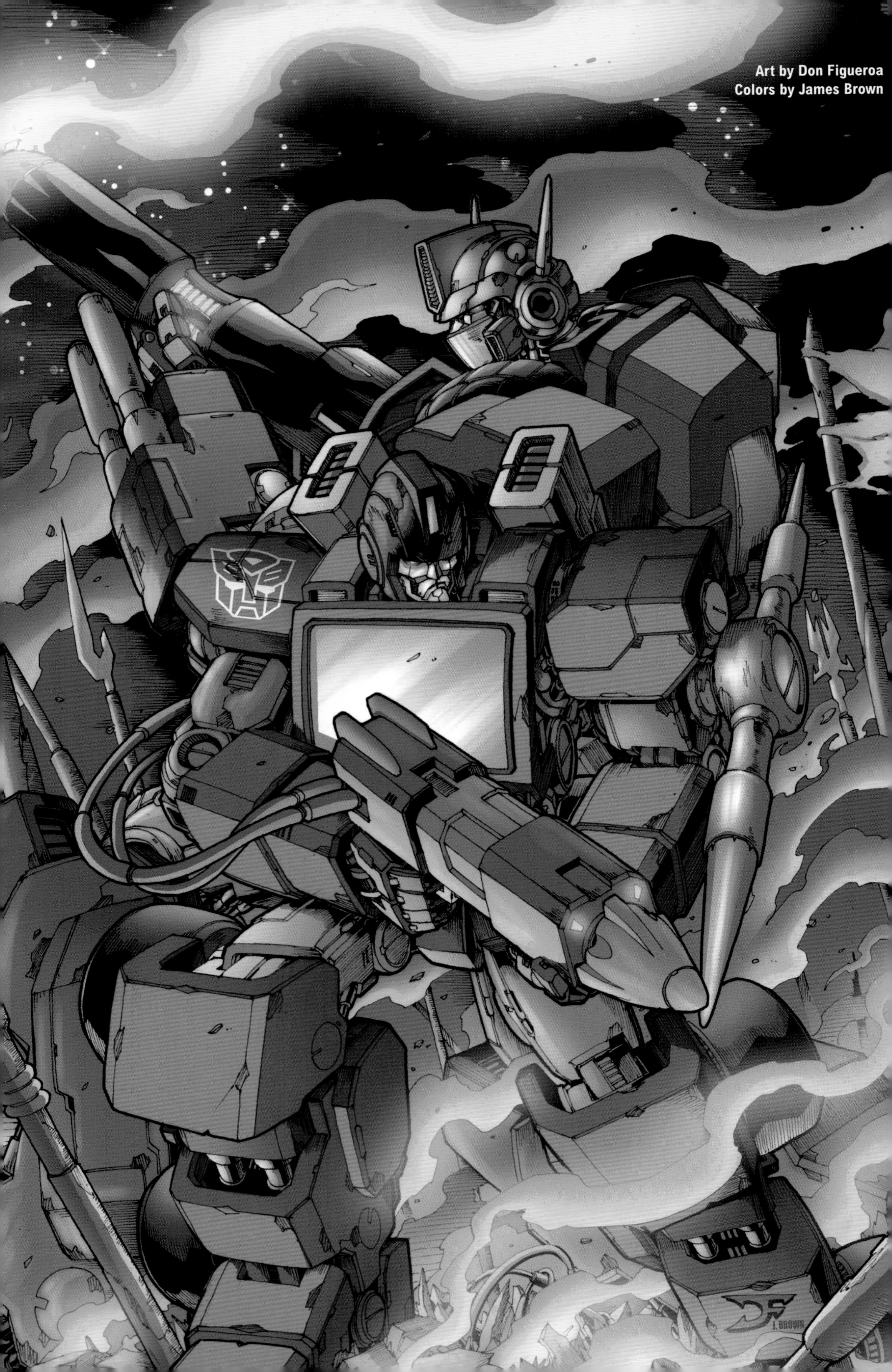

Art by Don Figueroa
Colors by James Brown

Art by Chee Yang Ong
Colors by Moose Baumann

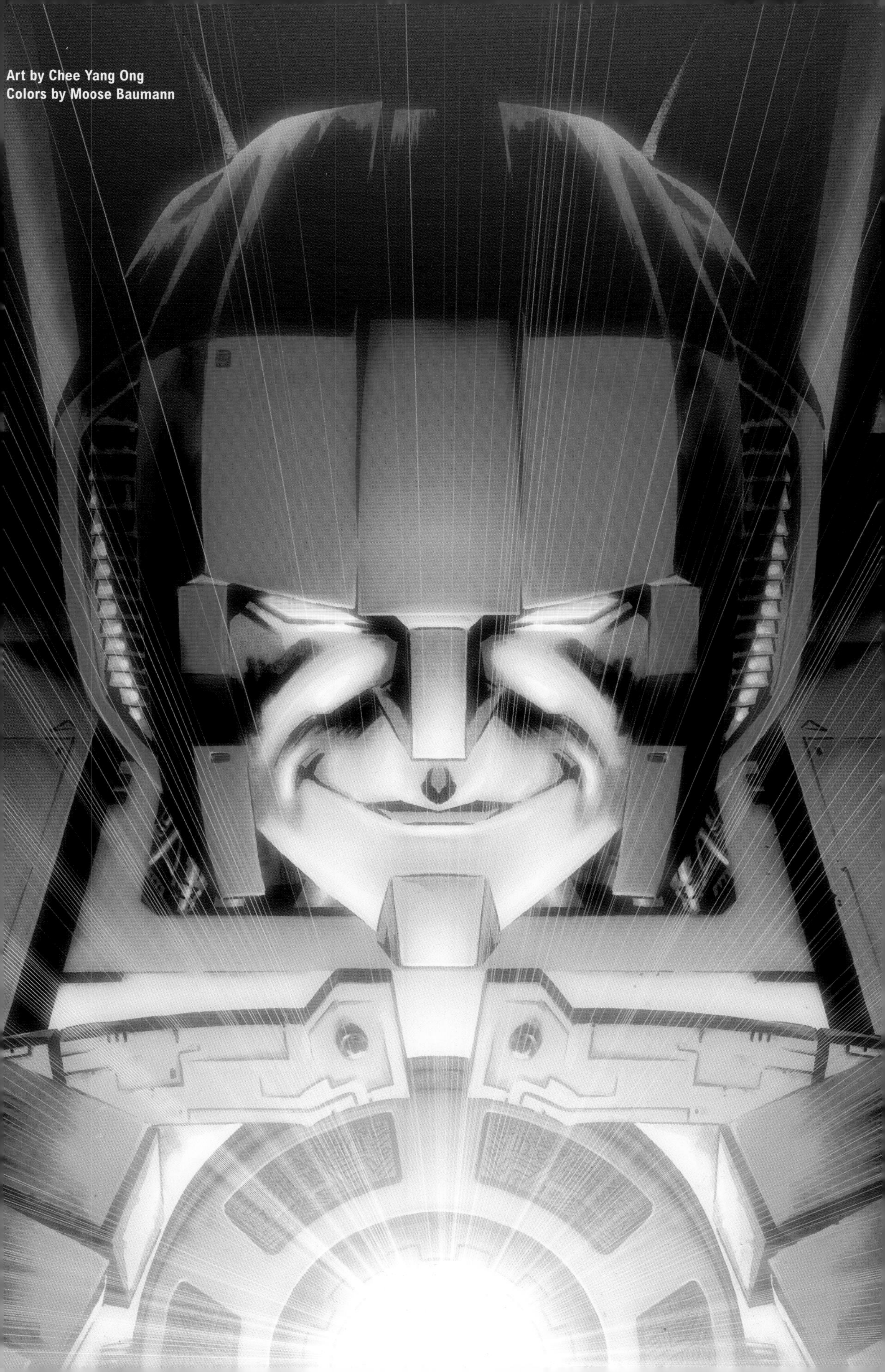

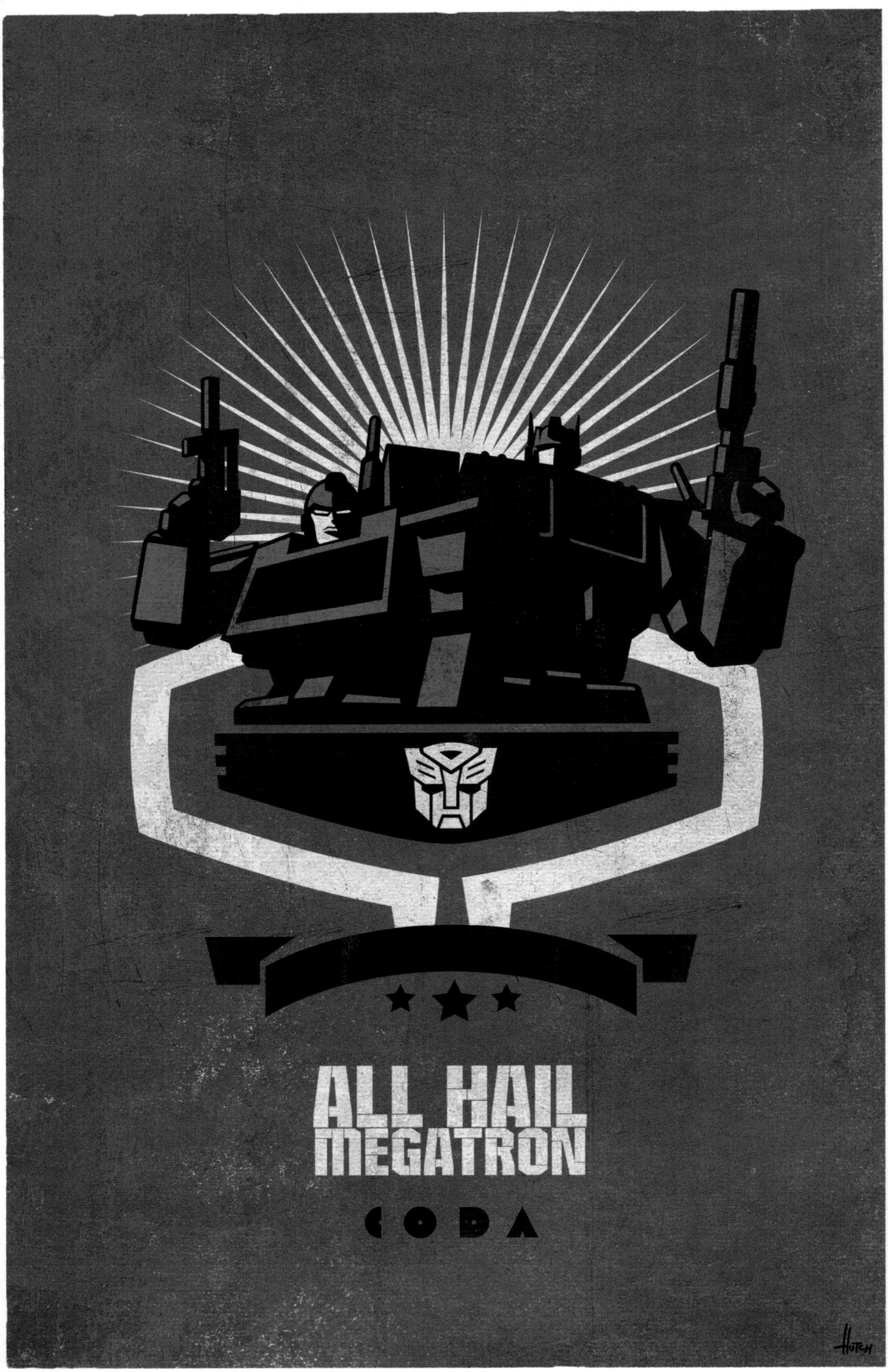
ALL HAIL
MEGATRON
CODA
HUTCH

Art by Trevor Hutchison

Art by Emiliano Santalucia
Colors by Josh Burcham

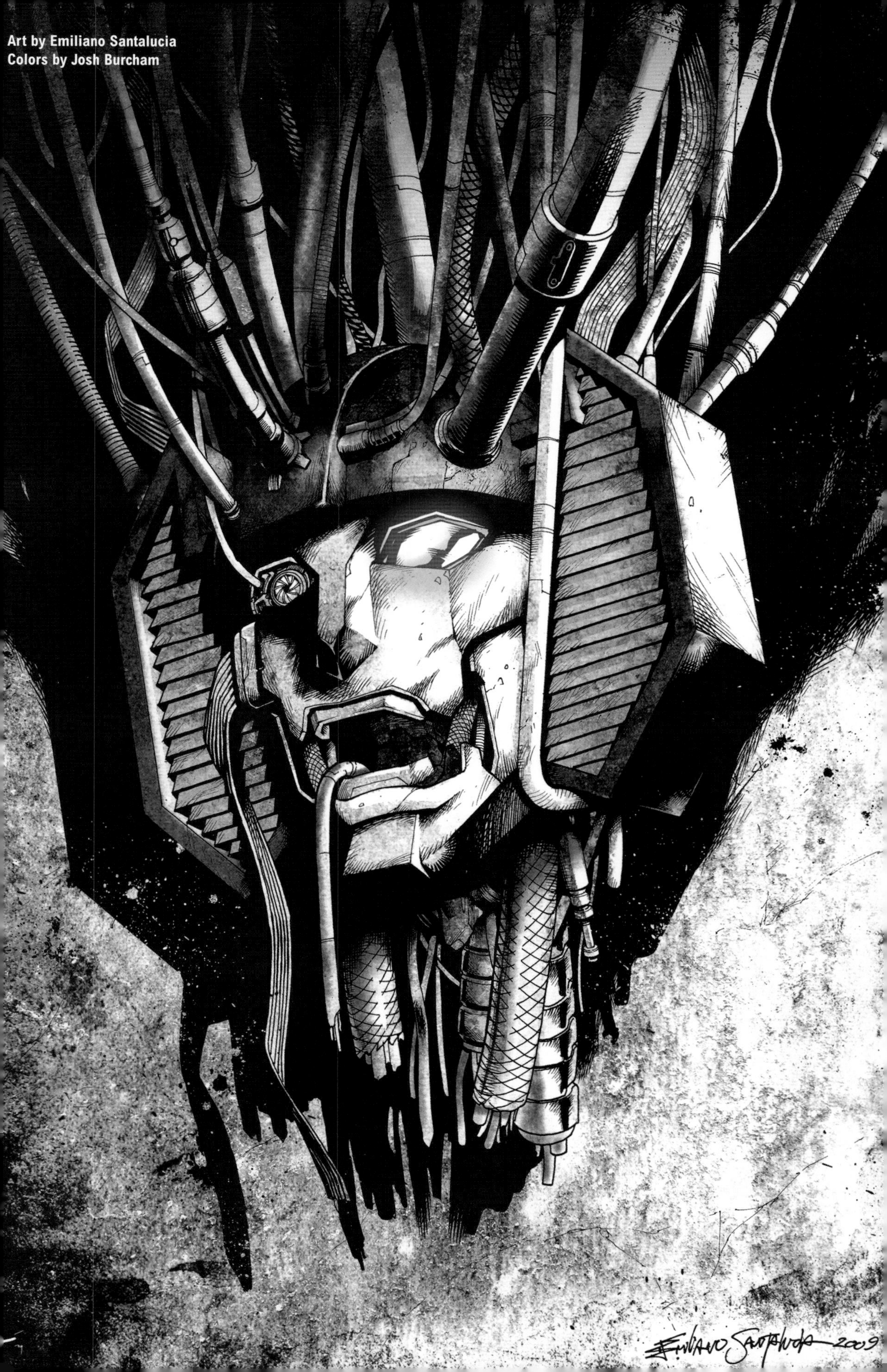

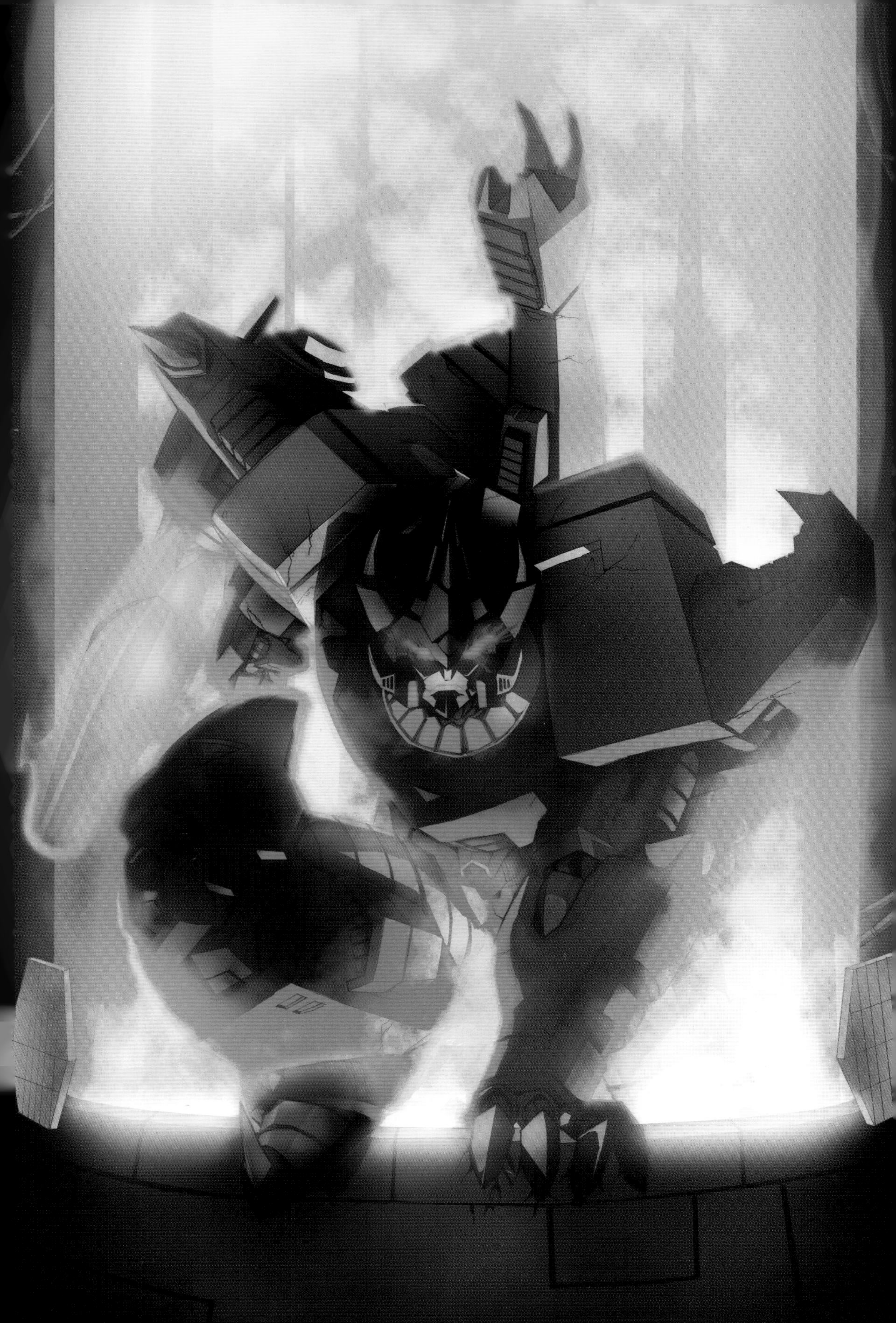

Art and Colors by Andrew Griffith

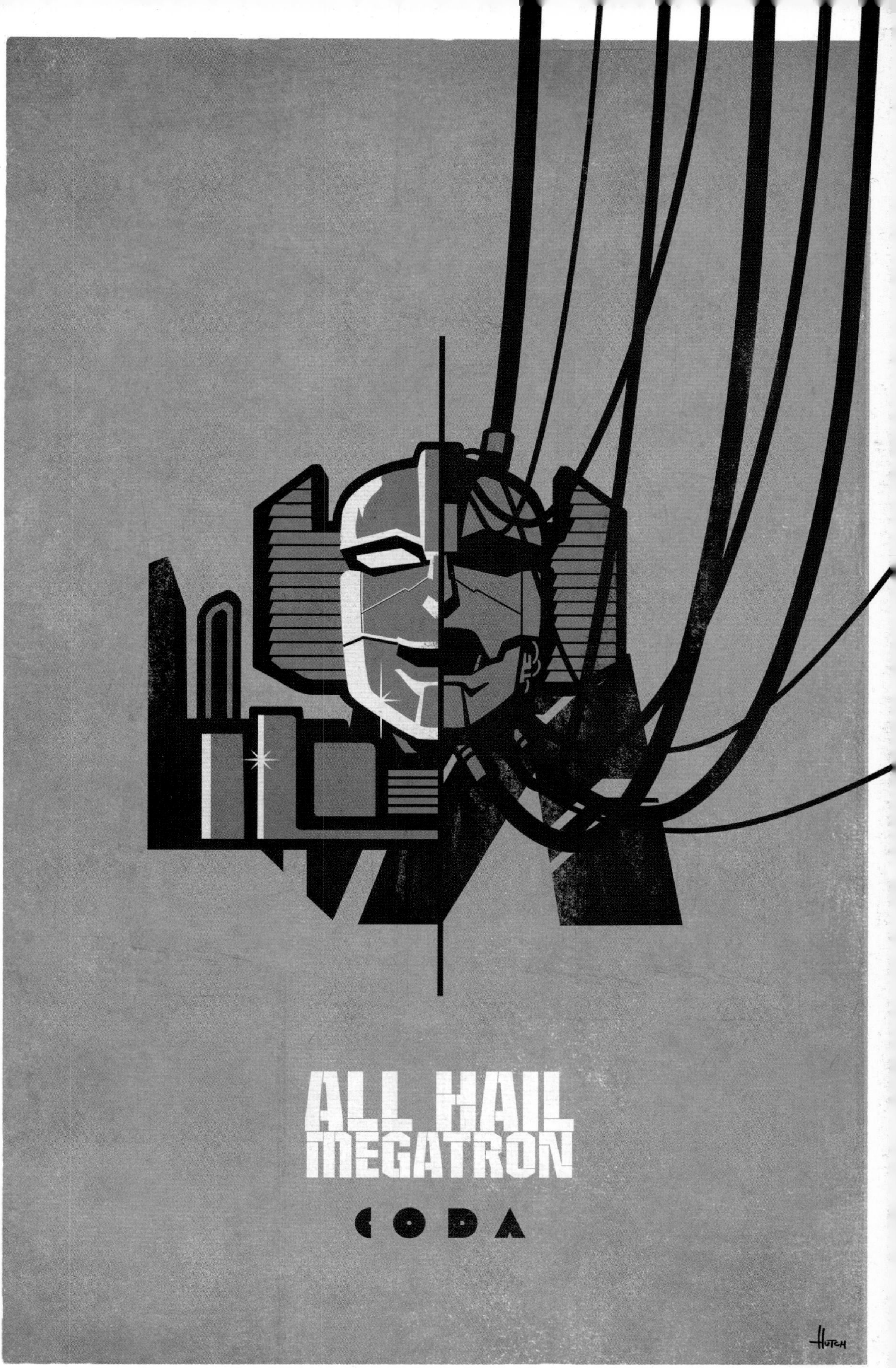
ALL HAIL
MEGATRON
CODA
HUTCH
Art by Trevor Hutchison

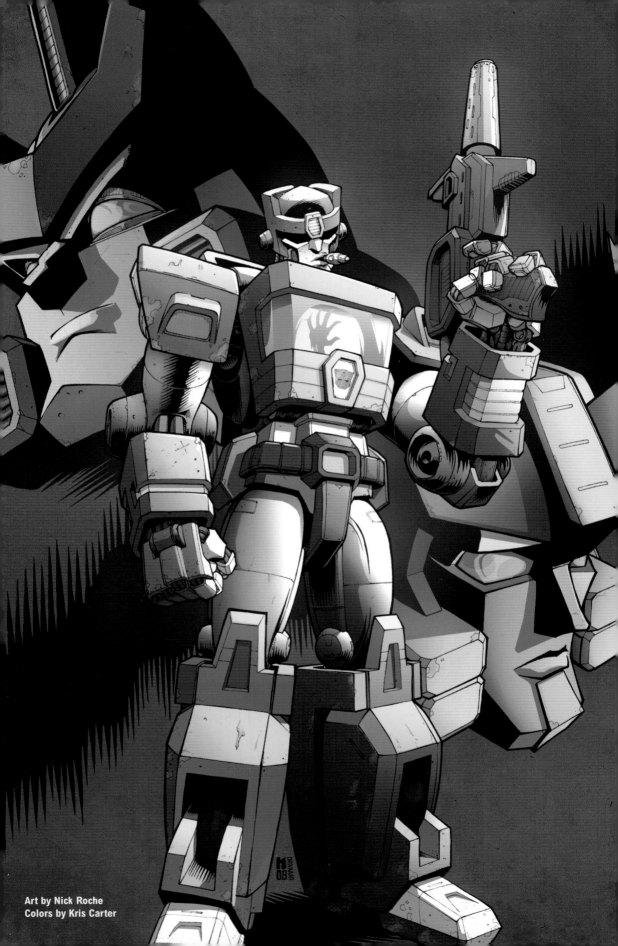

Art by Nick Roche
Colors by Kris Carter

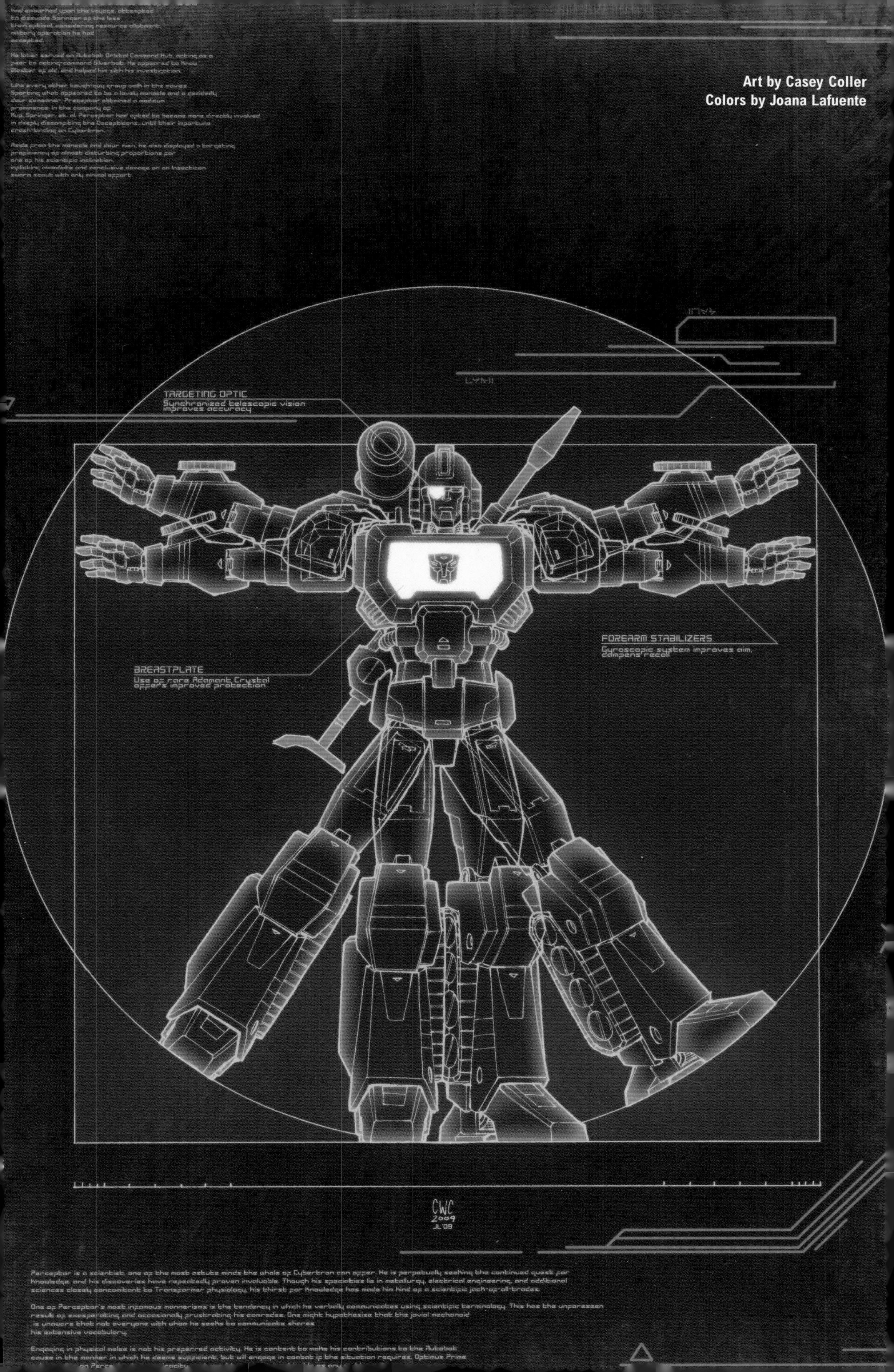
had embarked upon the voyage, attempted
to dissuade Springer of the less
than optimal, considering resource allotment,
military operation he had
accepted.
He later served on Autobot Orbital Command Hub, acting as a
peer to acting-command Silverbolt. He appeared to know
Blaster of old, and helped him with his investigation.
Like every other tough-guy group walk in the movies.
Sporting what appeared to be a lovely monocle and a decidedly
dour demeanor, Preceptor obtained a modicum
prominence. In the company of
Kup, Springer, et. al, Perceptor had opted to become more directly involved
in deeply discomfiting the Decepticons...until their importune
crash-landing on Cybertron.
Aside from the monocle and dour mien, he also displayed a targeting
proficiency of almost disturbing proportions for
one of his scientific inclination,
inflicting immediate and conclusive damage on an Insecticon
swarm scout with only minimal effort.
TARGETING OPTIC
Synchronized telescopic vision improves accuracy
FOREARM STABILIZERS
Gyroscopic system improves aim, dampens recoil
BREASTPLATE
Use of rare Adamant Crystal offers improved protection
CWC 2009
JL'09
Perceptor is a scientist, one of the most astute minds the whole of Cybertron can offer. He is perpetually seeking the continued quest for knowledge, and his discoveries have repeatedly proven invaluable. Though his specialties lie in metallurgy, electrical engineering, and additional sciences closely concomitant to Transformer physiology, his thirst for knowledge has made him kind of a scientific jack-of-all-trades.
One of Perceptor's most infamous mannerisms is the tendency in which he verbally communicates using scientific terminology. This has the unforeseen result of exasperating and occasionally frustrating his comrades. One might hypothesize that the jovial mechanoid
is unaware that not everyone with whom he seeks to communicate shares
his extensive vocabulary.
Engaging in physical melee is not his preferred activity. He is content to make his contributions to the Autobot
cause in the manner in which he deems sufficient, but will engage in combat if the situation requires. Optimus Prime

Art by Casey Coller
Colors by Joana Lafuente

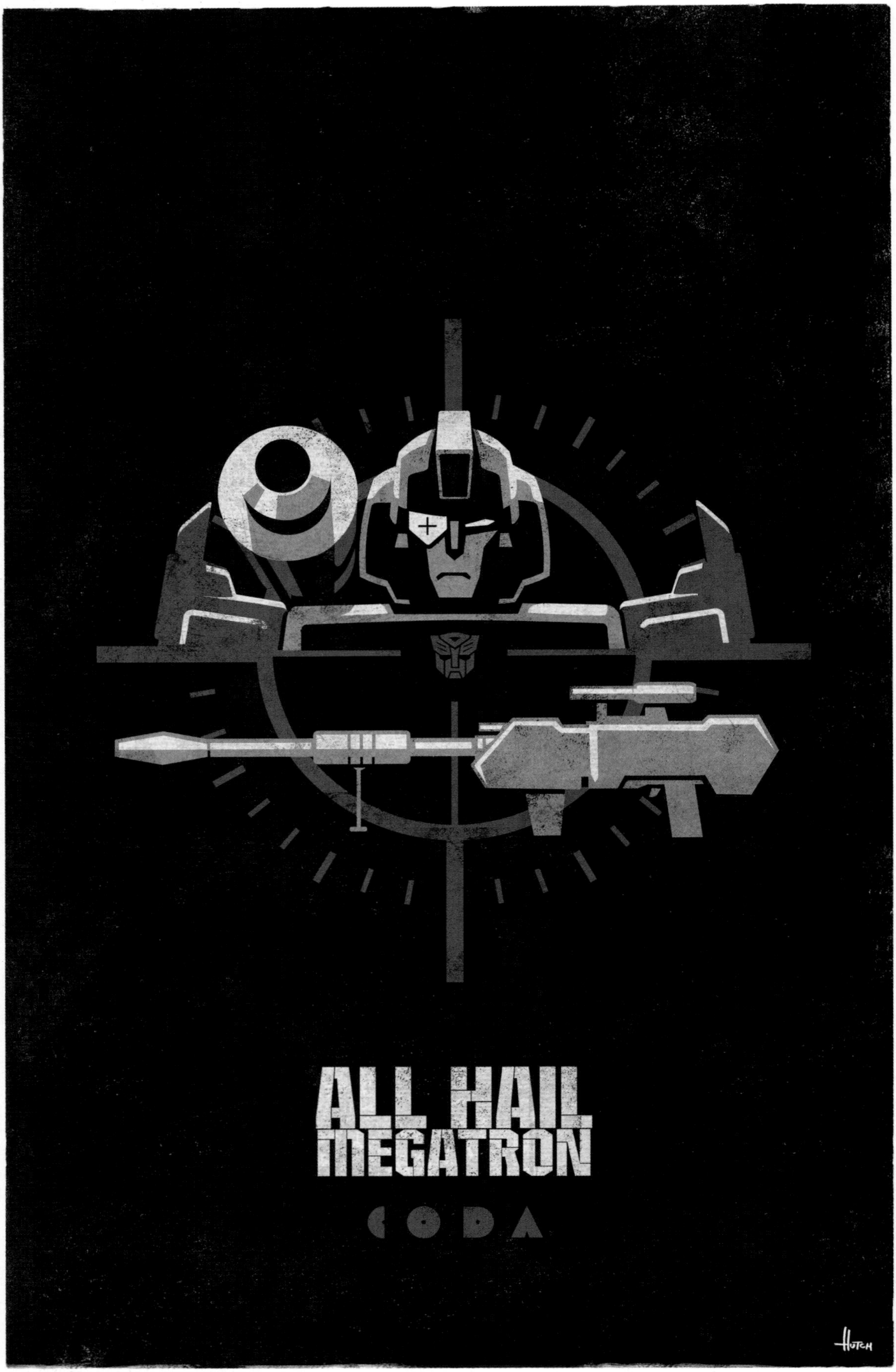
ALL HAIL
MEGATRON
CODA
HUTCH

Art by Trevor Hutchison

Art by Guido Guidi
Colors by Josh Burcham

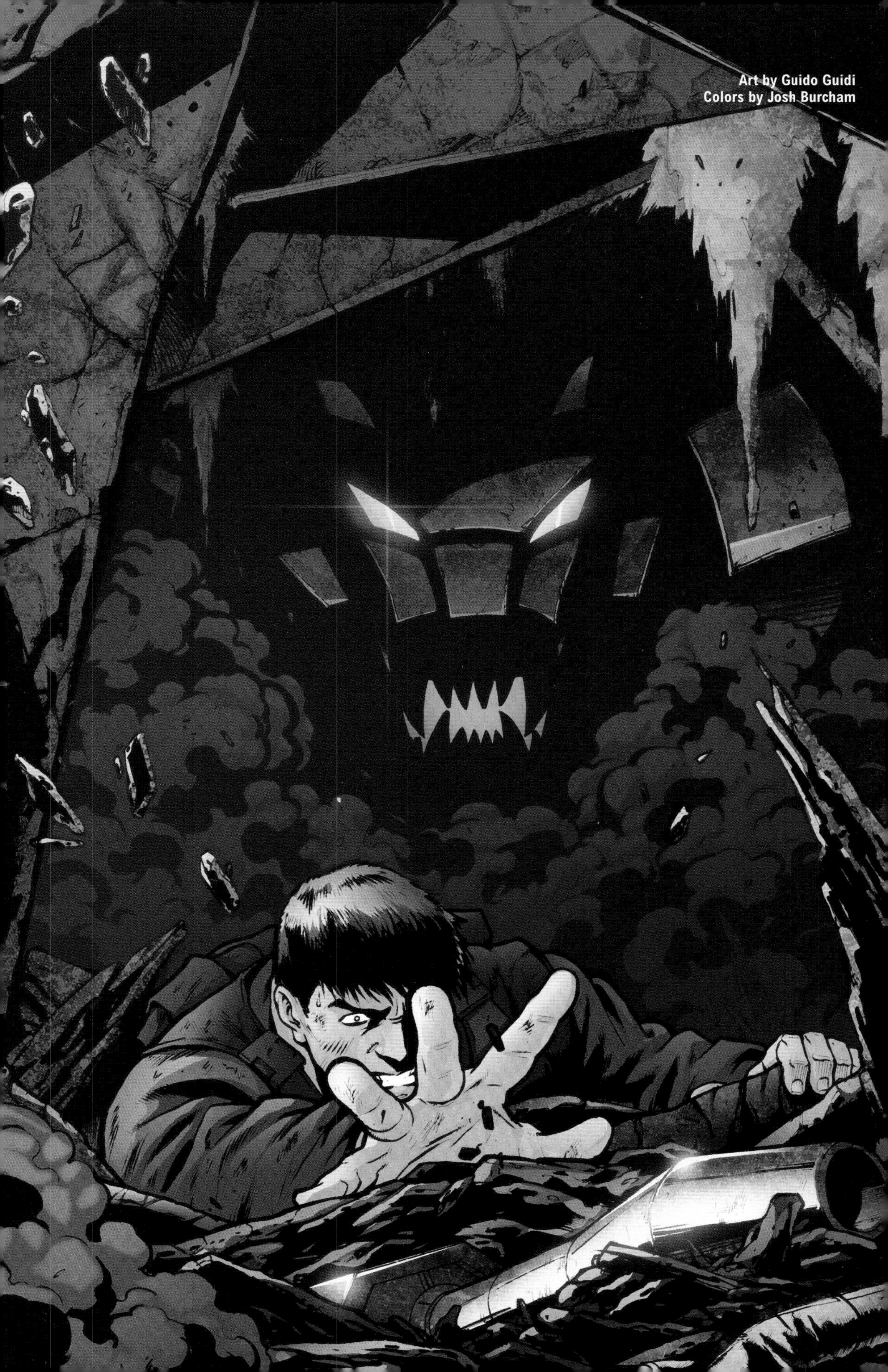

Art by Chee Yang Ong
Colors by Moose Baumann

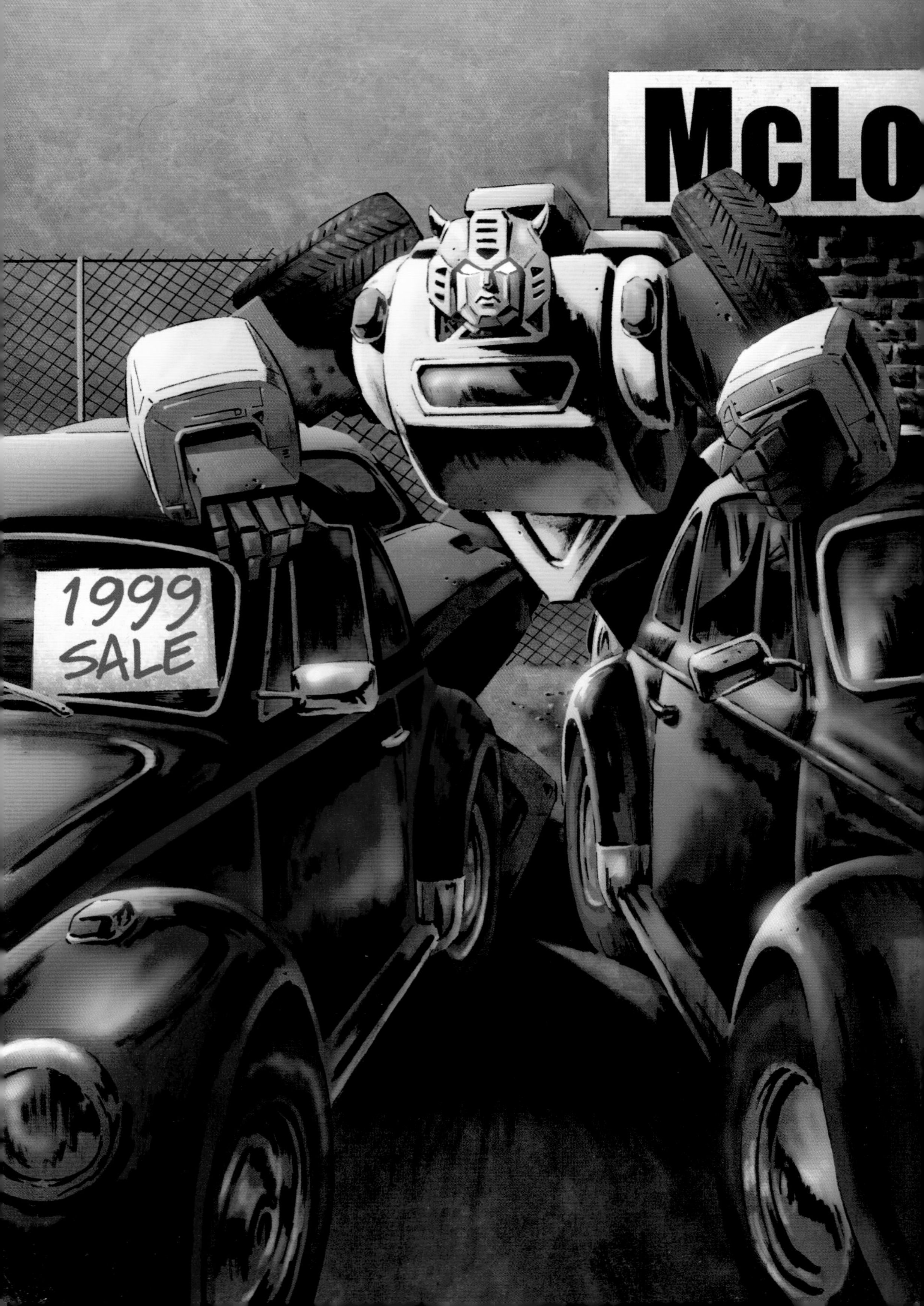
McLo
1999
SALE

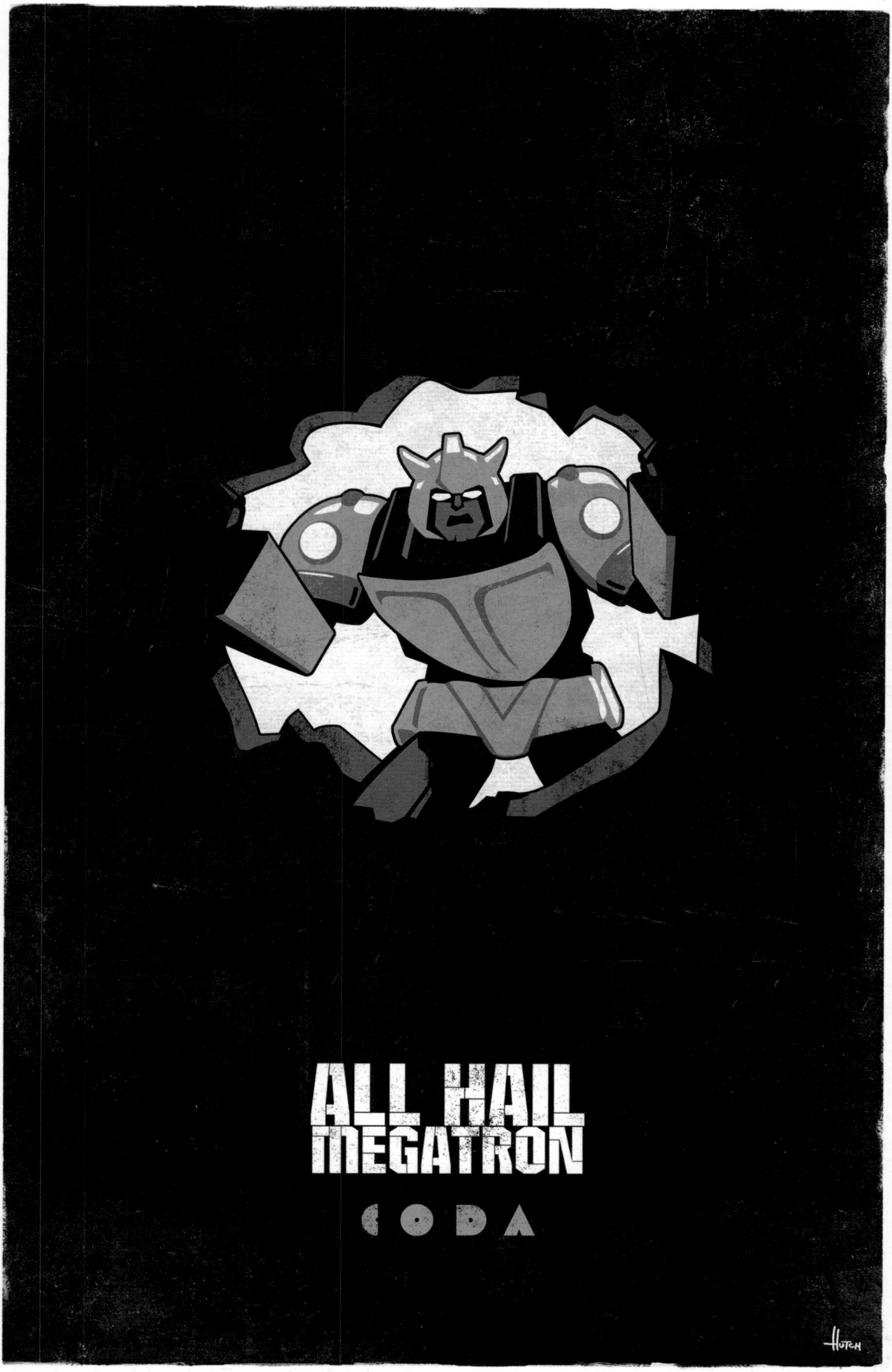
ALL HAIL MEGATRON
CODA
HUTCH

Art by Trevor Hutchison